D0984498

Faces of Intention

Selected Essays on Intention and Agency

This collection of essays by one of the most prominent and internationally respected philosophers of action is concerned with deepening our understanding of intention and agency.

In Bratman's view when we settle on a plan for action we are committing ourselves to future conduct in ways that help support important forms of coordination and organization both within the life of the agent and interpersonally. These essays enrich that account of commitment involved in intending and explore its implications for our understanding of temptation and self-control, shared intention and shared cooperative activity, and moral responsibility. The essays offer extensive discussions of related views by, among others, Donald Davidson, Hector-Neri Castañeda, J. David Velleman, Christine Korsgaard, Harry Frankfurt, and P. F. Strawson.

This collection will be a valuable resource for a wide range of philosophers and their students and will also be of interest to social and developmental psychologists, AI researchers, and game and decision theorists.

Michael E. Bratman is Howard H. and Jessie T. Watkins University Professor of Philosophy at Stanford University.

CAMBRIDGE STUDIES IN PHILOSOPHY

General editor ERNEST SOSA (Brown University)

Advisory editors:
JONATHAN DANCY (University of Reading)
JOHN HALDANE (University of St. Andrews)
GILBERT HARMAN (Princeton University)
FRANK JACKSON (Australian National University)
WILLIAM G. LYCAN (University of North Carolina at Chapel Hill)
SYDNEY SHOEMAKER (Cornell University)
JUDITH J. THOMSON (Massachusetts Institute of Technology)

RECENT TITLES

Faces of Intention

SELECTED ESSAYS ON INTENTION AND AGENCY

Michael E. Bratman

CAMBRIDGE
UNIVERSITY PRESS

PUBLISHED BY THE PRESS SYNDICATE OF THE UNIVERSITY OF CAMBRIDGE
The Pitt Building, Trumpington Street, Cambridge, United Kingdom

CAMBRIDGE UNIVERSITY PRESS
The Edinburgh Building, Cambridge CB2 2RU, UK   http://www.cup.cam.ac.uk
40 West 20th Street, New York, NY 10011-4211, USA   http://www.cup.org
10 Stamford Road, Oakleigh, Melbourne 3166, Australia

First published 1999

Printed in the United States of America

Typeface Bembo 10.5/13 pt.   *System* Penta   [RF]

A catalog record for this book is available from the British Library.

Library of Congress Cataloging in Publication Data
Bratman, Michael.
Faces of intention : selected essays on intention and agency / Michael E. Bratman.
p.   cm. – (Cambridge studies in philosophy)
Includes bibliographical references.
ISBN 0-521-63131-9 (hardcover), – ISBN 0-521-63727-9 (pbk.)
1. Intentionality (Philosophy)   2. Agent (Philosophy)   I. Title.   II. Series.
B105.I56B73   1998
128'.4–dc21   98-26459
                                                CIP

ISBN 0 521 63131 9 hardback
ISBN 0 521 63727 9 paperback

For Susan

Contents

Acknowledgments

I have tried to acknowledge my many, many intellectual debts in each of the essays. I would like also to express my gratitude to a number of institutions for their support of my research. Some of my work has been generously supported by the Center for the Study of Language and Information. Several essays were written while I was a Fellow at the Stanford University Humanities Center. I learned much from discussions with participants in the National Endowment for the Humanities Summer Seminar for College Teachers that I directed in 1993. I made some progress while I was Olmsted Visiting Professor in the Yale University Program on Ethics, Politics and Economics. Most recently, a fellowship at the Center for Advanced Study in Behavioral Sciences has provided the occasion for calm reflection needed to bring this project to completion. I am grateful for financial support provided by the Andrew W. Mellon Foundation. Throughout I have benefited greatly from the stimulation and support of colleagues and students in the Stanford University Philosophy Department.

My deepest thanks go to my family – Susan, Gregory, and Scott. Without their support this book simply would not have been written.

All essays other than essay 1 have been previously published. I have updated references, corrected an occasional stylistic infelicity, and have also made minor changes in essays 2, 6, and 10. Essay 7 has been substantially shortened and somewhat revised. Some of these changes have been made to decrease repetition. A good deal of repetition remains, however. This is in part because I wanted to ensure that each essay continues to stand on its own, and in part because (with the exception of essay 7) I did not want to make large changes to essays that had already appeared and been the target of discussion. The notes in essay 10 have been renumbered to conform with the style of the other papers. In each case I am very grateful for permission to reprint the essays.

The original locations of the essays are as follows:

2. "Practical Reasoning and Acceptance in a Context," *Mind* 101 (1992): 1–14. By permission of Oxford University Press.

3. "Planning and Temptation," in Larry May, Marilyn Friedman, and Andy Clark (eds.), *Mind and Morals: Essays on Ethics and Cognitive Science* (Cambridge: Bradford/MIT, 1995), pp. 293–310. By permission of the MIT Press.

4. "Toxin, Temptation, and the Stability of Intention," in Jules L. Coleman and Christopher W. Morris (eds.), *Rational Commitment and Social Justice: Essays for Gregory S. Kavka* (Cambridge University Press, 1998), pp. 59–83.

5. "Shared Cooperative Activity," *The Philosophical Review* 101 (1992): 327–341. Copyright 1992 Cornell University. Reprinted by permission of the publisher.

6. "Shared Intention," *Ethics* 104 (1993): 97–113. Reprinted by permission of The University of Chicago Press (© 1993 by The University of Chicago. All rights reserved.)

7. "Shared Intention and Mutual Obligation" is from "Intention Partagée et Obligation Mutuelle," in Jean-Pierre Dupuy and Pierre Livet (eds.), *Les limites de la rationalité*, Volume 1. Trans. by Joelle Proust (Paris: Éditions La Découverte, 1997), pp. 246–266. By permission of Éditions La Découverte & Syros.

8. "I Intend That We *J*," in Raimo Tuomela and Ghita Holmstrom-Hintikka (eds.), *Contemporary Action Theory,* Volume 2: *Social Action* (Dordrecht: Kluwer, 1997), pp. 49–63. With kind permission from Kluwer Academic Publishers.

9. "Responsibility and Planning," *The Journal of Ethics* 1 (1997): 27–43. With kind permission from Kluwer Academic Publishers.

10. "Identification, Decision, and Treating as a Reason," *Philosophical Topics* 24 (1996): 1–18. By permission of *Philosophical Topics*.

11. "Davidson's Theory of Intention," in Bruce Vermazen and Merrill Hintikka (eds.), *Essays on Davidson: Actions and Events* (Oxford: Oxford University Press, 1985), pp. 13–26. By permission of Oxford University Press.

12. "Castañeda's Theory of Thought and Action," appeared in James E. Tomberlin (ed.), *Agent, Language and the Structure of the World: Essays Presented to Hector-Neri Castañeda, with His Replies* (1983), pp. 149–169. (Copyright by Ridgeview Publishing Co., Atascadero, CA.) Reprinted by permission of Ridgeview Publishing Company.

13. "Cognitivism about Practical Reason," *Ethics* 102 (1991): 117–128. Reprinted by permission of The University of Chicago Press (© 1991 by The University of Chicago. All rights reserved.)

14. "Review of Korsgaard's *The Sources of Normativity*," *Philosophy and Phenomenological Research* 58 (1998): 699–709. By permission of *Philosophy and Phenomenological Research*.

1

Introduction: Planning Agents in a Social World

I

We are planning agents. Our purposive activity is typically embedded in multiple, interwoven quilts of partial, future-directed plans of action. We settle in advance on such plans of action, fill them in, adjust them, and follow through with them as time goes by. We thereby support complex forms of organization in our own, temporally extended lives and in our interactions with others; and we do this in ways that are sensitive to the limits on our cognitive resources. These facts are, I believe, an important key to an adequate philosophical treatment of (1) the very idea of intention, (2) basic features of our agency, (3) important forms of shared agency, and (4) important forms of responsible agency.

I discussed planning agency, and its significance to (1) and (2), in my 1987 book, *Intention, Plans, and Practical Reason*.[1] Since then I have tried to elaborate and to deepen this approach, to extend it to (3) and to (4), and to explore its relations to the work of others. The present volume of previously published work includes eleven essays

Thanks to Elijah Millgram for comments on an earlier draft of this Introduction. It was completed while I was a Fellow at the Center for Advanced Study in Behavioral Sciences. I am grateful for financial support provided by The Andrew W. Mellon Foundation.

1 Cambridge, MA: Harvard University Press, 1987. My work was influenced particularly by work of Gilbert Harman. See p. 177, n. 22, for references.

that were the result of this effort, as well as a pair of earlier critical studies that also seemed useful to include.

At the heart of my theory is a model of our planning agency and the attempt to use it to understand intention. I call this the *planning theory of intention*. The main idea is to see intentions as elements of stable, partial plans of action concerning present and future conduct. In settling on prior, partial plans of action we commit ourselves to future conduct in ways that help support important forms of coordination and organization, both over time and interpersonally. A basic problem is to explain the nature of such commitments. Future-directed intentions and plans are, after all, revocable: They do not control one's future conduct by way of some mysterious action at a distance; and many times, in the face of new and relevant information, we recognize that it would be folly to stick rigidly with our prior intention. So in exactly what sense am I now committed to later action when I settle now on a plan so to act then?[2]

One might try to appeal to interpersonal commitments of the sort involved in assurances and promises, and then see intention as a kind of internalization of such social commitments. But, as Donald Davidson has argued, there is a basic disanalogy, since promising and the like involve a public act in a way in which intending need not.[3] Further, there seems strong pressure to have future-directed intentions and plans even before we consider the social. There are good reasons for Robinson Crusoe on a desert island to plan for the future. This suggests that we try to characterize basic structures of planning agency, including characteristic commitments to future conduct, without seeing social commitments as prior and more basic.[4]

But then we are back to our question: What is this present com-

---

2 See *Intention, Plans, and Practical Reason*, p. 5.

3 See his "Intending" in his *Essays on Actions and Events* (New York: Oxford University Press, 1980), p. 90. In this passage, however, Davidson also seems to suggest that there is *no* problem raised by a person who had intended to act in a certain way and "simply changed his mind." This runs the danger of hiding from view the kind of commitment over time I am trying to understand.

4 There may still be important analogies, or theoretical commonalities, between intending and acts like commanding, ordering, requesting. Indeed, such a purported theoretical commonality is central to Hector-Neri Castañeda's theory of intention,

mitment to future conduct? The planning theory aims to answer this and other, related questions. Here are some of the main ideas.[5]

Plans of action typically have a hierarchical structure: Ends embed means and preliminary steps, and general intentions embed more specific intentions. Such hierarchically structured plans are typically partial – we do not need, and usually do not want, to settle on a completely specified plan before beginning to act. This means that our plans will typically need to be filled in as time goes by and as new information is available. Failure to fill in plans as need be can lead to means–end incoherence. Given the need to avoid such incoherence, prior plans pose problems for further deliberation. They thereby establish standards of relevance for options considered in deliberation.

Prior plans also provide a filter on options to be considered in such further reasoning. This is because one's plans need to be both internally consistent and consistent with one's beliefs, since either kind of inconsistency can be expected to undermine coordination. In posing problems for further deliberation and in filtering options to be considered in that deliberation, prior, partial plans provide a background framework within which much deliberation takes place. This background framework helps make our deliberation more tractable.

which I discuss in essay 12. Such a commonality is expressed in his theory through the apparatus of "practitions."

5 Further details can be found in my *Intention, Plans, and Practical Reason*. Among the ideas in that book that I do not explicitly touch on here, but that are occasionally in the background in the essays that follow, are my rejection of the "simple view" of the relation between intention and intentional action in chapters 8 and 9, and my account of the distinction between what one intends and what one only expects to result from what one intends, in chapter 10. The former idea is especially important to the project of providing a general theory of intention, not solely a theory of intending. The latter account may be of use in thinking through basic issues in moral psychology raised by the Principle of Double Effect.

David J. Israel, Martha E. Pollack, and I have explored possible applications of aspects of the planning theory to related problems in artificial intelligence. See our "Plans and Resource-Bounded Practical Reasoning," in Robert Cummins and John Pollock, eds., *Philosophy and AI: Essays at the Interface* (Cambridge: Bradford/ MIT Press, 1991), pp. 7–22. See also Martha E. Pollack, "Overloading Intentions for Efficient Practical Reasoning," *Noûs* 25 (1991): 513–536, and id. "The Uses of Plans," *Artificial Intelligence* 57 (1992): 43–68.

The provision of such a background framework is part of the story of the commitment characteristic of intention; it explains how intentions and plans impose structure on practical reasoning. But this is not yet the whole story. Such a background framework, if it did not have a characteristic stability, would not amount to a commitment to action of the sort with which we are concerned – a commitment to action not just at a time but also over time.

Here we face the problem of providing a systematic account of reasonable stability. This was a main focus of Chapters 5 and 6 of *Intention, Plans, and Practical Reason.* My discussion there focused primarily on what I called the nonreflective reconsideration or non-reconsideration of a prior intention in the face of new and unanticipated information. Such cases are typical for agents who, like us, have needs for coordination but significant limits on their capacity constantly to be reconsidering complex prior plans and engaging in associated replanning. In that discussion I presented a two-tier, pragmatic theory – a theory I saw as part of what Herbert Simon had called the theory of bounded rationality.[6] We need general habits, strategies, and policies concerning such nonreflective (non)reconsideration. We can assess such general mechanisms in terms of their expected impact on our achieving what we (rationally) desire, given our needs for coordination and our cognitive limitations. We can then see the rationality of a particular case of nonreflective (non)reconsideration of a prior intention as dependent on the acceptability of the underlying general mechanism.

The problem is that it is not clear how to extend such an approach to important cases in which issues about our cognitive limitations are not germane and the challenge to a prior intention does not depend on unanticipated information. A simple extension of such a two-tier approach runs the risk of failing to respect the fact that a planning agent has rational control at the time of plan execution: Following through with a plan is not, as I say, like following through with a tennis swing. This problem is implicit in essay 3 and is the problem I try to take some steps toward solving in essay 4.

6 See, e.g., his *Reason in Human Affairs* (Stanford: Stanford University Press, 1983).

Let me now try to identify some further, broad themes of my approach to planning agency.

First, structures of planning agency of the sort I am trying to describe are basic and, perhaps, distinctive aspects of our agency. Many animals, human and nonhuman, are purposive agents – agents who pursue goals in light of their representations of the world. But we – normal adult human agents in a modern world – are not merely purposive agents in this generic sense. Our agency is typically embedded in planning structures.

Second, appeal to such planning structures allows us to articulate basic features of intention and decision, features that distinguish such phenomena both from belief and from ordinary desire. We characterize important and distinctive roles of intention and decision in shaping ongoing reasoning and action without appealing, as Davidson says, to "mysterious acts of the will."[7] In this way the planning theory provides the basis of a modest, nonmysterious theory of the will.

Third, such planning structures are universal means: useful in the pursuit of a wide range of ends whose complexity requires levels of organization and coordination made possible by planning agency. Indeed, as Elijah Millgram has emphasized, our planning capacities are frequently presupposed by the very specification of what we desire.[8]

---

7 "Intending" in his *Essays on Actions and Events*, p. 83.

8 Millgram makes this last point in an unpublished lecture. Millgram notes that this means that we should not see our planning capacities merely as means to ends we could have independently of those capacities. I agree, though I would want to note that there will also be desired ends in common between a planning and a nonplanning agent. When I say planning capacities are universal means I am not only trying to convince a nonplanning agent to become a planning agent. I am also, in part, trying to contribute to what, following T. M. Scanlon, we can call a planning agent's "enterprise . . . of self-understanding." I am trying to highlight ways in which a planning agent's planning capacities contribute to her ends, for a very wide range of ends and including ends whose very specification presupposes such capacities. [The quote is from Scanlon's discussion of the question "Why be moral?" in his "Self-Anchored Morality," in J. B. Schneewind, ed., *Reasons, Ethics, and Society:*

(Consider, for example, a desire to write a book.) We can agree on the significance to a good human life of such planning structures without agreeing on a particular, substantive conception of a good human life. Planning abilities are, then, candidates for the role of a primary good in a liberal political theory.[9]

A theory of planning agency is in large part a theory of rational planning agency and so will interact in complex ways with general issues about the nature and scope of practical reason. My strategy here, and this is my fourth theme, is to pursue a theory of rational planning agency that is to a large extent end-neutral. I seek to articulate rational structures of planning agency that apply to agents like us even given wide differences in specific, substantive conceptions of the good. I see demands for the coherence and consistency of plans as rational demands of this sort; and in seeking a theory of reasonable stability I seek a theory that is broadly end-neutral in this sense. I try to take no stand on the basic issue of whether practical reason, by itself, mandates specific ends or moral constraints. My aim is to provide a theoretical story about planning agency that is, in its essentials, neutral with respect to this fundamental issue.[10]

A theory of planning agency of the sort to which I am pointing is both similar to and different from theories that emphasize, along lines developed by Harry Frankfurt, our capacities critically to reflect on

---

Themes from Kurt Baier, with His Responses (Chicago: Open Court, 1996), pp. 197–209, at p. 198. In my remarks here I am indebted to this discussion.]

9 See John Rawls, *A Theory of Justice* (Cambridge: Harvard University Press, 1971), esp. pp. 92–93. This last sentence benefited from discussion with Bruce Ackerman.

10 See *Intention, Plans, and Practical Reason*, p. 22. Note that my remarks in these last two sentences are about practical reason quite generally, not about solely instrumental practical reason. Note also that my discussions of planning agency are not neutral with respect to the question of whether all practical reasoning is instrumental reasoning about how to achieve what one desires. It is my view that planning introduces further structures of practical reasoning. R. Jay Wallace notes the need to consider questions about "the explanatory *role* that desire plays in forms of practical reasoning that are neither instrumental nor maximizing but nevertheless, in some sense, begin from an agent's desires." ["How to Argue About Practical Reason," *Mind* (1990): 350–385, at p. 381.] I see the planning theory as a partial response to such questions.

our desires.[11] I seek to articulate structures of our rational agency that are basic but whose presence is compatible with diverging conceptions of the good. In this respect my approach is similar in spirit to Frankfurt's. However, whereas theories that focus on such critical reflection tend at least initially to focus on structures present at a given time, an emphasis on our planning agency leads us to focus on processes of commitment and planning over time. Of course, in the end these theoretical programs should be compatible with and support each other, since we are both planning agents and agents who reflect critically on our motivation. Indeed, it is a conjecture of essay 10 that a certain kind of decision or policy[12] – and so a certain kind of intention – plays an important role in such critical reflection.

A sixth theme is that we can expect to find structures of planning agency embedded in other important forms of our agency. In particular, we sometimes engage in forms of shared intentional activity, and we think of ourselves as responsible agents. A fruitful theory of our planning agency should help us say more about these further dimensions of our agency. It should articulate basic features of our agency that are significantly engaged in shared intentional agency and in what we take to be responsible agency. A theory of our planning agency should, that is, serve as a theoretical kernel, a kernel common to broader accounts of these other important forms of our agency.

Reflection on shared intentional agency reminds us that much planning plays a social role and is associated with commitments to others of a sort that are typically grounded in assurances and promises. As noted, I try to say what individual planning agency is without seeing it as, at bottom, a kind of internalization of such social commitments. This leaves open the question of how such social commitments are related to commitments involved in ordinary, individual

---

11 See Harry Frankfurt, *The Importance of What We Care About* (Cambridge: Cambridge University Press, 1988). I discuss Frankfurt's work in essay 10. My thinking about the relation between Frankfurt's work and my own has been aided by conversation with Bruce Ackerman.

12 I see policies as intentions that are appropriately general with respect to their occasions of execution. See *Intention, Plans, and Practical Reason*, pp. 87–91, and my "Intention and Personal Policies," *Philosophical Perspectives* III (1989): 443–469.

intentions and plans. My seventh theme favors a modest theory of planning (as well as the modest theory of the will alluded to earlier). Such a theory does not try to derive basic forms of interpersonal commitment and obligation directly from structures of planning agency.[13] Instead, it holds that the grounds of such social commitments require further principles of obligation – for example, principles of assurance-based obligation. To get at such interpersonal obligations and commitments we will need to do some more moral philosophy.

III

The essays that follow fall into four parts. Essays 2 through 4 aim to expand the 1987 theory of the intentions and plans of individuals. Essay 2 considers the place in intelligent planning agency of a cognitive attitude of acceptance in a context, an attitude that differs in important ways from belief. Essays 3 and 4 return to questions about the stability of intention. There are roughly two sets of issues here. There are, first, issues about reasonable stability in the face of new information and given limitations on our resources for reasoning and replanning. As noted, this is the target of my pragmatic, two-tier theory. Second, there are issues about the stability of a prior intention that arise in certain cases in which things are just as the agent had envisaged them when she formed the intention in the first place, and issues about our limited capacities for reconsideration and replanning do not arise. These latter cases include both cases of anticipated temptation and cases (like Kavka's toxin case) in which there are potential benefits that would result from having an intention, but would not be a result of the execution of that intention. The second set of issues constitutes my main concern in essays 3 and 4. Here I seek a view of intention commitment and stability that has the following features. First, it respects the fact that a planning agent is not only a planner, she is also a temporally and causally located agent. This argues against a straightforward extension to these cases of the pragmatic two-tier

---

13 Though it encourages the conjecture that there are important interrelations, as I note briefly in my discussion of work of Thomas Scanlon in essay 7.

theory of plan stability. Second, it stays within end-neutral, instrumental practical reason. Third, it sometimes endorses the formation and retention of a general policy – for example, a policy to limit oneself to one drink at dinner – as a reasonable response to temptation. It is, however, difficult to put these three ideas together within a single view. (George Ainslie's theory can be seen as an attempt to do this for temptation cases, but I argue in essay 3 that it does not succeed.) I argue in essay 4 that we can do this by appeal to the significance to a planning agent of certain forms of future regret.

Essays 5 through 8 study shared agency. They attempt to draw on ideas from the planning theory of the intentions of individuals to provide useful conceptions of shared intention, shared intentional activity, and shared cooperative activity. The basic phenomenon, I conjecture, is shared intention – our shared intention, for example, to sing a duet together, or to have a conversation together. I argue, roughly, that such a shared intention consists in a public, interlocking web of appropriate intentions of the individuals. Shared intentional activity is activity suitably explainable by a shared intention and associated forms of mutual responsiveness. Shared cooperative activity requires, in addition, the absence of certain forms of coercion and commitments to mutual support in the pursuit of the joint activity.[14] Essay 5 develops this conception of shared cooperative activity; and essay 6 makes explicit and defends the underlying conception of shared intention. Both envisage a complex but modest story about the relation between shared intention and associated obligations, a story further defended in essay 7. Both draw on an appeal to the idea that I may intend that *we* act in a certain way. Essay 8 defends this appeal.[15]

---

14 My initial thinking about these matters benefited in particular from John Searle's essay "Collective Intentions and Actions," in Philip R. Cohen, Jerry Morgan, and Martha E. Pollack, eds., *Intentions in Communication* (Cambridge: MIT Press, 1990), pp. 401–415. I note differences in our views in various footnotes in essays 5, 6, and 8. For a wonderful example of shared cooperative activity in which barely a word is said, see Wallace Stegner's story, "Saw Gang," in *Collected Stories of Wallace Stegner* (New York: Penguin Books, 1991), pp. 69–74.

15 For a related discussion in the context of research in artificial intelligence, see Barbara J. Grosz, "Collaborative Systems" (AAAI-94 Presidential Address), *AI Magazine* (1996): 67–85.

Essay 9 asks how our capacities for planning agency are involved in our being (to borrow a phrase of Susan Wolf's) deeply responsible agents. It argues that there are important connections here, connections supported by reflection on Peter Strawson's observations about the significance of our capacities for participation in "ordinary interpersonal relationships." Essay 10 focuses on a different idea, but one that may well be important to our understanding of responsible agency, namely the idea of identification, as it has been discussed primarily by Harry Frankfurt. Here, drawing on an aspect of work of T. M. Scanlon, I argue for the importance of phenomena of deciding to treat, or having a policy of treating, a desire as a reason in one's practical reasoning and planning.[16] In the background is the idea that we can shed light on the nature of such decisions and policies by exploiting the resources of the planning theory of intention.

The fourth part consists of a quartet of studies of important alternative treatments of intention and agency. Donald Davidson sees practical reasoning as primarily a matter of weighing conflicting evaluative considerations for and against different courses of action. Intention is a special kind of evaluation that can be a conclusion of such (nondeductive) reasoning. Perhaps my most basic concern with this view is noted at the end of essay 11: It provides an apparently quite limited story concerning the role of prior intentions and plans as inputs to further practical reasoning.[17]

Hector-Neri Castañeda, in contrast with Davidson, saw intending as the basic first-personal practical attitude – a practical analogue to belief – and emphasized its role as input to practical reasoning.[18] Essay

16 I explore further developments in a work in progress tentatively titled "Reflection, Planning, and Temporally Extended Agency."

17 But see Davidson's reply to my paper in Bruce Vermazen and Merrill B. Hintikka, eds., *Essays on Davidson: Actions and Events* (Oxford: Oxford University Press, 1985), and my response in an appendix added to my paper when it was reprinted in *Companion to Action and Events*, edited by Ernest LePore and Brian McLaughlin (Oxford: Basil Blackwell, 1986), pp. 14–28. See also Olav Gjelsvik, "Intention and Alternatives," *Philosophical Studies* 82 (1996): 159–177. (My use of "future intention" in this essay on Davidson corresponds to my use of "future-directed intention" in my later work.)

18 Christine Korsgaard has a somewhat similar view of intending, rather than desir-

12 discusses Castañeda's theory in detail and offers some criticisms.[19] Here I add two general remarks. The first is that Castañeda's theory is primarily concerned with what one's intentions at a time commit one to at that time, and does not directly grapple with the idea that intending involves a commitment over time. Second, in my judgment Castañeda did not provide an adequate story of how reasoning whose primary inputs are prior intentions is connected with the sort of practical reasoning emphasized by Davidson (and those in the tradition of so-called decision theory), namely, the weighing of reasons provided by conflicting desires and values. My planning theory tries to make room for both kinds of practical reasoning and to explain how they are related: Prior intentions and plans provide a (normally) stable background framework within which one weighs reasons provided by conflicting desires and values.[20]

J. David Velleman and I agree that intentions and planning are basic features of our agency. But Velleman, in his 1989 book, tries to develop this theme within an approach I label "cognitivism about practical reason." In essay 13, I try to explain what seem to me to be important difficulties for this approach.[21]

Essay 14 discusses Christine Korsgaard's sketch of a broadly Kantian view of the will, as part of her Kantian account of reflective endorsement and of "the sources of normativity." Korsgaard highlights two main views in the theory of action: first, a Humean view that sees desires as causes of action, and the will as at most a by-

ing, as the basic first-personal practical attitude. See her "The Normativity of Instrumental Reason," in Garrett Cullity and Berys Gaut, eds., *Ethics and Practical Reason* (Oxford: Oxford University Press, 1997), pp. 215–254, at pp. 248–9 n.69.

19 For Castañeda's responses see his "Reply to Michael Bratman: Deontic Truth, Intentions, and Weakness of the Will," in James E. Tomberlin, ed., *Agent, Language and the Structure of the World* (Indianapolis: Hackett, 1983), pp. 395–409.

20 See *Intention, Plans, and Practical Reason*, p. 35.

21 But see Gideon Yaffe's response on behalf of Velleman in "Velleman on Intentions as Reasons for Action," *Analysis* 55 (1995): 107–115. Velleman's views have developed in important ways since his 1989 book. See for example his "The Possibility of Practical Reason," *Ethics* 106 (1996): 694–726 – pages 719–726 are directly relevant to my concerns. It is not clear to me, however, whether developments and clarifications indicated there solve the problems I point to in essay 13.

product of the underlying causal processes; and, second, a Kantian view that emphasizes the role of the agent, the will, and universal principles of action in the reflective endorsement of desires as potential grounds for action. Now, Davidson's theory might well be seen as a sophisticated representative of the Humean tradition. But I think that certain other approaches discussed in these essays do not fit well into either category. I think, in particular, this is true of the planning theory (and its modest theory of the will) and Frankfurt's views about identification and agency. Such views may provide materials for a theory of agency and the will located in the territory between Humean and Kantian approaches. This, anyway, is a conjecture I plan to explore in future research.

IV

I collect these essays under one cover because there seems to me to be a broad coherence in their overall conception and a synergy in their philosophical impact. Though there are significant tensions and gaps – and no doubt many underdiscussed and unresolved issues – I believe that the essays go some way toward filling in, extending, and deepening the theory described in my 1987 book. I see these essays and the earlier book, taken together, as providing an argument for the fecundity of the basic approach to intention and planning agency. What emerges, I think, is an outline of a useful framework for understanding important features of our temporally extended and socially interlocking agency.

PART ONE

ACCEPTANCE AND STABILITY

2

Practical Reasoning and Acceptance in a Context

In practical reasoning and action we seek to realize our intentions and satisfy our desires in the light of what we believe. Or so we are taught to say. In this essay I question the last clause and suggest that the cognitive attitudes guiding practical reasoning and action go beyond our beliefs. I begin by locating my problem within the planning conception of practical reasoning I have developed elsewhere (Bratman 1987).

I. PRIOR PLANS AND THE BACKGROUND OF DELIBERATION

As I see it, prior intentions and partial plans play central roles as inputs into the practical reasoning and action of intelligent agents like us: agents with serious resource limitations and with basic needs for coordination, both social and intrapersonal. In particular, prior plans

Thanks to A. Appiah, D. Brink, M. Crimmins, F. Dretske, R. Fogelin, R. Foley, P. Greenspan, J. Heil, D. Israel, H. Kyburg, A. MacIntyre, R. Moran, M. Pollack, J. Pollock, J. Raz, and audiences at the University of Maryland, Cornell University, the University of Miami, the 1988 AAAI workshop at Stanford University on models of limited rationality, and the Rational Agency working group at CSLI. I was particularly helped by Carl Ginet, who served as commentator when I presented an earlier version of this essay at Cornell University in 1988. My research was supported, in part, by the Center for the Study of Language and Information and by the Stanford Humanities Center. Support from the Center for the Study of Language and Information was made possible in part through an award from the System Development Foundation.

structure and guide further practical reasoning in two major ways. First, one's plans are subject to demands for coherence, given one's beliefs.[1] Prior plans are typically partial, but as time goes by they must be filled in in appropriate ways in order to avoid incoherence. Second, one's plans need to be consistent both internally and with one's beliefs. These consistency constraints create a filter on options to be considered in further deliberation as potential solutions to problems posed by threats of incoherence in one's partial plans.

This gives us a three-stage model of practical reasoning. First, one's prior partial plans generate problems, given threats of incoherence. Second, one tries to specify options that would be at least partial solutions to the problems posed and would satisfy the cited consistency constraints. Third, one engages in deliberation aimed at deciding between these options. Decision theory, as traditionally conceived, tends to focus solely on this last stage, the stage of deliberation. But once we take seriously the role of prior partial plans as inputs to further reasoning we need more carefully to model the stages that lie behind and frame such deliberation.

Here is a humdrum example: My plan for today includes reading a certain book tonight, in preparation for my seminar tomorrow. But I know that I do not at present have a copy of this book; so I must somehow build into my plans a sub-plan for getting the book – say, by stopping at the bookstore on the way home from school, or by going to the library after dinner. Further, since I plan to meet with you at lunch today, I cannot solve my problem about the book by planning to skip lunch and take a trip to the bookstore then. In this way demands for coherence and consistency lead me to a set of options among which I deliberate.

Suppose I deliberate between stopping at the bookstore on the way home and going to the library after dinner. In this deliberation I may well be concerned with the likelihood of the needed book being at the bookstore or the library. But there are other propositions that I will not think about in this broadly probabilistic way. Consider the proposition that my seminar is tomorrow. In my deliberation I simply take that for granted. This assumption is part of the cognitive back-

---

1 I called this "means–end coherence" in Bratman (1987).

ground that, together with my plans, frames my deliberation. And I treat the proposition that I do not now have the needed book in a similar fashion. I *take these things for granted* in my deliberation; I *accept* these propositions in the cognitive background of my deliberation. It is in part because I accept these propositions that I find myself faced with a practical problem.

What is it to take something for granted, to accept it, in the background of one's deliberation? In Bratman (1987), esp. §§3.2–3.4, I assumed that what one takes for granted in this way one believes, and I called such belief "flat-out belief." I now think that this supposition is overly simple and hides important complexities. In this essay I want to say why and to sketch an alternative way of thinking about the cognitive background of deliberation.[2] Before I can do this, however, I need to say more about belief.

II. BELIEF

I have beliefs about what books I own, about the day of my seminar, about the weather. I want a relatively noncontroversial list of features of belief. Before trying to provide such a list, however, I need to note an issue that I will not try to resolve.

We sometimes think about belief as an all-or-none affair, and sometimes as essentially a matter of degree. It may seem most natural to characterize my belief that my seminar is tomorrow as all-or-none. In contrast, it may seem more natural to think of my expectation of rain this afternoon as essentially a matter of degree – as a degree of confidence between 0 and 1. It is tempting to assume that one of these belief-like phenomena is somehow basic and that talk about the other is in some way derivative. Harman (1986, chap. 3), for example, thinks of all-or-none belief as basic;[3] whereas Bayesian decision theorists tend to see degrees of confidence, represented by subjective probabilities, as basic. It seems to me that both of these ways of classifying cognitive phenomena have their uses and that it is a mis-

2 My discussion owes much to Robert Stalnaker's suggestive discussion in Stalnaker (1984, chap. 5).

3 More precisely, Harman sees all-or-none "explicit" belief in this way.

17

take to try to reduce one to the other. Here I will simply refrain from any assumption that either is ultimately more basic than the other. In speaking of an agent's beliefs, then, I will include talk both of all-or-none belief and of degrees of confidence. I want to try to lay out what seem to me to be four quite general and interrelated features of belief, even given this flexibility.

(i) Reasonable belief is, in an important way, context independent: at any one time a reasonable agent normally either believes something (to degree n) or does not believe it (to that degree). She does not at the same time believe that p relative to one context but not relative to another.[4] Of course, one's beliefs can change as one moves from one context to another. Richmond Thomason (1986, p. 345) discusses an example of someone who, when he thinks about dentist appointments, believes he has a dentist appointment on Friday, but when he thinks about Friday does not believe this.[5] But such changes

4 Granted, we sometimes specify what a person believes in ways that involve a kind of context relativity. If I say "Sue believes that the book was here" what I am claiming that Sue believes will vary with my spatio-temporal location. But this is a context relativity in the way I specify what Sue believes, not in Sue's attitude itself. More complex issues are raised by the suggestion that whether Sue assents to a proposition may depend on the sentence used, in the context, to express that proposition. In John Perry's example, if I ask Sue whether the meeting is at noon she will say yes; if I ask her whether the meeting is now she will say no; and yet it is now noon (Perry 1979). Such examples lead Perry to distinguish Sue's "belief states" – which correspond to sentences she would use in her context to express what she believes – and "what [she] thereby believes" (p. 18). If we follow Perry here we would need to express the point about the context-independence of belief in a more guarded way. We would need to say that once we fix both on a proposition and on an associated belief state, a rational agent will either believe (to a given degree) that proposition by way of being in that belief state or she will not. These qualifications noted, I will help myself to the simpler way of speaking and talk only of what it is that is believed; for the issues of indexicality that lie behind Perry's distinction, while fundamental, are orthogonal to present concerns.

5 It will be clear from my discussion below that, while I am sympathetic to Thomason's emphasis on "context-sensitivity," I think it is a mistake to locate reasonable relativity to context in belief, strictly speaking, rather than in what I will be calling acceptance. Still, my discussion has benefited from Thomason's paper.

will likely get this person in trouble in his planning, and are not a case of *reasonably* believing that *p* in one context but not in another. My advice to this person would be to wear a string round his finger to remind him of his appointment, even when he is thinking about Friday. Or again, perhaps I earlier believed that I had a copy of the book at home and now no longer believe it. But this is a change of mind; it is not that I now believe this relative to one context but not relative to another.

(ii) Reasonable belief is shaped primarily by evidence for what is believed and concern for the truth of what is believed. Thus the slogan: belief aims at truth. Normally, if one's belief is shaped not by a concern for its truth but instead by what one wants to be the case one is subject to criticism for wishful thinking or its kin.[6]

(iii) Belief is not normally subject to direct voluntary control. We do not normally just choose our beliefs. As Bernard Williams (1973) has emphasized this is not just a contingent limitation of the will; it is not like our inability directly to raise our hair. It is tied, rather, to the ways in which belief aims at truth. If I could just choose what to believe at will I could do so independent of whether the content of that belief is true. But if I know of an attitude of mine that it is not shaped by a concern with the truth of its content it seems I could not regard it as a belief.

(iv) An agent's beliefs are subject to an ideal of integration. Other things equal one should be able to agglomerate one's various beliefs into a larger, overall view; and this larger view should satisfy demands for consistency and coherence.

I offer these four conditions as ones that are part and parcel of our ordinary conception of belief – be it all-or-none or a matter of degree. While more could be said about each of these conditions, for

6 J. David Velleman has argued forcefully that these issues, and those discussed below in *(iii)*, become more complex when we consider certain kinds of self-fulfilling predictions. But I will not try to address these complexities here. See Velleman (1989) and my discussion in Bratman (1991).

present purposes what I have said should suffice. My claim is that when we look at the framing of the deliberation of intelligent agents like us we discover at work a cognitive attitude that diverges from belief with respect to these general features. In particular, we discover a cognitive attitude that exhibits an important context-relativity.

III. VARIETIES OF ACCEPTANCE

Return to the phenomenon of taking something for granted in the cognitive background of one's deliberation. Could this just be belief? If we see beliefs as, at bottom, degrees of confidence, and treat such degrees of confidence as subjective probabilities, then this becomes the question of whether to take it for granted that p is to assign p a probability of 1. And the answer seems to be "no." I take it for granted in the background of my deliberation that my seminar is tomorrow. But about this I am not, in the requisite sense, certain: I would not bet the farm on this proposition should you offer me such a bet.

But what if we are willing to talk about ordinary all-or-none beliefs that need not involve certainty? In this sense I believe that my seminar is tomorrow, that there is a university library, and so on. Is taking it for granted that p in the background of my deliberation simply having an all-or-none belief that p? I think not. This is primarily because what we reasonably take for granted, in contrast with what we believe, can vary across different contexts and be in part shaped by various practical considerations.

Let me begin with a general statement of the view I will defend. There are various kinds of practical pressures for accepting a given proposition in the background of one's deliberation. These pressures are context-relative in the sense that they apply in only some of the practical contexts in which this proposition is relevant. Such pressures can sometimes make it reasonable for an agent to accept a proposition in a given context, even though she reasonably would not (or, indeed, does not) accept that proposition in a different context in which it is relevant.[7] Such reasonable acceptance need not include all of

---

7 Stalnaker makes a similar point: "A person may accept something in one context, while rejecting it or suspending judgment in another. There need be no conflict

what one believes; nor need it be limited to what one believes; nor can it be identified with mere supposition; nor is it mere pretence. We need to distinguish such context-relative acceptance from belief, and we need to make room for both in our model of practical reasoning.[8]

Or, anyway, that is my conjecture. My argument proceeds by considering a series of examples, examples illustrating a range of practical but context-relative pressures on acceptance. I will classify these examples in terms of the different practical pressures they illustrate. In each case my example echoes similar examples in the literature: I make no claim to originality here. The contribution I hope to make is to provide a natural and plausible way of thinking about practical reasoning and planning that does justice to such cases.

1. Simplification of One's Reasoning

Strategies of reasoning that simplify and thereby help us economize in our use of scarce reasoning resources have an obvious attractiveness.[9] One such strategy involves acceptance in a context, as illustrated by the following example:

---

that must be resolved when the difference is noticed, and he need not change his mind when he moves from one context to another" (Stalnaker 1984, pp. 80–81).

8 van Fraassen (1980) emphasizes a distinction between believing that a scientific theory is true and accepting that theory. In van Fraassen's view, to accept a theory "*involves as belief only that it is empirically adequate*" (p. 12); but acceptance of a scientific theory also involves a commitment to a corresponding research program. van Fraassen's distinction concerns our cognitive attitudes toward scientific theories and is not intended to apply to our views "about the observable things and events in this world" (p. 12). In contrast, it is primarily with respect to more or less observable phenomena that I want to distinguish belief from acceptance. In the main examples to follow, all – with the exception of example (8) – concern matters that are clearly observable in the relevant sense.

9 A point emphasized by Harman (1986). John Harsanyi (1985) develops a similar point. Harsanyi sees strategies of simplification as aimed at already formed decision problems. In my view, however, simplification can enter into the prior stages of practical reasoning in which problems are posed and options specified, thereby shaping the basic structure of the decision problem itself.

(1) In planning my day – a June day in Palo Alto – I simply take it for granted that it will not rain even though I am not certain about this. If I were instead figuring out at what odds I would accept a monetary bet from you on the weather I would not simply take it for granted that it will not rain. But in my present circumstances taking this for granted simplifies my planning in a way that is useful, given my limited resources for reasoning.

In this example, largely because of practical pressures in favor of simplification, what I accept/take for granted reasonably varies across different practical contexts. Perhaps I find myself in these different contexts at different times in the day, and what I accept shifts as I change contexts. Perhaps I even move back and forth from planning my day to betting with you. In the former context I accept that the weather will be good; in the latter context I do not. It is not that I have a context-independent cognitive attitude that keeps changing; instead, I accept something relative to one context that I do not accept relative to another.

This example does not, however, show that we accept things we do not believe. It may seem reasonable to say that I flat-out believe that there will be no rain, that this belief helps frame my planning for today, but that, reasonably enough, it does not frame my reasoning about the bet. So we need to turn to a second example.

2. Asymmetries in the Costs of Errors[10]

(2) I am planning for a major construction project to begin next month. I need to decide now whether to do the entire project at once or instead to break the project into two parts, to be executed separately. The rationale for the second strategy is that I am unsure whether I presently have the financial re-

10 Such pressures are discussed in Ullmann-Margalit (1983). Ullmann-Margalit argues that "presumption rules" are typically grounded in part in "the differential acceptability of the relevant sorts of expected errors . . ." (p. 162). Thomason (1986, pp. 343–4) suggests that pressures of risks typically shape what one believes; I claim, instead, that such pressures typically shape what one accepts in the context.

sources to do the whole thing at once. I know that in the case of each subcontractor – carpenter, plumber, and so on – it is only possible at present to get an estimate of the range of potential costs. In the face of this uncertainty I proceed in a cautious way: In the case of each subcontractor I take it for granted that the total costs will be at the top of the estimated range. On the basis of these assumptions I determine whether I have at present enough money to do the whole project at once. In contrast, if you offered me a bet on the actual total cost of the project – the winner being the person whose guess is closest to the actual total – I would reason differently.

In this example I take for granted, in a certain practical context, something which I do not believe. Further, my taking the top of the estimated range for granted seems reasonable of me even though I would not take this for granted in a different context. I proceed in this way largely because of my uncertainty and the high costs of certain kinds of errors in prediction. Of course, I thereby run an increased risk of unnecessarily delaying the completion of my project. But I have made a judgment that the error of going ahead with the total project when it turns out to cost too much is less acceptable than the error of not going ahead when I could in fact have afforded to.[11] When I bet with you on the actual total cost, in contrast, there isn't such an asymmetry; for here there is no relevant difference between errors of overestimating and errors of underestimating the costs.

In a variant of this example,[12] a cautious strategy is supported also by my special concerns about the reliability in the context of my own reasoning powers:

(3) I am called on to make the decision described in (2) in the evening after a difficult day. My doubts about my abilities in

11 Another example, which makes a similar point, comes from John Horty, who attributes it to John McCarthy: Driving down a narrow, winding mountain road it is wise to assume that there is a car coming up on the opposite side even if you do not believe this. Here again there is an obvious asymmetry in the costs of errors.

12 Derived from an example used for different purposes in Raz (1975, p. 485).

such circumstances fully to comprehend all the complexities lead me to a cautious strategy: I reason on the assumption that the costs from each subcontractor will be at the top of the estimated range.

Here again what I take for granted in the context is not something I believe in a context-independent way. And I might well not have taken this for granted in a different context.

A related example makes it clear that reasonable acceptance in such cases really is affected by asymmetries in the costs of errors, and not solely by relevant degrees of confidence:

(4) I have a chair and a two-storey ladder. In each case I think it equally and highly likely that it is in good condition. Indeed, if you offered me a monetary bet about whether the chair/ladder was in good condition I would accept exactly the same odds for each object. But when I think about using the chair/ladder things change. When I consider using the chair I simply take it for granted that it is in working order; but when I am about to use the ladder I do not take this for granted.

When I am considering using the objects the differential costs of error with respect to a chair and a two-storey ladder explain differences in what I accept in the context. It is one thing to fall off a chair, another to fall off the top of a two-storey ladder.

3. Needs of Social Cooperation

Examples (1)–(4) highlight individualistic pressures for acceptance. But there can also be important social pressures:[13]

(5) The three of us need jointly to decide whether to build a house together. We agree to base our deliberations on the assumption that the total cost of the project will include the top of the estimated range offered by each of the subcontractors. We facilitate our group deliberations and decisions by agreeing

13 As Stalnaker emphasizes in Stalnaker (1984, p. 80). See also Stalnaker (1974).

24

on a common framework of assumptions. We each accept these assumptions in this context, the context of our group's deliberations, even though it may well be that none of us believes these assumptions or accepts them in other, more individualistic contexts.

4. Special Relations to Others

H. H. Price (1954, p. 14) notes that it has been "held that there was a moral obligation to believe that all the members of one's family were persons of the highest excellence, or at least of great excellence." Price tries to make sense of this idea (though in the end he is skeptical about such obligations on moral grounds) by interpreting it as an appeal to obligations to "direct one's attention" in ways that will support such beliefs (p. 18). John Heil (1992, p. 58) has suggested that such practical and moral considerations might also support raising one's relevant "doxastic thresholds, the point at which an appreciation of evidence carries over into belief" (see also Heil, 1983). In each case the concern is with the impact of such special relations on one's context-independent beliefs. In contrast, I want to consider the relevance of such special relations to context-relative acceptance. Here is an example once suggested to me by Michael Dummett:

> (6) My close friend has been accused of a terrible crime, the evidence of his guilt is strong, but my friend insists on his innocence. Despite the evidence of guilt, my close friendship may argue for assuming, in my ordinary practical reasoning and action, that he is innocent of the charge. In making plans for a dinner party, for example, such considerations of loyalty might make it reasonable for me to take his innocence for granted and so not use this issue to preclude inviting him. Yet if I find myself on the jury I may well think that I should not take his innocence for granted in that context for reasons of friendship.

So, again, we have context-relative acceptance driven by a certain practical concern, in this case a concern grounded in one's special relation to one's friend.

5. Pre-conditions for any Practical Reasoning at All

Paul Grice (1974) has suggested that there are kinds of conditions – such as simply being alive – which are assumed in the background of almost any planning even if the agent lacks strong reasons for confidence that those conditions will actually obtain. An example suggested to me by Thomas Hill helps make this point:

> (7) A soldier in a war zone has his doubts that he will make it through the day and expresses these doubts in a letter he writes in the morning. Nevertheless, after writing his letter he proceeds to make plans for his daily tour of the battlefield; and in so doing he takes it for granted that he will be around to execute these plans. After all, how else could he plan for the day? Since he needs to make such an assumption in order to get his planning off the ground, such acceptance may be reasonable even in the face of his doubts.

The soldier accepts that he will be around later in the day to execute his plans, despite his doubts about this proposition, and despite the fact that he does not accept this in the context of writing his letter. The main rationale for this acceptance is that he needs to take this for granted if he is to engage in planning for the day at all. Now, in engaging in such planning an agent needs to accept not only that she will be alive; she also needs to accept that what she will do is to some extent up to her. This leads us to a final, Kantian example:

> (8) Having reflected on issues about free will I am perplexed about whether I have it. Yet I still must on occasion deliberate about what to do. When I do I need to accept that what I will do is to some extent up to me. I need to accept that I have a kind of free will I do not believe I have. And it is hard to see how such acceptance could fail to be practically rational; for its absence would preclude any practical reasoning at all.[14]

14 So for someone with such philosophical doubts, acceptance in practical reasoning that she has free will can be a special case of the general phenomenon of acceptance that is driven by practical reasons.

26

IV. CONTEXT-RELATIVE ACCEPTANCE AND THE ADJUSTED COGNITIVE BACKGROUND

Examples (1)–(8) argue that there is an important phenomenon of acceptance that is context-relative in a way in which belief is not. I will not reasonably and at one and the same time believe that p relative to one context but not relative to another. In contrast, I might reasonably accept that p relative to one context but not relative to another. Such acceptance can be driven by a wide range of practical considerations, considerations that provide practical reasons for acceptance rather than evidence for the truth of what is accepted. And there can be a gap between such practical grounds for acceptance and the demands of theoretical reason on belief. One may believe (have a high degree of confidence in) a proposition and still reasonably not accept it in certain contexts. And even in the absence of belief (high degree of confidence) that p I can sometimes reasonably accept that p in an appropriate practical context.

Belief has four characteristic features: (a) it is, in the sense explained, context-independent; (b) it aims at the truth of what is believed; (c) it is not normally in our direct voluntary control; and (d) it is subject to an ideal of agglomeration. In contrast, what one accepts/takes for granted (a) can reasonably vary, in ways illustrated, across contexts; (b) can be influenced by practical considerations that are not themselves evidence for the truth of what is accepted; (c) can be subject to our direct voluntary control; and (d) is not subject to the same ideal of agglomeration across contexts. So acceptance in a context is not belief.

Is such context-relative acceptance mere pretense?[15] I do not think it is. In accepting that p I do not simply behave as if I think that p: I also reason on the assumption that p. So there is not the kind of indirect, circuitous connection between reasoning and action that is characteristic of presence. Nor is context-relative acceptance mere supposition.[16] "Suppose I had a million dollars," I ask myself. "What should I do with it?" Such a question may trigger contingency plan-

---

15 A query from both Carl Ginet and Alan Strudler.
16 Stalnaker, in contrast, sees mere supposition as a species of acceptance.

ning based on the mere supposition that I have such wealth. But this planning will not directly shape my action. If I conclude, for example, that with such wealth I should invest in General Motors my conclusion will not lead directly to my calling up my broker. In contrast, when I accept (in the context) that the costs will be at the top of the range I take this for granted in my reasoning about what to do, and this directly shapes my subsequent conduct. Context-relative acceptance is tied more directly to action than is mere supposition; and it is tied more directly to practical reasoning than is mere pretence.

A caveat: I have emphasized a distinction between an agent's context-independent and context-dependent cognitive attitudes. But I still can allow that the latter may be ultimately explainable by the former. Perhaps my acceptance that the project costs will be at the high end can itself be explained by various context-independent attitudes of mine, including my belief that given such asymmetric costs of error one should be cautious.[17] But to explain is not to explain away: such explanations would not show that context-relative acceptance is not psychologically important.

What one accepts in a context can be shaped by practical demands that should not in the same way shape one's context-independent beliefs. This challenges a theme in Levi (1980), for Levi rejects such a gap between the demands of practical reason on acceptance in a context and the demands of theoretical reason on degrees of confidence. Levi grants that an agent will typically treat some possible circumstances as non-serious possibilities. If in a certain context I treat the possibility of not-p as non-serious I am (to use my terminology) accepting, in that context, that p. Levi claims that a rational agent should "be committed to a single standard for serious possibility both for theoretical inquiry and for practical deliberation" (p. 16). So one should treat not-p as a non-serious possibility in a certain decision context (and so, in my terminology, accept p in that decision context) only if one adds p to the corpus of propositions to which one assigns a probability of 1 for purposes of theoretical inquiry. Practical pressures for acceptance should not override this constraint:

17 I was helped here by David Brink.

Once X's corpus at t is fixed, the distinction between what is and what is not a serious possibility according to X at t should be fixed. Variation in the problems X addresses and the goals and values he seeks to promote should not justify alteration of the distinction as long as the corpus remains fixed. (p. 4, note)

In contrast, I maintain that practical pressures can make it reasonable of me to accept that p in a certain practical context even if it is not reasonable of me to assign p a probability of 1 in my theoretical reflections.[18]

These reflections, taken together, suggest the following model of the cognitive background of deliberation. An agent's beliefs provide the *default cognitive background* for further deliberation and planning. This background has the quartet of properties I have cited as characteristic of belief. Most importantly, this cognitive background is, in the sense explained, context-independent. But practical reasoning admits of adjustments to this default cognitive background, adjustments in what one takes for granted in the specific practical context. Simply put, one may adjust the default cognitive background in two main ways: one may *posit* that p and take it for granted in one's practical context even though p is not believed (or given a probability of 1) in the default background; or one may *bracket* p in one's practical context even though p is believed in the default background. Positing and bracketing are two ways in which there can arise important differences, at the margins, between one's default cognitive background and one's *context-relative adjusted cognitive background*.[19] And it is this

---

18 Levi does go on to say that "a change in X's problems, goals, and values could alter his assessment of which serious possibilities are relevant possibilities to be taken into account in X's deliberation" (Levi, 1980, p. 4, note). Levi offers this example: If my problem is whether to bet on a coin's coming up heads I might reasonably see the possibility that a Republican will be elected president as serious but irrelevant. But this qualification does not touch the main point here. After all, if the proposition that it will rain must be seen by me as serious, since I do not assign the proposition that it won't a probability of 1, how could I reasonably see it as irrelevant to my planning for the day?

19 We cannot in general see the issue of whether to posit p (or bracket a belief that p) as yet another decision problem about which to deliberate. Here, as elsewhere,

adjusted cognitive background that, together with one's plans, frames one's further practical deliberation.

To be accepted in a context is to be taken as given in the adjusted cognitive background for that context. If one has a relevant all-or-none, context-independent belief that p, and this belief is not bracketed, then one accepts that p in that context. And similarly concerning a context-independent degree of confidence of 1. But one may also accept in a context propositions one does not believe in a context-independent way. And one may believe that p in a context-independent way and yet not accept that p in a certain context. In general there can be reasonable differences between one's adjusted cognitive background for a given practical context and one's context-independent, default cognitive background. So the explanation of decision and action will in general need to appeal to a cognitive attitude that itself neither guarantees nor is guaranteed by corresponding belief.[20]

---

practical reasoning will need to draw on subtle nondeliberative mechanisms. The distinction between the default and the adjusted cognitive backgrounds helps us pose questions about what these mechanisms should be.

20 Cohen (1989) also emphasizes a distinction between belief and acceptance: he highlights the passivity of belief, in contrast with acceptance; and he notes that "the reasons for accepting that p need not always be epistemic ones: they might be ethical or prudential" (p. 369). On these points we agree. But we may be in disagreement with respect to my claim that acceptance is context-relative. Cohen says that "[t]o accept that p is to adopt the policy of taking the proposition that p as a premiss in appropriate circumstances, and you either adopt that policy or you do not" (p. 374). This suggests that – contrary to what I have been urging – one either accepts that p or one does not, though one's acceptance will involve taking p as a premiss only in "appropriate circumstances." A further difference resides in Cohen's claim that belief is tied very closely to special feelings: "Belief that p . . . is a disposition to feel it true that p. . . . You answer the question whether you believe that p by introspecting or reporting what you are disposed to feel about the matter" (p. 368). In contrast, I want to characterize both belief and acceptance primarily in terms of their (related but different) roles in an appropriate psychology of practical reasoning and action. Finally, whereas Cohen sees acceptance as a "mental act" and belief as a "disposition" (p. 368), I see both as inner states, states to be distinguished from mental acts of positing and bracketing.

V. INTENTION AND DECISION, BELIEF AND ACCEPTANCE

Some theorists (Grice 1971; Velleman, 1989) argue that to intend to *A* I must believe I will *A*. In my judgment, however, this condition is too strong.[21] I might, for example, intend to stop on my way home to get the book, not believe I will fail to stop, but also not believe I will stop, given my absentmindedness and my tendency to go into automatic pilot once I get on my bicycle. There is, however, a plausible line of argument for the view that intention requires corresponding belief. I want to say what that argument is and show how the notion of context-relative acceptance can help us identify the rather different conclusion to which it points when it is properly understood.

Suppose that as a way of settling on means to getting the book I deliberate between stopping at the bookstore and going to the library. Suppose that both options are consistent with my prior plans and beliefs. But suppose that I do have some doubts about whether I would stop at the bookstore if I decided to; for I know of my absentmindedness. If I simply consider the pros and cons of stopping at the bookstore I risk losing track of this suspected gap between decision and action.[22] Given my doubts perhaps I should instead consider in deliberation the more complex option of taking steps to try to make it likely that I will stop at the bookstore. About this option I do believe that I would so act if I so decided.

It is tempting to be led by such considerations to the view that the options in rational deliberation should be such that one believes one would so act if one so decided.[23] But this is quite close to the idea that intentions – at least those intentions that are the upshot of deliberation and decision – require corresponding beliefs. If in deciding to

---

21 Here I agree with Davidson (1980).
22 Paul Weirich (1983) discusses a similar problem.
23 Weirich (1983, p. 176) suggests that something quite close to certainty is needed here. And Patrick Maher (1986, pp. 377–8) suggests that a rational deliberator should ignore an option in deliberation only if she is certain that she cannot so act. As will be clear below, I reject both views.

A I must believe that if I decide to A I will, then in deciding to A I am but a short step from believing I will A.

I think, however, that we should reject the proffered belief condition on options in deliberation; for my deliberation might reasonably concern the option of stopping at the bookstore despite my doubts about whether I would stop if I so decided. I propose, instead, an alternative condition on options in deliberation, one that does justice to the intuitions mooted but stops short of requiring the belief that one will do what one decides. What is required of an option in deliberation is that one's so acting be consistent with one's intentions and beliefs, and that one accept in that context that one will so act if one so decides.

Let us see how this proposal might work. Suppose that my stopping at the bookstore and my stopping at the library are each consistent with my prior plans and beliefs. However, given my absentmindedness I have doubts both about whether I would stop at the bookstore if I so decided and also about whether I would stop at the library if I so decided. Given the symmetry of the case, and to keep things simple, I bracket these doubts and take it for granted in my deliberation that I would perform whichever option I decided on: I deliberate between bookstore and library. While I do not believe I will stop at the bookstore if I so decide, I do accept this in the context of my deliberation. That seems enough for me reasonably to consider the cited options in my deliberation. But since acceptance is not belief, even if I decide to stop at the bookstore I may not be in a position to believe that I will stop.

This highlights the need for a distinction between decision and intention. Decisions that are the upshot of deliberation between options themselves involve a kind of context-relativity: These decisions are made against, and should be evaluated with respect to, a specific background of acceptances; and these acceptances may reasonably be peculiar to the specific context in which the decision is made. Intentions, in contrast, will be context-independent in a way that parallels the context-independence of belief. A decision issues in an intention which then needs to be compatible both with the agent's relevant beliefs and with the agent's other intentions, intentions themselves the results of various other decisions. The fact that these various decisions were made in different contexts does not relieve the pressure on the resulting intentions to be mutually compatible; for the agent needs to coordinate her various activities over time.

So we have, in practical reasoning, a context-dependent pair – decision and acceptance – and a context-independent pair – intention and belief.[24] Each pair has a primarily cognitive member – acceptance[25] or belief – and a primarily practical member – decision or intention. And each pair plays different but interrelated roles in planning agents like us. The context-relativity of acceptance, and the resulting context-relativity of decision, allow us to be sensitive to various special practical pressures on how we set up our decision problems. But we also need to ensure continuity and coordination of our activities at one time, over time, and in the world as we find it. And that is a major role of our context-independent intentions and plans, taken together with our context-independent beliefs.

Bratman, M. E. 1987. *Intention, Plans, and Practical Reason*. Cambridge, Mass.: Harvard University Press.

—1991. "Cognitivism About Practical Reason." *Ethics*, 102, pp. 117–28. [This volume, essay 13.]

Cohen, L. J. 1989. "Belief and Acceptance." *Mind*, 98, pp. 367–89.

Davidson, D. 1980. "Intending" in his *Essays on Actions and Events*. New York: Oxford University Press, pp. 83–102.

Grice, H. P. 1974. "Reply to Davidson on Intending." Delivered to the 1974 University of North Carolina Colloquium.

—1971. "Intention and Uncertainty." *Proceedings of the British Academy*, 57, pp. 263–79.

24 Here I put aside desire. I also ignore ways in which belief can involve kinds of context dependence. (See note 4.) My suggestion is that there is a useful analogy between the intention/decision distinction and the belief/acceptance distinction. This suggestion should not be conflated with Cohen's suggested "parallelism between the desire/goal-seeking distinction and the belief/acceptance one" (1989, p. 381). As Cohen sees it, both decision and intention (and other things as well) will fall on the same, "goal-seeking" side of his former distinction.

25 Though, as already emphasized, acceptance is shaped in part by practical concerns.

Harman, G. 1986. *Change in View*. Cambridge, Mass.: MIT Press.

Harsanyi, J. 1985. "Acceptance of Empirical Statements: A Bayesian Theory without Cognitive Utilities." *Theory and Decision*, 18, pp. 1–30.

Heil, J. 1983. "Believing What One Ought." *Journal of Philosophy*, 80, pp. 752–765.

—1992. "Believing Reasonably." *Nous*, 26, pp. 47–62.

Levi, I. 1980. *The Enterprise of Knowledge*. Cambridge, Mass.: MIT Press.

Maher, P. 1986. "The Irrelevance of Belief to Rational Action." *Erkenntnis*, 24, pp. 363–84.

Perry, J. 1979. "The Problem of the Essential Indexical." *Nous*, 13, pp. 3–21.

Price, H. H. 1954. "Belief and Will." *Proceedings of the Aristotelian Society* suppl. vol. 28, pp. 1–26.

Raz, J. 1975. "Reasons for Actions, Decisions, and Norms." *Mind*, 84, pp. 481–99.

Stalnaker, R. 1974. "Pragmatic Presuppositions" in Munitz, M. K., and Unger, P. K., eds., *Semantics and Philosophy*. New York: NYU Press, pp. 197–213.

—1984. *Inquiry*. Cambridge, Mass.: MIT Press.

Thomason, R. 1986. "The Context-Sensitivity of Belief and Desire" in Georgeff, M., and Lansky, A., eds., *Reasoning about Actions and Plans*. Los Altos: Morgan Kaufmann, pp. 341–60.

Ullmann-Margalit, E. 1983. "On Presumption." *The Journal of Philosophy*, 80, pp. 143–163.

van Fraassen, B. C., 1980. *The Scientific Image*. Oxford: Oxford University Press.

Velleman, J. D. 1989. *Practical Reflection*. Princeton: Princeton University Press.

Weirich, P. 1983. "A Decision-Maker's Options." *Philosophical Studies*, 44, pp. 175–86.

Williams, B. 1973. "Deciding to Believe" in his *Problems of the Self*. Cambridge: Cambridge University Press, pp. 136–51.

3

Planning and Temptation

Much of our behavior is organized. It is organized over time within the life of the agent, and it is organized interpersonally. This morning I began gathering tools to fix the bicycles in the garage. I did this because I was planning to go on a bike trip tomorrow with my son and knew I needed first to fix the bikes. Just before I gathered the tools, I was on the telephone ordering tickets for a trip to Philadelphia next week. I did that because I was planning to meet my friend in Philadelphia then. If all goes well, each of these actions will be part of a distinct coordinated, organized sequence of actions. Each sequence will involve coordinated actions, both of mine and of others. These sequences will also need to be coordinated with each other. Such coordination of action – between different actions of the same

An earlier and shorter version of the discussion of George Ainslie's book was presented at a symposium on his book at the Pacific Division of the American Philosophical Association, April 1994. There I benefited from discussion with Ainslie and the other contributors: Ronald De Sousa and Alfred Mele. Versions of this paper were presented at the April 1994 Conference on Mind and Morals and at the December 1994 Conference on Methods in Philosophy and the Sciences. Margaret Gilbert provided helpful comments on the latter occasion. I have benefited from the discussions at these conferences. I have also learned from written comments from Peter Godfrey-Smith and Alfred Mele, and discussion with Gilbert Harman, John Pollock, and Brian Skyrms. My work on this chapter was supported in part by the Center for the Study of Language and Information.

agent and between the actions of different agents – is central to our lives.

How do we accomplish this organization? It seems plausible to suppose that part of the answer will appeal to commonsense ideas about planning. It is part of our commonsense conception of ourselves that we are planning agents (Bratman 1983, 1987). We achieve coordination – both intrapersonal and social – in part by making decisions concerning what to do in the further future. Given such decisions, we try to shape our actions in the nearer future in ways that fit with and support what it is we have decided to do in the later future. We do that, in large part, by planning.

I decide, for example, to go to Philadelphia next week. This gives me an intention to go, which then poses a problem for further planning: How am I to get there? My prior intention helps frame that further planning: It provides a test of relevance (only various ways of getting there are relevant options), and it provides a filter on options to be considered in my planning. It filters out, for example, an option of going instead to Chicago. Or at least this is how my intention functions if it is sufficiently stable and is not reconsidered. In functioning in these ways, my prior intention helps explain why certain options get into my deliberation and others do not.

Why do we need stable intentions and plans to support coordination? Why don't we simply figure out, at each moment of action, what would then be best given our predictions about what we and others will do in the future if we act in certain ways in the present? One answer echoes the work of Herbert Simon (1983): We are agents with significant limits on the resources of time and attention we can reasonably devote to reasoning and calculation. Given these resource limits, a strategy of constantly starting from scratch – of never treating prior decisions as settling a practical question – would run into obvious difficulties. A second, related answer is that coordination requires predictability, and the actions of planning agents are more easily predicted.[1]

If we are to meet in Philadelphia next week, my friend needs to predict that I will be there then. The fact that I am planning to be

---

1 Velleman (1989, 225ff.) makes a similar point.

there then helps support such a prediction. His prediction that I will be in Philadelphia next week need not depend on his detailed knowledge of my deepest values or on a prediction of complex calculations I will make just before leaving. He knows I am now planning to go, and that such a plan will normally control my conduct; in normal circumstances that will suffice to support his prediction.

I need not only coordinate with my friend and with my son; I also need to coordinate my own activities over time. Frequently this involves acting in certain ways now on the assumption that I will act in certain ways later. I would not bother with the tools in the garage if I were not fairly confident I would use them later. Just as my planning agency makes me more predictable to others, it also makes me more predictable to me, thereby supporting the coordination of my various activities over time.

I see such planning as a key to the phenomenon of intention; I call this the planning theory of intention.[2] Here I want to explore the relation between such views about intention and planning and some recent psychological theorizing about temptation – about the phenomena of giving into it at times and at other times overcoming it. I am interested, in particular, in the work of the psychiatrist George Ainslie, especially his recent and important book (Ainslie 1992). Ainslie seeks to describe what he calls a "mechanism for willpower" (144), and his discussion is fascinating and suggestive. But in the end, it does not take intentions and plans sufficiently seriously.

II

Suppose I am a pianist who plays nightly at a club. Each night before my performance, I eat dinner with a friend, one who fancies good wines. Each night my friend offers me a fine wine with dinner, and – as I also love good wine – each night I am tempted to drink it. But I know that when I drink alcohol, my piano playing afterward suffers.

---

2 I distinguish plans as mere recipes from plans in the sense of "planning to." I might have a plan in the first sense for cooking lamb and yet in no way intend to cook it. It is plans in the second sense that involve intentions: If I plan to do something, I intend to do it.

And when I reflect in a calm moment, it is clear to me that superior piano playing in my evening performance is more important to me than the pleasures of wine with dinner.[3] Indeed, each morning I reflect on the coming challenges of the day and have a clear preference for my turning down the wine. Yet early each evening when I am at dinner with my friend, I find myself inclined in the direction of the wine. If I were to go ahead and drink the wine, mine would be a case of giving into temptation.

Austin once warned us not to "collapse succumbing to temptation into losing control of ourselves" (1961, 146). Ainslie would agree. On his view, when I give into temptation, I do not lose control of my action. I control my action in accordance with my preference at the time of action; but this preference is itself at odds with central preferences of mine at different times. I proceed to sketch this story.

Begin with the idea that we frequently discount goods simply because they are in the future. Think of the utility of a certain good to me at a certain time as a measure of my preference for that good as compared with competitors. In temporal discounting, the utility to me today of a good that I would certainly get tomorrow is less than the utility it would have for me tomorrow, and this difference in utility is due solely to the temporal difference. Bill, for example, prefers cake now to ice cream now, yet he prefers ice cream now to cake tomorrow. If this shift in preference is not due to uncertainty about getting the cake tomorrow if he so chose, but is rather due solely to the different times at which Bill would get the desserts, then Bill's case is one of temporal discounting.

---

3 Ainslie would put this point by saying that the reward of better piano playing is larger than the reward of wine drinking, where reward tends to be understood hedonistically. But the central issues here do not depend on such a hedonistic approach, so I am trying to avoid it.

Note also that what Ainslie would call the "reward" of better piano playing on any given evening is larger than that of drinking the wine at dinner, whether or not I resist the temptation to drink the wine on earlier days or on later days. Playing the piano well on a single, given night does not become a wasted effort if I play poorly on other nights. This feature of the example is built into most of Ainslie's discussion (see, for example, figures 3.3–3.5 in his chap. 3), and I will take it for granted in my discussion.

For such cases we can speak of the discount rate – the rate at which the utility of the future good is diminished solely by the perception that the good lies in the future. Perhaps such temporal discounting is irrational.[4] Still, many, including Ainslie, suppose it is pervasive. If so, we can expect certain cases of giving into temptation. If, for example, my discount rate is steep enough, the utility to me at dinner of my playing well that evening will be substantially reduced from its utility to me later that evening. The utility to me at dinner of drinking wine may then be above the utility to me at dinnertime of playing well later. If my action at dinner is determined by such preferences, I will drink the wine.

This story provides for some cases of giving into temptation but does not explain why earlier in the day I had a clear preference not for the wine but for the superior performance. According to Ainslie, if my discount rate for the wine is the same as my discount rate for the piano playing, if that discount rate is linear or exponential, and if at dinner I really do prefer to drink the wine, then I will prefer at breakfast that I drink wine at dinner. Merely by appeal to temporal discounting we do not yet account for the temporary reversal of my preference prior to dinner.

Ainslie argues that we can account for such preference reversals if the discount functions – representable by curves that map the utility to me of a certain event as a function of the time prior to that event – are not linear or exponential but, rather, sufficiently bowed so that the utility curves cross prior to the earlier event.[5] Suppose that my discount rate concerning wine is the same as that concerning piano playing,[6] and suppose that mine is a highly bowed discount function. (Ainslie's version is a hyperbolic discount function, grounded in Herrnstein's (1961) "matching law.") Then we can expect the fol-

---

4 See Lewis (1946, 493), Rawls (1971, 420). See also Parfit (1984, 158ff.).

5 We can ask in what sense this is an explanation of such preference reversals, but I put such matters aside here.

6 A nonobvious assumption, but one that Ainslie makes throughout. However, as Green and Meyerson (1993, 40) write, "The exponential model may predict a preference reversal if the value of the discount rate parameter is inversely related to amount."

lowing: From temporally far away, I prefer superior piano playing to wine at dinner. But at some time before dinner the utility curves may cross; there may be a reversal of preference. This reversal, however, is temporary; at some time after dinner, I again prefer superior piano playing to the wine.[7] If I have drunk the wine, I will then regret it. Ainslie claims that such highly bowed discount functions are pervasive and that they explain why temptation – understood as temporary preference reversal – is a common feature of our lives.[8]

Ainslie then asks how a rational agent can overcome the temptation predicted by such highly bowed discount functions. What rational strategies for resisting temptation are available?[9]

There are a number of ways I might try to respond to my knowledge this morning that at dinner my preference may change in the direction of the wine. I might, for example, make a side bet with you that I will turn down the wine, thereby generating new reasons for doing so, reasons that may block the reversal of preference. But there may also be available to me a way of thinking of my situation at dinner that will by itself enable me to overcome the temptation in favor of wine without a public side bet or its ilk.

When I compare at dinner

(a) drinking the wine now

---

7 I am supposing that after dinner I can compare playing the piano well later with my having had the wine. I can ask which I now, at a time between the two, prefer. Ainslie does not talk this way, perhaps because he sees preference as tied to choices one can still make. But it seems to me we need something like this way of talking.

8 Indeed, Ainslie claims that an enormous range of phenomena can be seen as instances of preference reversal associated with hyperbolic discount functions. Some of the supposed applications of this model (e.g., to certain cases of psychological compulsion – see Ainslie 1992, 225–227) seem to me problematic. Austin claimed that Plato wrongly collapsed succumbing to temptation into losing control of oneself. I wonder if Ainslie sometimes wrongly collapses losing control into succumbing to temptation.

9 I think it is fair to put the question this way. Ainslie might object, however, that he is also interested in strategies that themselves involve forms of irrationality but still help us resist certain temptations. These would be cases of so-called rational irrationality (Parfit, 1984). My discussion, however, seeks "mechanisms for willpower" that do not involve irrationality.

with

(b) not drinking now and, as a result, playing well later tonight,

I prefer (a). But since I know I will be in a similar situation on many (let us say, thirty) future occasions, I can also compare the following sequences of actions, present and future:

(c) my drinking the wine each of the next thirty occasions

and

(d) my refraining from drinking on each of those occasions.

On natural assumptions, at dinner on day 1 I will prefer (d) – the sequence of nondrinkings – over (c) – the sequence of drinkings; and I will have this preference even while, at dinner, I prefer (a) – drinking now – to (b) – not drinking now. This is because at dinner on day 1 I am still far enough away from dinner the next twenty-nine nights for my preferences concerning wine versus piano on those nights still to rank piano over wine. If I could choose the nondrinking *sequence*, (d), and if that choice would control my conduct, I could resist the temptation of wine each night and thereby achieve the preferred sequence.

Ainslie calls this approach to overcoming temptation the tactic of "personal rules."[10] This tactic depends on the agent's being able in some sense to "choose a whole series of rewards at once" (147). I agree with Ainslie that this is an important tactic. But to understand what this tactic involves, we need to ask what such a present choice or intention concerning future rewards or actions is.

The standard expected-utility model of rational action does not seem to have clear room for such a commitment to future action. On this model, an agent will have preferences, representable in terms of utilities, concerning present or future options or goods. An agent will have various expectations concerning the future – some conditional on present choices and some specifically concerning future preferences. An agent makes a choice about what to do now. There is,

10 Though it seems to me more aptly called a tactic of "personal policies." See Bratman (1989).

41

however, no further, distinctive state of the agent, which is her present choice or intention – and not merely her preference – concerning future action. Choice and intention are, strictly speaking, always of present conduct.[11] So we are faced with the question, What sense are we to make of the very idea of a choice or intention in favor of (d)?

One response would be to abandon the constraints of the standard model and to try to spell out how future-directed intentions function in a rational agent. That is the strategy of the planning theory of intention, and I will return to it. The more conservative strategy is to seek a substitute, while staying within the basic resources of the expected-utility model. This, I take it, is Ainslie's approach.[12] I proceed to sketch his version of conservatism and then to argue against it.

III

At dinner on day 1 I must choose between

(a) drink wine at dinner tonight

or

(b) do not drink wine at dinner tonight, and as a result play better later tonight.

My preference at dinner so far favors (a). But now I wonder what I will do the next twenty-nine nights: will I drink then, or not? When I try to answer this question, it is natural for me to see my present choice about whether to drink now as a "precedent": if I drink tonight, I will drink the other twenty-nine nights; and if not, not. That is, I believe

(i) if I choose (a) then I will drink on each of the thirty nights,

11 This powerful idea is not limited to expected-utility theory. Consider the nineteenth-century John Austin: "It is clear that such expressions as 'determining,' 'resolving,' 'making up one's mind', can only apply in strictness to 'volitions': that is to say, to those desires which are instantly followed by their objects" (1873, 451).

12 See especially his central discussion on pp. 147–162.

and

(ii) if I choose (b) then on each of the thirty nights I will refrain from drinking.

My belief in (i) allows (a) to take on the expected-utility of (c), the sequence of thirty drinkings; and my belief in (ii) allows (b) to take on the expected utility of (d), a sequence of thirty nondrinkings. And my preference now concerning these sequences favors a sequence of nondrinkings, (d), over a sequence of drinkings, (c). So once I see things this way, I will prefer (b) over (a), and so refrain from drinking tonight. That, Ainslie supposes, is how I can use personal rules to overcome temptation. I "choose a whole series of rewards at once" in the sense that I choose a present option in part because of an expectation that if I choose that option I will choose a corresponding series of future options. My belief that (ii) "works by putting additional reward at stake in each individual choice" (Ainslie 1992, 153).

On this picture there is choice of present action, in part on the basis of beliefs that connect such choices with later choices of what will then be present actions. However, there is, strictly speaking, no choice or intention on day 1 to refrain from drinking on each of the next thirty nights. Or anyway, if there is such a choice, it is reduced to a choice of present action (namely, (b)) together with a *belief* connecting that choice to later choices (namely, a belief that (ii)). Such beliefs allow me to overcome my temptation to drink now. "The will," Ainslie says, "is created by the perception of impulse-related choices as precedents for similar choices in the future" (161). This story about overcoming temptation is conservative; it stays within the confines of the standard model. The choices and intentions that it countenances are, strictly speaking, limited to present action. There can be a series of future choices – a series one can try to predict – but not strictly a choice of a future series.[13]

---

13 This, anyway, is the most natural reading of most of what Ainslie says. Consider, for example: "But how does a person arrange to choose a whole series of rewards at once? In fact, he does not have to commit himself physically. The values of the alternative series of rewards . . . depend on his expectation of getting them. As-

I think that this account runs into a problem.

Consider my belief that if I choose (b) then I will abstain on each of the thirty nights, but if I instead choose (a) I will drink on all those nights. Is this a belief in the causal efficacy of a choice of (b) – that is, a belief that a choice of (b) would lead causally to later actions of nondrinking? Or is this, rather, only a belief that a choice of (b) would be good evidence that I am the sort of person – an abstainer – who will continue to choose nondrinking?[14]

Suppose my belief is only that a choice of (b) would be a predictor of analogous choices later.[15] Would this belief really give me reason to choose (b)? The problems here are familiar from discussions of Newcomb's problem.[16] On this interpretation of my belief I am

---

suming he is familiar with the expectable physical outcomes of his possible choices, the main element of uncertainty will be what he himself will actually choose. In situations where temporary preferences are likely, he is apt to be genuinely ignorant of what his own future choices will be. His best information is his knowledge of his past behavior under similar circumstances, with the most recent examples probably being the most informative" (147, 150).

It seems clear here that Ainslie understands the choice of a series not as a present choice of future action or rewards but instead as a series of future choices, a series one may try to predict on the basis of one's knowledge of one's past choices. To "arrange to choose a whole series of rewards at once" is to arrange that there be a series of future choices.

14 In his recent discussion of Ainslie's views, Robert Nozick asks a similar question, but answers it differently (Nozick 1993, 19).

15 As Ainslie suggests at the top of p. 152. See also his remarks on p. 203, where he notes the relevance of Newcomb's problem.

16 This problem was originally described in Nozick (1969). This essay is reprinted, with a number of other useful essays on the subject, in Campbell and Sowden (1985). In the original example discussed by Nozick, a person, call her Sue, is faced with a choice between two boxes. The first box contains $1,000; the second box contains either $1,000,000 or nothing. Sue can choose either just the second box or both boxes. Sue knows all of the following about her situation. First, there is an extremely reliable predictor who has predicted what choice Sue will make. Second, if the prediction is that she will choose only the second box, the predictor has put the money in that box. Third, if the prediction is that she will choose both boxes, the predictor has put no money in the second box. But, fourth, the

thinking like a so-called one-boxer if I reason from this belief to a choice in favor of (b). That is, in treating this belief as giving me reason to choose (b) I am choosing (b) not because this choice will have a desired result, but only because this choice is evidence of something else, something not affected by the choice itself. In choosing (b) I give myself evidence of, but do not cause, an underlying trait that will lead me to abstain later. There is a large literature that discusses whether such reasoning is legitimate (e.g., Campbell and Sowden 1985). A common view, which I share but will not try to defend here, is that it is not legitimate. I will assume that, at the least, an account of rational "willpower" should not be forced to sanction such one-boxer reasoning. One-boxer reasoning is, at best, controversial in a way in which rational willpower should not be.

For Ainslie's approach to work, then, it should explain why I should see my choice to abstain on day 1 as a cause of later choices to abstain. Further, since we want a model of rational willpower, we need to explain how my choice to abstain on day 1 affects my reasons for choice on the later days, in a way that will lead me rationally to refrain on those days.

This is where the theme of "the strategic interaction of successive motivational states" is supposed to do work.[17] Ainslie wants to exploit a supposed analogy between a single-person case calling for willpower and a two-person repeated prisoner's dilemma. Ainslie writes: "A repeated prisoner's dilemma makes players predict each other's future moves on the basis of known past moves. . . . This is true whether the players on different days are two people, or a single person, . . . as

---

predictor has already done whatever he is going to do: When it comes time for Sue to choose, the money is already there or it is not. A choice of only the second box is good evidence that the $1,000,000 is there; but it does not cause the money to be there. A person who supposes that the rational choice for Sue is to choose only the second box has been labeled a "one boxer." Nozick has recently returned to this problem in Nozick (1993, chap. 2). I will not discuss here Nozick's new approach to this problem.

17 Nozick notes that "doing the action now may have a minor effect on the probability of repetition in accordance with the psychologist's 'law of effect' " (1993, 19). But Ainslie's view needs a causal influence more significant than this. That is what the analogy with the interpersonal case is supposed to accomplish.

long as each plays repeatedly. Whether or not Monday's player is a different person from Tuesday's player, Monday's move will be the Tuesday player's best predictor of Wednesday's move and subsequent moves" (161).

Let us see how this analogy is supposed to work. Consider first a two-person case. Suppose Jones and Smith are in a situation of a repeated prisoner's dilemma in which each acts on alternate days. By performing the cooperative option on Monday, Jones may lead Smith reasonably to believe that he, Jones, will, at each of his turns, cooperate so long as Smith cooperates. Jones thus affects a belief of Smith's – a belief about how Jones would behave if Smith were to cooperate – and thereby gives Smith new reason for cooperating. And similarly for Smith, when Tuesday arrives. This may reasonably lead each to cooperate so long as the other cooperates on the previous day.[18]

Now return to me and the wine. Ainslie's idea is that by choosing not to drink on day 1 I give myself on day 2 evidence that if (but only if), on day 2, I do not drink then, as a result, I will not drink on day 3. It is as if I, on day 1, am trying to engage myself, on day 2, in a mutually beneficial cooperative scheme. On day 1 I am like Jones on Monday; on day 2 I am like Smith on Tuesday. On day 1 I try to get me-on-day-2 to believe I am a kind of tit-for-tatter. My choice to abstain on day 1 causes me on day 2 (by giving me appropriate evidence) to believe that if I abstain on day 2, then, as a result, I will also abstain on day 3; and that belief helps provide practical reason for a choice to abstain on day 2. So my choice not to drink on day 1 is a cause of my rational choice on day 2, not mere evidence that I will make that choice on day 2. That, anyway, is the supposed analogy. It is in his use of this analogy that Ainslie sees himself as arguing that "the study of bargaining supplies the concepts needed for adapting behavioral psychology to apply to intraphysic conflict" (xiii).

Note that Jones and Smith are assumed to be rational agents. Their problem is how to cooperate given the reward structures and their rationality. Analogously, it is being assumed that on each day I am a

---

18 I put aside, in both this case and the single-person case, issues raised by the fact (if it is a fact) that it is known of a specific, last day that after that day there will be no further occasions for cooperation.

rational agent. My problem is how, consistent with my rationality, I can overcome the temptation of temporary preference reversals. Ainslie's answer is that the solution in the intrapersonal case is analogous to a solution supposedly available in the interpersonal case when the "dilemma" is known to be a repeated one.

I agree with Ainslie that there are useful analogies between interpersonal strategic interaction and intrapersonal willpower. Jones and Smith each prefers the situation in which both cooperate over that in which neither does. Analogously, on each of the thirty days I prefer the situation in which I refrain from wine on all days to that in which I drink on all days. But I doubt that this analogy can do all the work Ainslie wants it to do. It is one thing to explain what is to be achieved by willpower, another to explain how it is rationally achieved. When it comes to explaining the latter, the analogy between one-person and two-person cases seems to break down. Or so I want now to argue.

It is important to be clear about what is needed here. It needs to be shown that my choice to abstain on day 1 is not merely evidence of an underlying tendency to make similar choices in the future but also a cause of such future choices. Ainslie tries to do this by seeing my choice on day 1 as evidence for, and so a cause of, a belief to be held on day 2. This belief on day 2 must satisfy two demands: it must be a belief that can function as part of a practical reason for a choice, on day 2, to abstain; and it must be a belief that is to some extent confirmed by the choice to abstain on day 1. The belief, on day 2, that may well be to some extent confirmed by the choice to abstain on day 1 is the belief that I tend to abstain. But that is not a belief that normally gives me, on day 2, practical reason to choose to abstain on day 2. The belief that if I had it on day 2 would give me reason to abstain on day 2, is the belief that if I abstain on day 2, then as a result I would continue to abstain. The problem is to say why that belief is confirmed by my choice on day 1.

Ainslie's purported solution to this problem depends on the analogy with the two-person case. On Monday Jones can, while performing the cooperative option, indicate that his continued cooperation is conditional on Smith's cooperation: he can indicate that he, Jones, is a conditional, not simply a nonconditional, cooperator. And even if Jones does not explicitly indicate this, it may be clear to Smith that this is true, given the payoff structure: for he and Smith are two different agents who, it is being assumed, have no intrinsic concern for each other; and Smith knows that Jones awaits his, Smith's, choice. My choice on day 1 to abstain is supposed, by Ainslie, to be analogous to Jones's cooperative act on Monday. When I come to decide on day 2, I am supposed to be like Smith on Tuesday. I can see that my abstaining on day 1 indicates a willingness to continue to abstain so long as I abstain on day 2, just as Smith can see that Jones's cooperation on Monday indicates a willingness to continue to cooperate so long as he, Smith, cooperates on Tuesday.

But it seems to me that here the analogy breaks down. Suppose that on day 2, I recall having chosen to abstain on day 1. Why would I suppose that the person who made the choice on day 1 is waiting around to see if I will "reciprocate" on day 2 and will, only then, continue to "cooperate" on day 3? Unlike the two-person case, there is no other person. There is only me. Simply to suppose that I am waiting around to see what I do on day 2 before I decide what to do on day 3 is to beg the question at issue; for the question is why my earlier choice to abstain gives me reason for later choices to abstain. You can, if you want, talk of the earlier "person-*stage*" who decided on day 1 to abstain, and distinguish that stage from the present, day 2 stage. But that earlier person-stage is no longer around at all, let alone waiting to see what I do on day 2.[19] So we are still without an explanation of why I should reasonably see my present choice to abstain on day 1 as a cause of future, rational abstentions.

It might be replied that on day 2 I will know that if I do not abstain on that day, I will cease believing I am an abstainer. But even if this is true, it is not clear how it can help. A belief on day 2 that I am an abstainer does not give me practical reason for a choice on day 2 to abstain. That fact is not changed by the fact – if it is a fact – that if I choose on day 2 not to abstain, I will cease to have this belief. That the continuation of my belief that I am an abstainer is itself causally dependent on my choosing to abstain on day 2 does not show

---

19 In this sentence I was helped by Döring (1997), which makes a similar point in discussing work of E. F. McClennen.

that my belief is really a belief that my abstaining later is causally dependent on my choice to abstain now. A belief that is itself causally dependent need not be a belief in causal dependence.

Consider a final reply: I know on day 1 that if I were to choose to drink the wine, then on day 2 I would believe I am not an abstainer. This would tend to make me, on day 2, discouraged about the possibility of my abstaining on day 2 and would thereby tend to make me more likely not to abstain. In that way I may see my choice on day 1 as causally influencing analogous choices later.[20]

The first point to note about this reply is that it does not involve the analogy with the two-person case. I am no longer seen as trying to convince my later self that I am a kind of tit-for-tatter. Rather, I am simply taking into account, on day 1, the psychological impact on myself of my choice. The second, related point is that the impact I am focusing on – becoming pessimistic and discouraged – is not seen by me as giving me a new practical reason to drink on day 2.[21] This is a genuine disanalogy with the two-person case, in which information about earlier choices is supposed to provide a rational basis for later choices. Instead, what I am worrying about, on day 1, is that on day 2 I would be led to drink as a result of psychological causes that are not reasons for drinking. But the project is to explain how a

---

20 Ainslie suggests this reply on pp. 150 and 203. See also Nozick (1993, 19). Ainslie, for example, writes: "Acts governed by willpower evidently are both diagnostic and causal. Drinking too much is diagnostic of a condition, alcoholism out of control, but it causes further uncontrolled drinking when the subject, using it to diagnose himself as out of control, is discouraged from trying to will sobriety" (203).

21 Alfred Mele helped me see that there may be cases in which this is not true. These will be cases in which the value to me of resisting a temptation depends on my resisting it most or all of the time. In Mele's example, the "reward" of not smoking on a particular occasion may depend on my generally not smoking; otherwise it may be a wasted effort. In such a case, if I am pessimistic about the likelihood of my resisting a certain temptation on later occasions, I may reasonably see my resisting this one time as a wasted effort. But, as noted above in note 3, this is not the structure of the cases Ainslie focuses on. In any case, for such cases we have no need for an elaborate story about the analogy with the interpersonal case.

rational agent overcomes temptations created by temporary reversals of preference.[22] That I have earlier failed to refrain from the wine is not normally a practical reason to fail again,[23] though it may be evidence that I will fail again. To see my earlier failure as ineluctably leading to my later failure is to be guilty of a kind of "bad faith" rather than to be functioning as a rational agent. So this last reply does not accomplish what we want.

So I am skeptical about Ainslie's "mechanism for willpower." The analogy between the intrapersonal and the interpersonal case does shed light on a parallel structure of payoffs. And we do sometimes treat our choices in some sense "as precedents for similar choices in the future" (Ainslie 1992, 161). But it is one thing to explain what is to be achieved by willpower, another to explain how it is rationally achieved. Absent an appeal to controversial forms of reasoning, Ainslie's model seems not to provide such a rational mechanism.

V

Return to the choice I face on day 1. Ainslie assumes that, strictly speaking, what I must choose between is (a) and (b). This assumption leads to a problematic story about a "mechanism for willpower." This suggests that we reconsider the assumption that the proper objects of choice and intention are limited to present options. Why not take more seriously the idea – supported by the planning theory of intention – that I really can choose between the sequences, or policies, cited in (c) and (d)? Given my clear preference for (d) over (c) I choose, and so come to intend, (d).[24] I make this choice believing that

---

22 Anyway, that is my project. Ainslie seems sometimes unclear whether it is his, as in the earlier quoted remarks from p. 203. (See above, note 20.) But this seems to me a conception of his project that coheres with his overarching idea that "the study of bargaining supplies the concepts needed for adapting behavioral psychology to apply to intrapsychic conflict" (xiii).

23 But see note 21.

24 There is an important complication. At dinner on day 1, after the preference reversal, I prefer the sequence consisting of drinking tonight and abstaining on the rest of the evenings (call it sequence (d')) to sequence (d). (See Ainslie's table 5.2

(iii) if I choose (c) then, as a result, I will drink on each of the thirty nights,

and

(iv) if I choose (d) then, as a result, on each of the thirty nights I will refrain from drinking.

My intention in favor of (d) normally leads me rationally to abstain on day 1, and so on. That is how intentions normally function. This intention is a basic part of the relevant rational mechanism, a mechanism that is a part of our planning capacities.

Ainslie says: "The will is created by the perception of impulse-related choices as precedents for similar choices in the future" (161). On the alternative planning theory, the "will" is expressed also in choices of (and intentions concerning) future options, not merely in the perception of choices of present options as precedents for future choices. The primary basis for such choices and intentions is the desirability of those future options. Choices and intentions concerning the future pervade our lives as planning agents. Such choices and intentions concerning the future help structure the planning we depend on to achieve the benefits of coordination.

Ainslie and I agree on the importance of choosing a whole series of rewards at once. The issue is how to model such choices. I have considered three different models. On model 1, what is chosen is strictly a present option, but this choice is seen as evidence of a general tendency to choose similarly. This model sees a person with willpower as a one-boxer. On model 2, which I take to be Anslie's preferred model, I am still limited to choosing only present options. But that choice – for example, to abstain now – can be seen by me as causing later beliefs, which then ground later, similar choices. Finally, on model 3, the model suggested by the planning theory, I can make a present choice in favor of a valued sequence of future actions

---

on p. 161.) However, prior to the preference reversal I prefer (d) to (d'). So, other things equal, which I choose will depend on when I make the choice. But once I do make the choice, I have a new intention or policy that may help shape later action. (I was helped here by discussion with William Talbot.)

or a valued policy to act in certain ways on certain occasions. Such a choice issues in an intention concerning future conduct, and this intention is, normally, causally responsible for specific, future actions.

Once we take future-directed intentions seriously as basic elements of the psychology, we face a host of questions. We need a general account of how such intentions function in the practical reasoning of intelligent agents like us. We need an account of when an intelligent agent will settle, in deliberation, on certain intentions for the future, and of when she will later reconsider such prior intentions. This latter will be an account of the stability of intention (Bratman 1987, chap. 5; 1992). Part of an account of intention stability will focus on relevant mechanisms of salience and problem detection, for we do not want, as limited agents, constantly to be reflecting in a serious way on whether to reconsider our prior intentions. Finally, these accounts – of practical reasoning and of intention stability – will be linked: rationally to decide now, on the basis of present deliberation, to A later in circumstances in which I expect to have rational control of my action, I must not suppose that when the time and circumstance for A arrive I will, if rational, abandon that intention in favor of an intention to perform some alternative to A. (Call this the linking principle.)

Let us reflect briefly on the stability of intention. We are agents with important needs for coordination over time, both social and intrapersonal; and we are agents with limited powers of knowledge and limited resources we can devote to planning and reasoning. Given these needs and limits, what should be our strategies, habits, and/or mechanisms of reconsideration of prior plans?

We can begin by noting that there are criticizable extremes. On one extreme is the person who always seriously reconsiders his prior plans in the face of any new information, no matter how trivial. Such a person would constantly be starting from scratch and would be unlikely to achieve many of the benefits of planning. On the other extreme is the overly rigid planner – one who almost never reconsiders, even in the face of important new information. Most of us, of course, are somewhere in the middle between these two extremes, and that is in part why we are able to achieve the benefits of planning.

A theory of intention stability will need to say more about where in the middle instrumentally rational but limited planners like us should be. This is a big project. Without arguing in detail, however, I think we can reasonably make a conjecture concerning cases of temporary preference change. The conjecture is that instrumentally rational planners will not endorse a habit or strategy of always reconsidering a prior intention to A at t whenever they find themselves, at t, temporarily preferring an alternative to A. After all, such a habit or strategy would frequently undermine a valued kind of intrapersonal coordination, and it would do this in the service of a merely temporary preference. An instrumentally rational planner will have mechanisms and strategies of reconsideration that sometimes block reconsideration of a prior intention in the face of merely temporary preference change. (This is not to say that she will always resist all temporary temptations.)[25] This means that prior intentions and plans can have an independent role in rational motivation: once in place they can sometimes rationally control conduct even in the face of a temporary preference change to the contrary. (If, however, one does go ahead and act as planned, in the face of temporary preference change, there will also be a sense in which that is what one preferred to do. But that sense of "prefer" need not get at what explains one's action.)

A model of planning agency will differ in basic ways from a model of the agency of nonplanning agents – mice, perhaps. We may share with mice the generic characteristic of being purposive agents, and that may be an important commonality. But we are also a distinctive kind of purposive agent: We are planning agents. This is central to our ability to achieve complex forms of organization and coordination over time. It is a point familiar from discussions of free will that purposive agency does not ensure the kind of responsible agency we care about when we reflect on matters of moral praise and blame. The point here is a related one: Purposive agency does not ensure planning agency.[26] We have as much reason to suppose that we have

<hr />

25 A point David Gauthier helped me appreciate.
26 This raises the general issue of how to understand the relation between planning agency and morally responsible agency. Consideration of our planning capacities

intentions and plans as we have to suppose that we have beliefs and desires; so we should resist the temptation to settle for a model of agency that ignores the difference between us and nonplanning, purposive agents.[27]

I have so far followed Ainslie's lead and focused on cases of temporary preference reversal.[28] But a full story about planning will also need to consider cases in which one's preferences and evaluations concerning one's options are instead coherent and stable. We can expect reasonable strategies of (non)reconsideration of prior intentions to respond differently in these different kinds of cases.

More generally, we can distinguish two aspects of reasonable intention stability (Bratman 1992; 1998; but see DeHelian and McClennen 1993). First, we want mechanisms and strategies of reconsideration that over the long run will suitably promote our efforts to achieve what we want and value, given our needs for coordination and our limits. But, second, if in a particular case, it is clear to the agent that, taking everything into account (including costs of reconsideration, replanning, reputation effects, and so on), she does better, in the light of her longstanding, coherent, and stable desires and values, by abandoning some prior intention, then that is what she should do. If appeal to the usefulness of some general rule of (non)reconsideration were allowed to block reconsideration even in such a case, we would be sanctioning a kind of planworship that would be unac-

---

contrasts with consideration of distinctions (Frankfurt 1971) between first- and second-order desires, in emphasizing the temporal spread of our agency. So a focus on planning may be useful in understanding a relevant kind of unity of agency over time. (Frankfurt makes a similar point in Frankfurt 1988, 175).

27 A temptation in the direction of, as we might say, a kind of genus-envy.

28 There are also cases in which the preference change is temporary if it is resisted, but permanent if it is not resisted. I might now decide not to accept a job offer I expect next week. But I might know that at the time of the offer I will be tempted and experience a preference change. Will that change be temporary? It depends on what I do. If I resist and turn down the offer, I will soon be glad I did. But if I accept the offer, the effects of the job itself will be reinforcing in ways that will make me glad I accepted. So my preference change is, in such a case, only conditionally temporary – that is, temporary only if I resist. Some versions of the story of Ulysses and the Sirens also have this structure. I will not try to discuss such cases here.

ceptable for a reflective agent.[29] The first aspect of intention stability helps explain why a reasonable planner may resist temporary preference changes of the sort that Ainslie emphasizes. The second aspect ensures that planners need not be overly rigid.

This supposes that longstanding, coherent, and stable desires and values may reasonably play a different role in rational reconsideration than merely temporary desires and preferences. Though I cannot argue for this here, it does seem to me a reasonable supposition, and one that Ainslie may want to share. For me to stick with my prior plan in the face of a clear, stable, longstanding, and coherent on-balance preference and evaluation to the contrary seems overly rigid. But if what conflicts with the plan is merely a temporary preference, the result of a temporary preference reversal, the charge of rigidity may lose its force, and a pragmatic argument in favor of a general strategy of sticking with one's plan in such a case may be cogent.

Rational nonreconsideration can, then, depend in part on the temporariness of a preference change. Consider, in contrast, Kavka's toxin case (Kavka 1983). A billionaire will give me a lot of money on Tuesday if I form the intention on Monday to drink a disgusting but nonlethal toxin on Wednesday. To get the money, I do not need to drink the toxin; I just need to intend, on Monday, to drink it. But I need to form this intention without exploiting any external mechanisms (such as a side bet) or forms of self-obfuscation. According to the linking principle, I can rationally form this intention only if I do not suppose that I will, if rational, abandon it when the time to drink arrives. However, it seems I would rationally abandon it; for on Wednesday I would have no good reason to drink the stuff.[30] Nevertheless, some philosophers have suggested that a pragmatic approach to rational reconsideration can justify a strategy that would lead to not reconsidering such an intention: such a strategy would, after all,

---

29 This terminology aims to highlight the parallel with J. J. C. Smart's (1967) famous criticism of rule utilitarianism as potentially guilty of sanctioning "rule worship."

30 This assumes that on Monday my mere intention, even in the special, science-fiction circumstances of the toxin case, does not by itself amount to an assurance to the billionaire of a sort that induces an obligation to drink the toxin.

help me to become rich.[31] But I think the second aspect of reasonable reconsideration will block this move. If I were to be faced with the toxin on Wednesday and were clear-headed about my situation, I would see that my longstanding, coherent, and stable ranking overwhelmingly supports my not drinking it; this is not merely a temporary preference reversal. So I should then reconsider and abandon a prior intention to drink, despite the attractions of a policy of not reconsidering in such cases. Knowing this, I will not be in a position on Monday rationally to decide to drink on Wednesday. So there are crucial differences between such cases and Ainslie's cases of temporary preference change. Planning agency, properly understood, provides a mechanism of willpower for cases of temporary preference reversal without a commitment to unacceptably rigid planning.

REFERENCES

Ainslie, George. 1992. *Picoeconomics: The Strategic Interaction of Successive Motivational States within the Person.* New York: Cambridge University Press.

Austin, John. 1873. *Lectures on Jurisprudence.* Vol. 1. 4th ed. London: John Murray.

Austin, J. L. 1961. "A Plea for Excuses." In J. L. Austin, *Philosophical Papers.* Edited by J. O. Urmson and G. J. Warnock. Oxford: Oxford University Press.

Bratman, Michael, E. 1983. "Taking Plans Seriously." *Social Theory and Practice* 9: 271–287.

— 1987. *Intention, Plans, and Practical Reason.* Cambridge, Mass.: Harvard University Press.

— 1989. "Intention and Personal Policies." *Philosophical Perspectives* 3: 443–469.

— 1992. "Planning and the Stability of Intention." *Minds and Machines* 2:1–16.

— 1998. "Following through with One's Plans: Reply to David Gauthier." In Peter Danielson, ed., *Modeling Rational and Moral Agents.* Oxford: Oxford University Press.

Campbell, Richmond, and Sowden, Lanning, eds. 1985. *Paradoxes of Rationality and Cooperation.* Vancouver: University of British Columbia Press.

DeHelian, Laura, and McClennen, Edward. 1993. "Planning and the Stability of Intention: A Comment." *Minds and Machines* 3.

Döring, Frank. 1997. "Le 'Choix résolu' selon McClennen." In Jean-Pierre Du-

---

31 See Gauthier (1994, 1998), DeHelian and McClennen (1993), and McClennen (1990, chap. 13). What we say here may have implications for our understanding of rational, interpersonal cooperation; but I will not try to discuss these matters here.

puy and Pierre Livet, eds., *Les limites de la rationalité* Paris: Éditions la Découverte, Vol. 1, pp. 111–117.

Frankfurt, Harry. 1971. "Freedom of the Will and the Concept of a Person." *Journal of Philosophy* 68:5–20.

— 1988. "Identification and Wholeheartedness." In Harry Frankfurt, *The Importance of What We Care About*, pp. 159–176. New York: Cambridge University Press.

Gauthier, David. 1994. "Assure and Threaten." *Ethics* 104:690–721.

— 1998. "Intention and Deliberation." In Peter Danielson, ed., *Modeling Rational and Moral Agents*. Oxford: Oxford University Press.

Green, Leonard, and Myerson, Joel. 1993. "Alternative Frameworks for the Analysis of Self Control." *Behavior and Philosophy* 21:37–47.

Herrnstein, Richard. 1961. "Relative and Absolute Strengths of Response as a Function of Frequency of Reinforcement." *Journal of the Experimental Analysis of Behavior* 4:267–272.

Kavka, Gregory. 1983. "The Toxin Puzzle." *Analysis* 43:33–36.

Lewis, C. I. 1946. *An Analysis of Knowledge and Valuation*. La Salle, Ill.: Open Court Publishing Co.

McClennen, E. F. 1990. *Rationality and Dynamic Choice: Foundational Explorations*. Cambridge: Cambridge University Press.

Nozick, Robert. 1969. "Newcomb's Problem and Two Principles of Choice." In Nicholas Rescher et al., eds., *Essays in Honor of Carl G. Hempel*. Dordrecht: Reidel.

— 1993. *The Nature of Rationality*. Princeton: Princeton University Press.

Parfit, Derek. 1984. *Reasons and Persons*. Oxford: Oxford University Press.

Rawls, John. 1971. *A Theory of Justice*. Cambridge, Mass.: Harvard University Press.

Simon, Herbert. 1983. *Reason in Human Affairs*. Stanford: Stanford University Press.

Smart, J. J. C. 1967. "Extreme and Restricted Utilitarianism." In Philippa Foot, ed., *Theories of Ethics*. Oxford: Oxford University Press.

Velleman, J. David. 1989. *Practical Reflection*. Princeton: Princeton University Press.

4

Toxin, Temptation, and the Stability of Intention

I. INSTRUMENTALLY RATIONAL PLANNING AGENCY

We frequently settle in advance on prior, partial plans for future action, fill them in as time goes by, and execute them when the time

An earlier version of this essay was presented at the conference held in honor of Gregory Kavka ("Rationality, Commitment, and Community," Feb. 10–12, 1995, University of California, Irvine). A revised version was presented at the March 1995 Pacific Division meeting of the American Philosophical Association, and parts of that version were presented in my 1995 Potter Lecture at Washington State University. The present essay is a substantially revised version of the APA paper. A number of the ideas in this essay were also presented, and usefully criticized, in yet-earlier papers given at Yale University, the University of North Carolina at Chapel Hill, NYU, Rutgers University, John Hopkins University, the University of Maryland, and the University of Arizona. The paper, in very roughly its present form, was presented and usefully criticized in March 1996 at Davidson College and Duke University, and at the University of California at Berkeley School of Law Workshop on Rationality and Society in November 1996. I have greatly benefited from the comments and criticisms of many people, including Bruce Ackerman, Nomy Arpaly, Lawrence Beyer, John Broome, Daniel Farrell, Claire Finkelstein, Gerald Gaus, Olav Gjelsvik, Jean Hampton, Gilbert Harman, John Heil, Thomas Hill, Frances Kamm, Keith Lehrer, Edward McClennen, Alfred Mele, Elijah Millgram, Christopher Morris, Michael Pendlebury, John Pollock, Samuel Scheffler, Tim Schroeder, J. David Velleman, and Gideon Yaffe. I have learned a lot from a series of exchanges – formal and informal – with David Gauthier. Special thanks go to Geoffrey Sayre-McCord for a long and extremely helpful discussion. Final work on this essay was completed while the author was a Fellow at the Center for Advanced Study in the Behavioral Sciences. I am grateful for financial support provided by the Andrew W. Mellon Foundation.

comes. Such planning plays a basic role in our efforts to organize our own activities over time and to coordinate our own activities with those of others. These forms of organization are central to the lives we want to live.[1]

Not all purposive agents are planning agents. Nonhuman animals who pursue their needs and desires in the light of their representations of their world may still not be planning agents. But it is important that we are planning agents. Our capacities for planning are an all-purpose means, basic to our abilities to pursue complex projects, both individual and social.

Why do we need to settle on prior plans in the pursuit of organized activity? A first answer is that there are significant limits on the time and attention we have available for reasoning.[2] Such resource limits argue against a strategy of constantly starting from scratch – they argue against a strategy of never treating prior plans as settling a practical question. A second answer is that our pursuit of organization and coordination depends on the predictability to us of our actions.[3] Coordinated, organized activity requires that we be able reliably to predict what we will do; and we need to be able to predict this despite both the complexity of the mechanisms underlying our behavior and our cognitive limitations in understanding those mechanisms. In treating prior plans as settling practical questions we make our conduct more predictable to cognitively limited agents like us by simplifying the explanatory structures underlying our actions.

Intelligent planning agents may differ in their desires, cares, commitments, and concerns. They may, in particular, endorse various noninstrumental, substantive ideals of steadfastness, of sticking to one's prior plans in the face of challenge.[4] But we can ask what

1 This is a major theme in my *Intention, Plans, and Practical Reason* (Cambridge, MA: Harvard University Press, 1987).

2 This is in the spirit of work by Herbert Simon. See, e.g., his *Reason in Human Affairs* (Stanford: Stanford University Press, 1983).

3 A similar point is made by J. David Velleman in his *Practical Reflection* (Princeton: Princeton University Press, 1989), pp. 225–6.

4 Jordon Howard Sobel emphasizes the possibility that an agent may "put a premium on steadfastness"; see his "Useful Intentions" in his *Taking Chances: Essays on Ra-*

"instrumental rationality" – rationality in the pursuit of one's desires, cares, commitments, and concerns – requires of planning agents, despite possible differences in those desires, cares, commitments, and concerns.[5] A theory of instrumentally rational planning agency may not exhaust all that is to be said about rational intentions and plans. But it will, if it is successful, characterize important structures of rational planning agency that are, as it is said, neutral with respect to diverging conceptions of the good.

Such a theory needs to be responsive to a fundamental tension. On the one hand, a planning agent settles in advance what to do later. On the other hand, she is an agent who, whatever her prior plans, normally retains rational control over what she does when the time comes. Following through with one's plan is not, after all, like following through with one's tennis swing. We need to do justice to both these aspects of planning agency.[6]

tional Choice (Cambridge: Cambridge University Press, 1994), pp. 237–54, esp. p. 249. Wlodek Rabinowicz, in a complex and subtle discussion, also emphasizes that a rational agent may "assign value to resoluteness and to commitment to previously chosen plans." "To Have One's Cake and Eat It Too: Sequential Choice and Expected-Utility Violations," _Journal of Philosophy_ 92 (1995), 586–620, at p. 611. Matters here are delicate: Such valuations may lead to odd forms of bootstrapping, as I argued in my _Intention, Plans, and Practical Reason_, ch. 2. But here I want simply to put such views to one side, for my interest is in an account of instrumentally rational planning agency that does not begin by presupposing such intrinsic valuations.

5 "Instrumental" is here understood broadly: It is not limited solely to causal means to an end. For example, my going to a concert tonight might be promoted by my going to hear the Alma Trio, though my going to hear the Alma Trio is not a causal means to my going to a concert. (See Bernard Williams, "Internal and External Reasons," in his _Moral Luck_ [Cambridge: Cambridge University Press, 1981], p. 104.) The crucial point is that I am trying to discuss structures of planning agency in a way that appeals to the nature of such agency and to demands of instrumental reason but does not depend on arguing that practical reason, by itself, mandates certain ends.

6 This problem is similar to the problem posed by the trilemma I discuss in _Intention, Plans, and Practical Reason_, p. 5. See also Paisley Livingston, "Le dilemme de Bratman: Problèmes de la rationalité dynamique," _Philosophiques_ 20 (1993), 47–67.

II. A BASIC MODEL

A planning agent, we may suppose, has a background of values, desires, cares, and concerns.[7] These support considered rankings of various kinds of alternatives, in light of relevant beliefs. I will call such rankings *evaluative rankings*. These rankings express the agent's considered ordering at a time, an ordering she sees as a candidate for shaping relevant choices.

A planning agent is in a position to have an evaluative ranking of alternative actions available beginning at a given time. She is also in a position to have an evaluative ranking of alternative plans for acting over time, and of alternative general policies. As a planning agent she will sometimes decide on a future-directed plan or policy. This involves settling on – and so, in an important sense, being committed to – ways of acting in the future. She might, for example, settle on a detailed plan for an anticipated job interview; and she might settle in advance on a general policy about, say, alcohol consumption. In settling on such plans or policies she comes to have relevant intentions to act in specified ways in specified future circumstances.

By settling now what she will do later a planning agent puts herself in a position to plan appropriate preliminary steps and means, and to filter options that are incompatible with planned action. This will work only if her plans are to some extent stable and she is not constantly reconsidering her prior decisions – not constantly starting from scratch. A theory of instrumentally rational planning agency is in part a theory of intention and plan stability: a theory of when an instrumentally rational planning agent should or should not reconsider and abandon a prior intention.

Many important issues about the rational stability of prior intentions concern appropriate strategies, given limitations of time and attention, for responding to unanticipated information that one's prior planning did not take into account.[8] Perhaps I settled on a plan

---

7 Much of the model to be described is discussed in my *Intention, Plans, and Practical Reason*, which also provides other details.
8 These were a primary concern in my discussions of stability in my *Intention, Plans,*

for an interview on the assumption that Jones would be the interviewer. When I get to the interview, I discover that Smith has taken her place. Should I stop to reconsider and, perhaps, replan? Here issues about our resource limits and the costs of reconsideration and replanning loom large. And here it seems natural to have a broadly pragmatic, two-tier model: we seek general habits and strategies of reconsideration that are, in the long run, effective in the pursuit of what we (rationally) desire. In a particular case we reasonably implement such pragmatically grounded general habits and strategies and, depending on the case, reconsider or refrain from reconsideration. This means that a planning agent may sometimes rationally follow through with a prior plan even though she would have rationally abandoned that plan if she had reconsidered it in light of relevant unanticipated information.

What about, in contrast, cases in which one's circumstances are, in all relevant respects, those for which one has specifically planned? Here it may seem natural simply to say that if one's plan was rational when formed, then surely it would be rational, barring relevant unanticipated information or change in basic desires or values, to execute it in those circumstances for which one specifically planned. But the issues here are complex.

III. AUTONOMOUS BENEFITS: TOXIN

Begin with Gregory Kavka's ingenious toxin case.[9] A billionaire has access to a technology that allows her to discern other people's intentions with almost flawless accuracy. She credibly offers to give me a lot of money on Tuesday if I form the intention on Monday to drink a disgusting but nonlethal toxin on Wednesday. I would be more than willing to drink the toxin to get the money. However, to get the money I do not need to drink the toxin; I just need to intend on Monday to drink it. But I need to arrive at this intention in a clear-headed way and without exploiting any external mechanisms (e.g., a

---

and *Practical Reason*, esp. chs. 5–6. See also my "Planning and the Stability of Intention." *Minds and Machines* 2 (1992), 1–16.

9 Gregory S. Kavka, "The Toxin Puzzle," *Analysis* 43 (1983), 33–6.

side bet). I would love to form this intention, but I have a problem. The benefit of the intention is, to use Kavka's term, "autonomous":[10] It does not depend causally on my actually executing the intention. I know that when Wednesday arrives I will already either have the money or I will not. In either case it seems that on Wednesday I will have no good reason to drink the stuff, and a very good reason not to, in precisely the circumstances in which I would have planned to drink it.[11] So it is not clear that I can rationally form the intention in the first place, despite its autonomous benefits.[12]

There are two ideas in the background here. The first is a principle that links the rationality of a prior intention with the rationality of

---

10 Gregory S. Kavka, *Moral Paradoxes of Nuclear Deterrence* (Cambridge: Cambridge University Press, 1987), p. 21.

11 This assumes that on Monday my mere intention, even in the special, science-fiction circumstances of the toxin case, does not by itself amount to an assurance to the billionaire of a sort that induces an obligation to drink the toxin. It also assumes that my intention to drink the toxin is not itself an intrinsic desire to drink toxin, an intrinsic desire of a sort that would give me an instrumental reason for drinking. Both assumptions are implicit in standard discussions of the toxin puzzle, and here I follow suit.

In his comments at the March 1995 Pacific Division meeting of the American Philosophical Association, Gilbert Harman challenged the second of these assumptions. (This challenge is also presented by Harman in his "The Toxin Puzzle" in Jules L. Coleman and Christopher W. Morris, eds., *Rational Commitment and Social Justice: Essays for Gregory Kavka* (Cambridge University Press, 1998), pp. 84–89, an essay that derives from his comments at the 1995 meeting.) Harman argues that the intention to drink toxin would be an intrinsic desire adopted for instrumental reasons. In this respect, he suggests, it would be like a new intrinsic desire to win a game, adopted because it is more fun to play when you care about winning.

I agree that if one does somehow come to have such a new intrinsic desire to drink, that may make it instrumentally rational to drink. But I do not see that an intention to drink toxin would generally be like this. After all, in coming to have the intrinsic desire to win, you come to care about winning – winning is now something that matters to you, if only temporarily. In intending to drink toxin in the kind of case we are discussing you would not in the same way care about drinking it.

12 Kavka writes that "you cannot intend to act as you have no reason to act, at least when you have substantial reasons not to act." ("The Toxin Puzzle," p. 35.) My remark in the text is in the same spirit, though it is offered as a remark about rational intention, rather than about intention *simpliciter*.

63

the later retention and execution of that intention. We may state this as a constraint on rational, deliberation-based intention: If, on the basis of deliberation, an agent rationally settles at t_1 on an intention to A at t_2 if (given that) C, and if she expects that under C at t_2 she will have rational control of whether or not she A's, then she will *not* suppose at t_1 that if C at t_2, then at t_2 she should, rationally, abandon her intention in favor of an intention to perform an alternative to A. Call this statement of a link between rational intention formation and supposed rational intention retention the *linking principle*.[13]

Second, there is the common idea that the instrumental rationality

---

13 I refer to versions of this principle also in my "Planning and Temptation," in *Mind and Morals*, ed. Larry May, Marilyn Friedman, and Andy Clark (Cambridge, MA: Bradford/MIT, 1995), pp. 293–310 [this volume, essay 3], and in "Following through with One's Plans: Reply to David Gauthier," in *Modeling Rational and Moral Agents*, ed. Peter Danielson (Oxford: Oxford University Press, 1998), pp. 54–65. Both Brian Skyrms, in remarks at the conference held in honor of Gregory Kavka, and Gilbert Harman, in his comments on my paper at the 1995 Pacific APA meeting, have suggested that the linking principle is challenged by cases of rational irrationality. (See Derek Parfit, *Reasons and Persons* [Oxford University Press, 1984], p. 13, and Thomas Schelling, *The Strategy of Conflict* [Cambridge, MA: Harvard University Press, 1980], p. 18.) These are cases in which it seems to be rational to cause oneself to have an intention to do something one knows it would be irrational to do. Now, it does not follow from the fact that it would be rational to cause oneself to intend to A if C that it would be rational so to intend. But in any case the formulation I have offered here of the linking principle is intended to circumvent these worries by limiting the cases to occasions on which the agent expects to retain rational control. These are, after all, the cases that are central here. (On this point I am in agreement with David Gauthier's remarks about rational irrationality in his "Commitment and Choice: An Essay on the Rationality of Plans," in *Ethics, Rationality, and Economic Behavior*, ed. Francesco Farina, Frank Hahn, and Stefano Vannucci [Oxford: Oxford University Press, 1996], pp. 217–43, at pp. 239–40.) My formulation also aims at forestalling complexities raised by Alfred Mele's case of Ted in his "Intentions, Reasons, and Beliefs: Morals of the Toxin Puzzle," *Philosophical Studies* 68 (1992), 171–94.

Both Skyrms and Harman indicated a preference for a principle that instead links a rational intention to A with a belief that one will A. I agree that a full story will include some appropriate belief condition (see my *Intention, Plans, and Practical Reason*, pp. 37–8), but I do not see this as precluding the linking principle formulated here.

of an action, in the kind of no-unanticipated-information cases of interest here, depends on the agent's evaluative ranking at the time of the action of options available then. Call this the *standard view*. On Wednesday my evaluative ranking will favor nondrinking over drinking. We infer, given the standard view, that even if I had earlier decided to drink toxin, when Wednesday arrives and the money is in the bank, instrumental rationality would require nondrinking. But then, given the linking principle and given that I am aware of these features of the case, I cannot rationally form the intention to drink in the first place. So there is a problem for rationally settling in advance on an intention to drink toxin despite the attractions of the autonomous benefit, a problem traceable to the joint operation of the linking principle and the standard view.

There is a complication. We have been supposing that in my prior deliberation on Monday about whether to drink toxin on Wednesday I take into account the autonomous benefit of an intention to drink. Does this mean that in my deliberation on Monday I am deliberating directly about the plan: intend on Monday to drink toxin on Wednesday, and then on Wednesday drink toxin? The problem with this is that my deliberation on Monday seems instead to be about what to do on Wednesday, not what to intend on Monday, though I know that a decision on Monday about what to do on Wednesday would involve an intention on Monday so to act. Granted, I might deliberate directly about whether on Monday to cause myself to intend to drink on Wednesday – for example, by taking a certain pill, or engaging in self-hypnosis. But that is a different matter.

Suppose, however, that on Monday I am directly deliberating about whether to drink toxin on Wednesday. I am not deliberating directly about the intention, on Monday, to drink. But this does not by itself show that I cannot include in my reasons for deciding to drink the fact that if I do so decide I win the money, whereas if I instead decide not to drink toxin I do not win the money.[14] The

14 In *Intention, Plans, and Practical Reason* I wrote that "in . . . deliberation about the future the desire-belief reasons we are to consider are reasons for various ways we might *act* later" (p. 103). This precluded appeal to autonomous benefits in delib-

barrier to winning the money in the toxin case is not a simple exclusion of the consideration of autonomous benefits in deliberation. If there is a barrier, it is, rather, the combination of the linking principle and the standard view.

IV. AUTONOMOUS BENEFITS: RECIPROCATION

Consider a second example. You and I are mutually disinterested, instrumentally rational strangers about to get off an airplane. We know we will never see each other – or, indeed, the other passengers – again. We also know that we each have a pair of suitcases, and that each of us would benefit from the help of the other in getting them down from the overhead rack. We each would much prefer mutual aid to mutual nonaid. Given our seating arrangements, however, you would need to help me first, after which I could help you. You will help me only if you are confident that I would, as a result, reciprocate. But we both see that once you help me I will have received the benefit from you that I wanted. My helping you later would, let us suppose, only be a burden for me. Of course, most of us would care about the plight of the other passenger, and/or have concerns about fairness in such a case. But let us here abstract away from such concerns, for our aim here is to determine what is required solely by

eration. I have changed my mind about this in response to criticisms from David Gauthier in his "Intention and Deliberation," in Danielson, *Modeling Rational and Moral Agents*, pp. 40–53. The linking principle I formulate here aims to retain a tight connection between rational intention and supposed rational execution of that intention, without precluding appeal to autonomous benefits in deliberation. T. L. M. Pink has offered a different criticism of my cited remark. See his "Purposive Intending," *Mind* 100 (1991), 343–59, and in more detail in his *Psychology of Freedom* (Cambridge: Cambridge University Press, 1996). Pink supposes that my remark disallows an appeal in deliberation to certain kinds of coordination benefits of a prior intention. Suppose, for example, that if I intend to go running tomorrow my intention will insure that I get a new pair of running shoes before then, thereby making my running more attractive. Pink thinks that my remark precludes appeal to this fact in my deliberation now about whether to run tomorrow. I am not sure that my remark has this implication. (In the example, note, the benefit of running with new shoes is a benefit of the act of running.) In any case I agree with Pink that we should allow appeal in deliberation to such coordination benefits.

instrumental rationality. Let us also suppose, again artificially, that my helping you or not would have no differential long-term effects (including reputation effects) that matter to me now. Given these special assumptions, it seems I would not have reason to reciprocate after you have helped me. Seeing that, you do not help me, so we do not gain the benefits of cooperation.[15]

In such a situation I might try to assure you I would reciprocate. But suppose I am not very good at deceit and will only be convincing to you if I really intend to reciprocate if you help me.[16] I would, then, very much like to provide a sincere assurance. Can I?

If an assurance from me issued in a moral obligation to reciprocate, then perhaps I could get a new reason to reciprocate simply by issuing such an assurance. But let us put direct appeal to such moral considerations to one side and see where the instrumental rationality of mutually disinterested agents would by itself lead. To achieve the benefits of a sincere assurance I must intend to reciprocate. But in the very special circumstances described, it seems that I will have, when the time comes, no reason to reciprocate. So it seems I cannot rationally intend to reciprocate, and so cannot gain the benefits of cooperation in such circumstances.

The point is not that there are no relevant considerations of fairness or of assurance-based obligation. The point is only that we may not get at such reasons, when, in such special cases, we confine our attention solely to instrumentally rational planning agency.

So we have two autonomous benefit cases: toxin and reciprocation. In each case I consider at t_1 whether to act in a certain manner (drink the toxin, help you if you have helped me) at t_2. I know that my so intending at t_1 would or may well have certain benefits prior to t_2 – my becoming richer; my being aided by you. But I also know that these benefits would be autonomous: they would not depend causally on my actually doing at t_2 what it is that at t_1 I would intend to do then. The execution at t_2 of the relevant intention would bring

15 Examples along these lines have figured prominently in the work of David Gauthier. See for example his "Assure and Threaten," *Ethics* 104 (1994), 690–721.

16 We could make this more realistic by assuming only that I know that a sincere assurance is considerably more likely to be successful than an insincere one.

with it only the burden of being sick or of helping you.[17] In each case, however, I prefer throughout the package of autonomous benefit and burden of execution over a package of neither.

Given my considered preference for such a package, can I in such cases rationally settle at t_1 on a plan that involves (conditionally or unconditionally) so acting at t_2? The linking principle tells us that rationally to settle on such a plan I cannot suppose that at t_2 I should, rationally, abandon my intention concerning t_2 – the intention to drink, or to reciprocate. But I know that under the relevant circumstances at t_2 my ranking would favor not drinking, or not helping. The standard view, then, says that at t_2 I should not execute my prior intention. If that is right then, given the linking principle, I cannot rationally and in a clearheaded way decide on the plan in the first place. Instrumental reason is an obstacle to gaining the autonomous benefits in such cases, even though I would gladly drink the toxin, or help you, in order to achieve those benefits.[18]

Is that right?

17 Recall that I am assuming in both of these cases that simply by forming the intention concerning t_2 I do not newly come to have a reason-giving intrinsic desire so to act.
18 These last two paragraphs draw (with changes) from my "Following Through with One's Plans: Reply to David Gauthier." For a trenchant discussion leading to a similar conclusion about the toxin case, see Daniel Farrell, "Intention, Reason, and Action," *American Philosophical Quarterly* 26 (1989), 283–95.

There is a possible complication concerning the reciprocation case (pointed out to me in different ways by Meir Dan-Cohen and David Gauthier). Suppose I do not follow through and so do not reciprocate even though you have helped me. I get the benefit of your help without the burden of my helping you. But I also get evidence about myself – evidence that I tend not to follow through in such cases. This evidence may make me in the future more skeptical than I would have been if I had followed through that I would follow through with such intentions in the yet farther future, and thereby make me less likely in the future to form intentions to reciprocate. I would, then, be in the future less likely to achieve associated autonomous benefits. So perhaps in those cases in which I expect to be in an indeterminate number of future situations of potential cooperation (even with different potential partners) I do have reason now to follow through and reciprocate.

This argument cites what we might call a *reflexive* reputation effect. I tried to

V. SOPHISTICATION AND RESOLUTION

An agent who adjusts her prior plans to insure that what she plans to do will be, at the time of action, favored by her then-present evaluative rankings has been called a "sophisticated" planner.[19] Given the conjunction of the linking principle with what I have termed the

---

abstract away from reputation effects in my characterization of our reciprocation case. But it might be objected that if we preclude even such reflexive reputation effects we are imposing an overly severe limitation on our discussion.

My response is, first, that if this argument succeeds, we should just grant that it is only a limited range of cases of potential reciprocation that are our concern here, namely, those cases that really do have the structure of the toxin case, a structure in which the primary consideration in favor of follow-through derives from the autonomous benefit of the prior plan rather than from the future effects of follow-through. But, second, I am skeptical that the argument succeeds. The argument depends in part on the claim that if I do follow through and reciprocate this time, I will as a result have reason to be more confident that I would follow through in the future and so will, as a result, achieve such self-confidence. But we are assuming that I am, and know I am, generally an instrumentally rational agent. So, for my present follow-through to support a rational belief in my own future follow-through, it needs to support the belief that such future follow-through would be instrumentally rational; otherwise I will tend to infer that my present follow-through is not a good predictor of my future conduct. But it is not clear how the appeal to the reflexive reputation effects of my present follow-through supports a claim about the rationality of future follow-through. (Perhaps what is crucial is not the reflexive reputation effects of my present follow-through but rather that my present follow-through gives me evidence that later follow-through would itself have certain reflexive reputation effects that would tend to make that later follow-through rational. But if my present follow-through only gives me evidence of that – if the rationality of later follow-through is not itself an effect of my present follow-through – it is not clear how this helps the argument.) A related concern is that the linking principle says that I can in the future rationally intend to reciprocate only if (roughly) I judge then that it would be *rational* in the farther future to follow through. It will, again, not be enough for me just to expect that I would (perhaps not rationally) follow through. And it is not clear how appeal to reflexive reputation effects of present follow-through can show that such follow-through in the farther future would be rational.

19 I learned this terminology, and much else, from Edward F. McClennen, *Rationality and Dynamic Choice: Foundational Explorations* (Cambridge: Cambridge University Press, 1990).

standard view, an instrumentally rational planning agent will be sophisticated, and so will not be in a position deliberatively to form the intention needed to get the autonomous benefits in our two cases.

The intuition that, to the contrary, instrumental rationality should not always stand in the way of such autonomous benefits suggests an alternative approach, one that retains the linking principle but abandons the standard view. The basic idea is that if it was best in prospect to settle on a prior plan, and if there is no unanticipated information or change in basic values, then it is rational to follow through with that plan in those circumstances for which one specifically planned. Settling on a plan to drink toxin, or to reciprocate if helped, might well be best in prospect, given relevant autonomous benefits. So it may be rational to follow through with such a plan in planned-for circumstances, even though, at the time of follow-through, one would thereby be acting contrary to one's then-present evaluative ranking of one's then-present options. So, instrumental rationality need not stand in the way of the money or of mutual aid. Borrowing a term from Edward McClennen, we may call this a version of "resolute choice."[20] In anticipation of a later distinction I will call it, more specifically, *strong resolution*.

Call the conjunction of the linking principle and the standard view *sophistication*. Both sophistication and strong resolution accept the linking principle, and both allow one to consider autonomous benefits in deliberation about plans for the future. Where they differ is in their view of rational intention retention and execution. Sophistication accepts the standard view; strong resolution says, instead, that a prior plan settling on which was – because of autonomous benefits – best in prospect, can trump a later, conflicting evaluative ranking concerning planned-for circumstances.

To these two approaches we may add a third, a qualified form of

---

20 Ibid. See also Laura DeHelian and Edward F. McClennen, "Planning and the Stability of Intention: A Comment," *Minds and Machines* 3 (1993), 319–33. I do not try to do justice to the complexity and subtlety of McClennen's detailed views here. In particular, his defense of his version of resolute choice is limited in important respects. My broad characterization of strong resolution will, I think, suffice for the purposes of the present discussion.

resolution defended by Gauthier.[21] Suppose that settling on a certain prior plan at t_1 is favored by one's evaluative ranking then. Suppose that the attractions of settling on this plan include expected autonomous benefits prior to t_2; and suppose that this plan specifically calls for one to A at t_2, given circumstance C. Suppose C does obtain at t_2; and suppose there is neither unanticipated information about this circumstance nor change in basic values. Gauthier proposes that one should stick with the plan if and only if one thereby does better than one *would have* done if one had not settled on the plan in the first place, at t_1.

This view qualifies strong resolution with a further, counterfactual test on rational follow-through. There are autonomous-benefit cases in which strong resolution would call for follow-through and yet Gauthier would not. These include certain cases of failed threats.[22] In the toxin case and the reciprocation case, however, Gauthier's view matches strong resolution. In drinking toxin or reciprocating one does better than one would have done if one had initially not settled on the plan to drink or to reciprocate. So one may rationally drink the toxin, and one may rationally reciprocate. Let us call Gauthier's view *moderate resolution*.

Both strong and moderate resolution focus on the evaluation of courses of action, as individuated by the agent's intentions and plans.[23] Strong resolution treats the prior evaluation of a course of action as critical, allowing it, in certain cases, to determine the rationality of later follow-through in planned-for circumstances. Gauthier adds a further, counterfactual test on rational follow-through, a test that

---

21 See his "Assure and Threaten," "Commitment and Choice," and "Intention and Deliberation."

22 This is a change from Gauthier's earlier views about deterrence. See his "Deterrence, Maximization, and Rationality," *Ethics* 94 (1984), 474–95. Gauthier's views about following through with a failed threat are complicated and involve consideration of general policies of issuing and carrying out certain kinds of threats. For a probing discussion and criticism see Joe Mintoff, "Rational Cooperation, Intention and Reconsideration," *Ethics* 107 (1997), 612–43.

23 Gauthier writes: "in deliberating rationally, one considers whether one's course of action is best . . . where a course of action is distinguished and demarcated by its intentional structure." "Assure and Threaten," p. 717.

concerns the comparative evaluation at the time of action of the overall course of action. But both views agree that if one's intentions and plans see one's conduct at t_2 as fitting into a larger course of action that began at t_1 (perhaps only with a decision), then it is the assessment of that larger course of action, a course of action some of which is already in the past, that is crucial. Strong resolution highlights the assessment at t_1 of that course of action; at t_2 one refers back to that assessment. Gauthier adds a role for a comparison at t_2 of that course of action with its t_1-through-t_2 alternatives. But both agree that it is the overall course of action that is one's concern, even at t_2. That is why, for Gauthier, one should follow through and reciprocate if one has been helped; for the course of action that began at t_1 with a sincere assurance that one would reciprocate if helped, and then includes reciprocating after having been helped, is seen at t_2 as superior to alternative courses of action available beginning at t_1.[24]

One evaluates, then, not simply alternatives from now on, but courses of action as individuated by one's intentions and plans. These courses of action can include elements already in the past, elements over which one no longer has causal control. On both views, then, intentional structure can trump temporal and causal location.

This is in tension with a basic fact about our agency. As time goes by we are located differently with respect to our plans. Along with a change in temporal location normally goes a change in the agent's causal powers. What is up to the agent is what to do from now on. So she will normally want to rank alternatives beginning from now on.

Granted, the agent may well rank her alternatives with respect to past events: she may, for example, be grateful for past benefits or want revenge for past harms. The point is not that a rational agent does not care about the past. The point concerns, rather, what is now under the control of the agent. What is now under her control are her

---

24 What about the sequence: Sincerely assure at t_1; do not reciprocate at t_2? This is not a sequence that one could decide on at t_1, since the intention not to reciprocate would mean that the assurance is not sincere. So it is not a "course of action" available beginning at t_1.

alternatives from now on.[25] So it seems she will want to rank those alternatives. Both versions of resolution concern themselves instead with courses of action that typically include elements no longer in the agent's causal control. This seems to me not to do justice to the significance of temporal and causal location to our agency. Strong and moderate resolution, in seeking a strong role for planning in achieving the benefits of coordination over time and across agents, seem not to do justice to the basic fact that as agents we are temporally and causally located.

A reply will be that in giving such priority to intentional structure a resolute agent employs a deliberative procedure that is, in the words of Gauthier, "maximally conducive to one's life going as well as possible."[26] One who employs such a procedure will win money in toxin cases and gain benefits of cooperation. But it is difficult to see why this shows that *at the time of action* one will not reasonably consult one's ranking of options that are at that time in one's control. If one is concerned with what is "maximally conducive to one's life going as well as possible," why wouldn't one be concerned with which action, of those presently in one's control, is "maximally conducive to one's life going as well as possible"? Faced with the toxin on Wednesday, however, the action presently in one's control that is maximally conducive to that benefit is, we may suppose, not drinking.

VI. TEMPORARY REVERSALS IN RANKINGS

I am skeptical, then, about strong and moderate resolution.[27] But I also think that sophistication is too simple.

25 Compare Bernard Williams's remark that "The correct perspective on one's life is *from now.*" *Moral Luck* (Cambridge: Cambridge University Press 1981), p. 13.

26 Gauthier, "Assure and Threaten," p. 701.

27 In a recent essay J. David Velleman tries to anchor a Gauthier-like view about reciprocation and assurance in a fundamentally different line of argument, one that appeals to the idea that action has a constitutive aim. I do not try to assess Velleman's alternative strategy here. See J. David Velleman, "Deciding How to Decide," in *Ethics and Practical Reason*, ed. Garrett Cullity and Berys Gaut (Oxford: Clarendon Press, 1997), pp. 29–52.

Consider Ann. She enjoys a good read after dinner but also loves fine beer at dinner. However, she knows that if she has more than one beer at dinner she cannot concentrate on her book after dinner. Prior to dinner Ann prefers an evening of one beer plus a good book to an evening with more than one beer but no book. Her problem, though, is that each evening at dinner, having drunk her first Pilsner Urquell, she finds herself tempted by the thought of a second: For a short period of time she prefers a second beer to her after-dinner read.[28] This new preference is not experienced by her as compulsive. If asked, she will say that right now she really prefers to go ahead this one time and have the second drink, despite the impact on her ability to concentrate later, though she will also acknowledge that even now she prefers that she resist similar temptations on future nights. As she knows all along, this change in ranking will be short-lived: after dinner she will return to her preference for a good read.

Prior to dinner on Monday Ann prefers

(1) one beer at dinner on Monday plus a book after dinner

to

(2) more than one beer at dinner on Monday and no book after dinner.

In the middle of dinner, after her first beer, this preference reverses, and she prefers (2) over (1). By the end of dinner, she again prefers (1) over (2), though by then this preference will express itself either in relief or in regret. Throughout dinner, however, Ann continues to prefer

(3) one beer at dinner and a book after, for all nights,

to

(4) more than one beer and no book for all nights.

28 I assume that there really is a preference shift, that she is not merely confused about what her preferences are. My discussion of the case of Ann owes much to George Ainslie, *Picoeconomics: The Strategic Interaction of Successive Motivational States within the Person* (Cambridge: Cambridge University Press, 1992).

But it is also true that during dinner on Monday Ann temporarily prefers

(3') more than one beer and no book on Monday, but one beer and a book on all other nights

to (3).[29]

What is Ann to do? We might say to Ann: "You should settle in advance on a policy of having at most one beer at dinner and then stick with that policy in the face of expected temptations. In that way you will achieve (3) rather than (4), thereby satisfying a preference you will have throughout. Granted, on each night there will be a slightly modified policy you will prefer to (3). On Monday, for example, you will prefer (3') to (3). But this will be only temporary. The preference that will persist throughout is for (3) over (4). By settling on a policy in favor of (3), that is what you can achieve."

Might this be sensible advice? Might Ann rationally settle on such a policy and then rationally stick with it in the face of a diverging preference?

Note that we are not asking whether it is always rational to resist all temptations. Nor are we supposing that if, in a particular case, it would be rational to stick with such a prior policy, that very fact ensures that one does. Note finally that I am understanding evaluative rankings as aspects of the real, explanatory story of action. Although such rankings are susceptible to a broadly functional characterization,

29 Ainslie, in *Pioeconomics*, tries to show that temporary preference reversals like Ann's would occur in agents who have certain – as he believes, extremely common – highly bowed temporal discount functions. But we do not need to discuss here Ainslie's diagnosis of such cases to agree that they are common. Our preferences for certain goods – be they beer, mystery novels, chocolates, or others you can cite from your own experience – do seem susceptible to this kind of temporary shift.

I consider Ainslie's views in "Planning and Temptation," where I discuss a wine-drinking pianist whose problem is similar to Ann's, except that whereas Ann's preference reversal is triggered by her drinking the first beer, the pianist's preference reversal is triggered by the arrival of dinnertime. Given this difference, Ann's case may not cohere with Ainslie's claim that the primary mechanism underlying such preference changes is generally one of temporal discounting.

they are not merely the reflection of actual choice and action. In this sense of "ranking" it is possible for Ann intentionally to stick with her policy and to act contrary to her present ranking (even though there is also a sense in which, if she so acts, that is what she most wanted).[30] Our question is whether this may be rational.

Sophistication answers in the negative. Despite her prior one-beer policy, at dinner Ann prefers a second beer. So, given the standard view, that is what instrumental rationality requires. A sophisticated Ann cannot even settle on the one-beer policy in the first place.

Such a blanket prohibition on settling on and sticking with such policies in the face of temporary rankings to the contrary seems to me mistaken. It seems to me that instrumentally rational willpower sometimes involves sticking with a sensible prior policy in the face of a diverging temporary preference. Can we make theoretical room for rational willpower of this sort?

We might distinguish here between a reversal of a mere preference and a reversal of an evaluative ranking.[31] Only the latter, we might say, trumps a prior policy. This may work for some cases of temptation, but I do not think that it does justice to all that is at stake. First, some versions of Ann's case may involve temporary changes in evaluative ranking. And second, for reasons that will emerge, there remain important issues about a planning agent's concern with her own future assessments.

Ann's case is in some respects similar to the toxin and reciprocation cases. In all three cases there is a prior plan or policy settling on which is best in prospect. And in all three cases the agent knows that when the occasion for action arrives her rankings of then-present options will argue against following through. But there is also a significant difference between the cases. The underlying desires and values that argue for abandoning a plan to drink toxin, or a plan to reciprocate,

---

30 Here I agree with similar remarks of Gauthier's in "Commitment and Choice," pp. 238–9. For a different approach to preference see Sarah Buss, "Autonomy Reconsidered," *Midwest Studies in Philosophy* 19 (1994), 95–121.

31 Compare Gary Watson, "Free Agency," *Journal of Philosophy* 72 (1975), 205–20. This appeal to Watson's distinction was a suggestion of J. L. A. Garcia, in conversation.

are stable. Ann's preference for two beers, in contrast, is temporary. I want to see whether an account of instrumentally rational planning agency should exploit this difference and, if so, how. But first I need to look at a different kind of case.

VII. SLIPPERY-SLOPE INTRANSITIVITIES

Consider Warren Quinn's example of the potential self-torturer who agrees to allow an extremely tiny medical device to be permanently attached to his body. The device generates a constant electric current of varying levels, from 0 (no current) to 1,000 (extremely high and extremely painful current). Each increment, from setting n to setting $n + 1$, is so small that he cannot feel the difference, though he can of course feel the difference between setting 0 and setting 1,000. The device begins at setting 0, and the potential self-torturer is given an initial ten thousand dollars for allowing it to be attached. He is also offered ten thousand dollars for each advance in the setting (something he can choose once each week) from setting n to setting $n + 1$, though he knows that once the device is advanced to a higher setting it cannot be returned to a lower setting.

This poses a problem:

Since the self-torturer cannot feel any difference in comfort between adjacent settings, he appears to have a clear and repeatable reason to increase the voltage each week. The trouble is that there *are* noticeable differences in comfort between settings that are sufficiently far apart. Indeed, if he keeps advancing, he can see that he will eventually reach settings that will be so painful that he would then gladly relinquish his fortune and return to 0.[32]

This potential self-torturer has intransitive preferences.[33] He prefers setting 1 to setting 0, setting 2 to setting 1, and so on. But he prefers

---

32 The example is from Warren Quinn, "The Puzzle of the Self-Torturer," in his *Morality and Action* (Cambridge: Cambridge University Press, 1993), pp. 198–209, at p. 198. Quinn provides references to relevant literature. Thanks to Liam Murphy for bringing Quinn's essay to my attention.

33 Quinn says that such intransitivities bar the potential self-torturer from saying that each setting is better than the preceding one, for *better than* is, Quinn says, a transitive relation. But Quinn also says that the preferential ranking may be

setting 0 to setting 1,000. Further, these intransitive preferences are there all along. This is not a case of preference change over time, though once the process gets going, different preferences are engaged at different times.

What is the potential self-torturer to do? Quinn suggests he should decide in advance on a "*reasonable* stopping point" and then stick with it when he gets there.[34] In that way he gets more than enough money to compensate for the discomfort but does not find himself in unacceptably extreme suffering.[35]

This is good advice. But to follow this advice the agent will need to stick with his prior decision in the face of a stable preference to go on. Suppose that he prefers 15 to 0, and 0 to 16: 15 is, so to speak, the *switch point relative to 0*. Suppose that for this reason the agent decides in advance to stop at this switch point – to stop at 15.[36] When he gets to 15 he will prefer to move to 16, and that is a preference that was there all along. To stick with his prior decision he must act contrary to his ranking of 16 over 15, and that would violate the standard view and so sophistication.

I have rejected strong and moderate resolution as applied to our

---

thoughtful and informed, and so an appropriate candidate for shaping choice (ibid., p. 199). So we may allow it to provide evaluative rankings in the sense relevant here.

34 Ibid., p. 206.

35 In his discussion Quinn seems to endorse "the principle that a reasonable strategy that correctly anticipated all later facts (including facts about preferences) still binds" (ibid., p. 207). We need to be careful, however, not to interpret this principle in a way that would justify sticking with a plan to drink toxin. (In an earlier essay Quinn had indicated that he would not welcome such a result. See "The Right to Threaten and the Right to Punish," in his *Morality and Action* [Cambridge: Cambridge University Press, 1993], pp. 52–100, at p. 98.)

36 I owe to David Gauthier the suggestion that such a switch point relative to 0 is a reasonable point at which to settle in advance on stopping. (In the absence of some such argument the agent might be in a Buridan situation: He might know that there is reason to decide in advance on a stopping point, but there might be no single point such that there is reason to decide to stop there rather than at some competitor.) Note that in reaching a decision to stop at the switch point relative to 0 the agent may know that there is also a later switch point *relative to 15* – a later point that is preferred to 15 but whose successor is dispreferred to 15.

autonomous-benefit cases. For these cases sophistication is a superior response to the fact that our agency is located temporally and causally. But as a view about cases of temptation, and of slippery-slope intransitivities, sophistication seems overly simple. We need to steer a path between resolution and sophistication.

VIII. PLANNING AGENCY AND FUTURE REGRET

Ann prefers, at the time of action, to drink a second beer; I prefer at the time of action not to drink toxin. Given, in each case, a prior intention to the contrary, why should Ann's drinking a second beer be a potential candidate for rational criticism whereas my refraining from drinking toxin is not? Why should rational intention stability distinguish in this manner between toxin and temptation?

Suppose that you are an adviser to Ann, or to the potential self-torturer. You might well say: "Stick with your plan or policy. If you do, you will be glad you did. And if you do not, you will wish you had." We can spell this out as an argument offered at the time of action:

(a) If you stick with your prior intention, you will be glad you did.

(b) If you do not stick with your prior intention, you will wish you had.

So, other things being equal,

(c) Though you now prefer to abandon your prior intention, you should nevertheless stick with it.

Statement (a) says, roughly, that the agent would not regret sticking with her prior intention; (b) says, roughly, that she would regret not sticking with her intention. Let us say that when (a) and (b), suitably interpreted, are true, following through with one's prior intention satisfies the *no-regret condition*.[37] Sophistication (since it accepts the standard view) holds that in our no-unanticipated-information cases

---

37 Note that this no-regret condition includes both the absence of regret at having followed through and the presence of regret if one did not follow through.

it is instrumentally rational to follow through with one's prior intention to A at t only if one's evaluative ranking at t favors A over one's other options at t. But consideration of the no-regret condition suggests an alternative view: In the kind of no-unanticipated-information cases we are considering, the agent's reasonable anticipation at the time of action that follow-through would satisfy the no-regret condition can sometimes make follow-through rational even in the face of a present ranking to the contrary.[38]

The agent, then, is to ask at the time of action, t_2, about her attitude at some appropriate later time, t_3, concerning options still available at t_2. I will say more shortly about what counts as an appropriate later time. Note, though, that the anticipated attitude at t_3 that is at issue concerns options still in one's power at t_2. We are not considering one's anticipation at t_2 of an assessment at t_3 of overall courses of action beginning *earlier* than t_2. We want the options being assessed to be options still available to the agent at the time of plan follow-through, t_2, for we are trying to be responsive to the fact that agency is located temporally and causally.

Such a view would continue to subscribe to the linking principle, but it would reject the standard view for some cases like that of Ann or of Quinn's potential self-torturer. I want to spell out how such a view would work.

Begin with Ann. She knows that she will be glad after dinner if she has stuck with her policy and had only one beer; and she knows that after a second beer, faced with the later part of the evening, she will wish that she had stuck with her one-beer policy. So she knows that in following through with a one-beer policy she would satisfy the no-regret condition.

---

38 Versions of the idea that anticipated future regret, or its absence, can matter to the rationality of present conduct appear in a number of studies. See, e.g., Graham Loomes and Robert Sugden, "Regret Theory: An Alternative Theory of Rational Choice under Uncertainty," *Economic Journal* 92 (1982), 805–24. (Note, though, that the regret that is central to the Loomes and Sugden theory is the result of new information that was not available at the time of the (regretted) action; my focus, in contrast, is on anticipated later regret that does not depend on such new information.) See also John Rawls, *A Theory of Justice* (Cambridge, MA: Harvard University Press, 1971), pp. 421–3.

The case of the potential self-torturer is more complicated. We need first to ask how far into the future he is to look. After all, very shortly after moving from 15 to 16, he may still be glad he gave up on a prior intention to stop at 15. However, at the time of his choice between 15 and 16, he can ask: "If I abandon my prior decision to stop at 15, what will then transpire?" And it seems he may reasonably answer: "I would then follow the slippery slope all the way to 1,000." His prior decision to stop at 15 was his best shot at playing the game without going all the way; if he does not stick with that decision, there is little reason to think he would stick with any other decision short of the bottom of the slippery slope.[39] Further, he can anticipate that were he to slide all the way to 1,000 he would then wish that he had instead stopped at 15: He would then wish he had earlier followed through with his yet-earlier decision and stopped at 15 rather than abandoning that decision and sliding all the way to 1,000. This line of reasoning can reasonably lead him to accept versions of (a) and (b), appropriately interpreted, concerning his following through with his plan to stop at 15: He would be glad later if he stuck with his plan and would regret it if he did not. So he can conclude at the time of action that his following through with his intention to stop at 15 satisfies the no-regret condition.

Now consider the toxin case. Suppose on Wednesday you try saying to me: "I know you prefer not to drink toxin, despite your prior intention to drink. But you will later be glad if you did drink it, and if you do not drink it you will later wish you had." I think I would surely object. On Wednesday I already either have the money or not. If I have the money and yet abandon an intention to drink, I will be *glad* I abandoned that intention and so avoided the pains of the toxin!

It might be replied that even after Wednesday I still prefer money and drink to no money and no drink. So perhaps I would later be glad I had stuck to my intention and drunk the toxin, given my

---

39 He need not think that his descending the slippery slope all the way to 1,000 would be *caused* by his failure to stop at 15. It is enough that he believe that if he does not stick with his plan to stop at 15 he will go all the way to 1,000. I return to related matters at the end of this section.

preference for the package of toxin plus money. But recall that we are considering my reflections at the time of action, on Wednesday. By this time the first part of the package – whether I have the money or not – is already fixed. My choice at that time – what remains under my control then – concerns the second part of the package: to drink or not to drink. What I want on Wednesday to know is how I will later assess *these* options. And it seems that I will reasonably conclude on Wednesday that at the end of the week, and holding fixed the past prior to my Wednesday decision, I would regret following through and drinking the toxin. Granted, if I did follow through I might later be glad that I am that kind of guy – the kind of guy who wins the money in such cases. But that is not later to favor the option on Wednesday of drinking over the option on Wednesday of not drinking, given that the money is, by Wednesday, already in the bank. So following through with an intention to drink toxin would not satisfy the no-regret condition, properly interpreted.

A similar point can be made for the case of reciprocation, as we have understood it. Suppose I intended to reciprocate, you have helped me with my luggage, and I am now considering reciprocating. Given the special assumptions we are making about the case, I will see that, after all is done, I would later favor not following through, for then I would have thereby gotten the benefit without the burden. As in the toxin case, if I did follow through I might be glad I am that kind of guy, but that seems a different matter.

The no-regret condition, then, seems to divide the cases in the manner we anticipated: It is reasonably believed by the agent at the time of action to be satisfied by follow-through in some cases of temptation and of slippery-slope intransitivity, but not to be satisfied by follow-through in our cases of toxin and reciprocation. In our temptation case, the agent can anticipate that looking back later she will be glad of earlier follow-through. In the toxin case the agent can anticipate that looking back later he would regret earlier follow-through.[40]

---

40 Consider the much-discussed case of Ulysses and the Sirens. (See, in particular, Jon Elster, *Ulysses and the Sirens: Studies in Rationality and Irrationality*, rev. ed. [Cambridge: Cambridge University Press, 1984].) Suppose Ulysses decides in ad-

To deepen our discussion we need to reflect further on regret. Regret should be grounded in some appropriate evaluative ranking. In particular, the agent's regret at t_3 concerning abandoning her prior intention at t_2 is, we may suppose, grounded in some appropriate evaluative ranking. What ranking?

In our temptation case, the answer is clear: Ann's later regret that earlier she had a second beer is grounded in her later ranking of one beer over two – a ranking she did not have at the time of drinking the second beer. Matters are more complex, however, for the potential self-torturer. He can see that if he abandons his intention and opts for 16 there is good reason to expect that he will continue all the way to 1,000. And he can see that when he gets to 1,000 he will wish he had stuck at 15: He will regret having abandoned his intention to stop at 15. But this regret is not grounded in a ranking of 15 over 16: There is no reason to think that he has reversed his ranking of 16 over 15. In what ranking, then, is the regret grounded?

Well, 15 is the switch point relative to 0. Is the relevant ranking his ranking of 0 over 16?[41] But we want the regret to concern what is still available to the agent at the time of choice between 15 and 16; for we want to respect the way in which agency is temporally and causally located. And 0 is no longer available at the time of choice between 15 and 16. This suggests that the ranking that is critical is, instead, his ranking of 15 over where he ends up, 1,000,[42] for both of those remain available at the relevant time. Perhaps, then, we can understand the relevant anticipated regret as grounded in *that* ranking: if he opts for 16, he will end up at 1,000; if he sticks with his intention, he will stay at 15; and he will regret his

---

vance to sail by the Sirens, but when he hears them his ranking changes in just the way he had anticipated. Ulysses is like Ann in one respect: He knows that if he sticks with his prior decision to sail by he will be glad he did. But on some versions of the Ulysses case, and unlike the case of Ann, it is also true that if he does not stick with his prior decision he will be glad he did not! So follow-through would satisfy one but not *both* parts of the no-regret condition. So there will be important cases of temptation and the like that are similar in certain respects to the one I have discussed but will need a different treatment.

41 A suggestion of Gideon Yaffe's.

42 I am assuming that this is indeed a ranking of our agent.

failure to stick with his intention to stop at 15 because he ranks 15 over 1,000.

But if that is the ranking that grounds the relevant regret, we have a puzzle about this case that does not arise in the temptation case. The ranking that grounds the later regret relevant to Ann's case is not a ranking that Ann has when she is faced with the temptation. But if the potential self-torturer ranks 15 over 1,000, that is a ranking that is there all along. In particular, it is there at the time of the choice between 15 and 16. If this ranking is relevant to the rationality of that choice, why isn't it relevant in a straightforward way, at the time of the choice itself? Why is there a need to look to later regret?

There is a good reason why this ranking, at the time of action, of 15 over 1,000 would not by itself support the choice of 15 over 16. The choice of 16 is *evidence* that one will go all the way to 1,000: it is, we are supposing, evidence that one's underlying psychology is such that one will likely go all the way. But the choice of 16 does not itself *cause* one's going all the way to 1,000; it is, rather, itself an effect of the mechanisms that will cause one's going all the way. There are large issues here, issues associated with "Newcomb's problem."[43] For present purposes let me just say that it seems to me that it is normally not a reason in favor of a choice that it is merely evidence of, and does not contribute to, something that is valued. At the time of the choice between 15 and 16 the agent could reasonably appeal to the ranking of 15 over 1,000 if he thought that the choice of 16 would cause his going all the way to 1,000. But that is not what the potential self-torturer thinks: he only thinks that a choice of 16 would be evidence that he will go all the way.

That explains why we cannot appeal to the ranking, at the time of action, of 15 over 1,000 to explain why it might be rational to stick with the intention to stop at 15. But if we cannot appeal to that ranking at the time of action, how can we appeal to it at the end, when the agent is in the throes of pain experienced at setting 1,000?

The answer seems to be that there is a kind of regret that is

43 See, for starters, Robert Nozick, "Newcomb's Problem and Two Principles of Choice," in *Essays in Honor of Carl G. Hempel*, ed. Nicholas Rescher et al. (Dordrecht: Reidel, 1969).

grounded in a ranking of what would have resulted from certain past conduct as compared with what has actually transpired.[44] At the end of the day the self-torturer sees that, indeed, after choosing 16 he did go on all the way to 1,000, and he sees that that would not have happened if he had stuck with his intention to stop at 15. If he had stopped at 15, he would, as a result, not have ended up at 1,000. He therefore regrets not having stuck with his intention to stop at 15. This regret seems to be grounded in his ranking of 15 over 1,000, even though he does not see his choice, instead, of 16 as causing his ending up at 1,000. Given his ranking of 15 over 1,000, it is enough to support this regret that he believes that if he had stuck with his intention to stop at 15 he would (as a result) not have ended up at 1,000 (which is in fact where he did end up). It is the potential self-torturer's anticipation of such later regret that supports the argument that it may be rational for him to stick with his intention to stop at 15.[45]

IX. WHY FUTURE REGRET CAN MATTER

Why should anticipated satisfaction of the no-regret condition matter to an instrumentally rational planning agent? Let us reflect on the

---

44 I do not say: "a ranking of what certain past conduct would have been evidence for (but not a cause of) as compared with what has actually transpired."

45 Gideon Yaffe has wondered whether there is an instability here. The potential self-torturer, let us suppose, sticks with his prior intention to stop at 15 in part because he believes that if he instead goes on to 16 he will (likely) go on to 1,000. But if he does stop at 15 he can, perhaps, reasonably believe that if he instead intended to stop at the (later) switch point *relative to 15* (supposing there is one) he might well pull that off. (After all, we have given reason to think it would then be rational to do so.) Suppose the agent had earlier decided on 15, the switch point relative to 0. Faced with the choice of 15 or 16, he wonders whether to stick with his prior decision. He sees that if he *does* stick with it, he *would* (probably) stick with a decision to stop at the (later) switch point relative to 15. So why not go on to that later switch point? The answer seems to be that if he does go on past 15 he will not have this evidence that he will stop at the later switch point. That seems sufficient to support his stopping at 15. Having stopped at 15, it may seem that one has available an argument for going on to the next switch point, but that argument would be undermined by one's going on and so seems not to have practical force.

very idea of a planning agent. Planning is future oriented. In being engaged in planning agency, one seems to be committed to taking seriously how one will see matters in the relevant future. One seems, in particular, to be committed to taking seriously how one will see matters at the conclusion of one's plan, or at appropriate stages along the way, in the case of plans or policies that are ongoing.[46] This gives anticipated future regret or nonregret on relevant future occasions a special significance to an agent engaged in settling on and following through with plans. That is a major reason why the anticipated satisfaction of the no-regret condition matters to an instrumentally rational planning agent. This also helps somewhat to clarify how far into the future the agent is to look. Implicit in one's planning is, normally, a rough conception of what counts as − as we might say − plan's end.[47]

The idea is not simply that anticipation of future regret or nonregret can change one's present evaluative ranking, though no doubt it can. The idea, rather, is that anticipation of future regret or nonregret can be relevant to the stability of a prior intention of a planning agent; it can be relevant to the question of when it is reasonable to reconsider and abandon a prior intention, and when not.[48] Our concern with stability, recall, is a concern with when it is rational to stick with a prior intention, given that one already has it; it is not simply a concern about the formation of a new intention from scratch.

This clarification helps defuse a possible objection. I have argued

---

46 This qualification concerning ongoing plans or policies should be understood throughout the discussion that follows.

47 These last two sentences benefited greatly from conversation with Elijah Millgram. For some suggestive remarks broadly in the spirit of this paragraph, see Gerald J. Postema, "Morality in the First-Person Plural," *Law and Philosophy* 14 (1995), 35–64, at pp. 56–7. See also Thomas E. Hill, Jr., "Pains and Projects," in his *Autonomy and Self-Respect* (Cambridge: Cambridge University Press, 1991). Hill writes that "the commitment to make my choices justifiable to myself later seems implicit in any project of deep deliberation" (p. 186). I am suggesting that a somewhat analogous commitment is implicit in planning agency more generally.

48 Of course, it may be that anticipated regret can play other roles in practical reasoning as well. See, for example, Robert Nozick, *The Nature of Rationality* (Princeton: Princeton University Press, 1993), p. 185, n. 21.

that anticipated future regret or nonregret can have a special relevance to a planning agent. But, faced with temptation, why couldn't an agent simply abandon any relevant planning and thereby escape the rational pressures of such anticipations?[49] The answer is that the agent comes to the temptation with relevant prior intentions, and so there is already an issue about whether she may rationally simply give them up. This is the issue of rational intention stability that we have been addressing. And so long as she has these intentions she is a planning agent in a manner that makes salient relevant, anticipated future regret.

In some cases, granted, one will reasonably side with one's present ranking and abandon one's prior plan, while recognizing that one will later regret it. Perhaps one now sees one's anticipated later regret as deeply misguided, or perhaps one anticipates that one's later regret will itself not be stable. The inference from (a) and (b) to (c) in the earlier argument is defeasible. Indeed, at the level of generality at which we have been proceeding there may be no simple principle that sorts out those cases in which this inference goes through from those in which it does not. But this inference can still have force in certain cases for a planning agent: that is what sophistication fails to see, and that is the key to our explanation of how rational intention stability distinguishes between toxin and temptation.

My claim is not that the no-regret condition has force simply because, in the words of Thomas Nagel, one sees "oneself as a temporally extended being for whom the future is no less real than the present."[50] Nagel argued that such a conception of oneself as temporally extended supports a concern with one's future desires. But that is not my argument. The force of the no-regret condition is not grounded simply in the recognition that one is a "temporally extended being." It is grounded, further, in one's actual engagement in relevant planning agency, and in the resulting significance to one of how one will see matters specifically at plan's end.

---

49 Tim Schroeder suggested an objection along such lines.
50 Thomas Nagel, *The Possibility of Altruism* (Oxford: Oxford University Press, 1971), p. 69. See also Rawls's remarks about seeing oneself "as one continuing being over time." *A Theory of Justice*, p. 422.

I am appealing to certain later attitudes toward now-available options, later attitudes one now anticipates that one will actually have if one proceeds with one's plan and completes it in a certain manner (or, alternatively, if one abandons one's plan). My appeal is not merely to some ranking one would have if one were to step back from pressures of present choice, nor is my appeal to regret or nonregret at the time of plan follow-through concerning one's earlier decisions, nor is it to a ranking made from some detached perspective on the whole of one's life.[51] Finally, the relevant, anticipated later attitudes concern courses of action that are still available to the agent at the time of the anticipation, at the time of plan follow-through. They are not rankings of general traits of character or of general procedures of deliberation.[52]

Earlier I indicated my endorsement of a broadly pragmatic, two-tier approach to plan stability and rational reconsideration in the face of resource limits and unanticipated new information. My main concern here, however, has been with perplexities about certain no-unanticipated-information cases in which one's ranking at the time of action argues against follow-through, and in which issues of resource limits are not germane. For some of these cases I have rejected the standard view, and so sophistication. But in doing this I have not appealed to a pragmatic, two-tier theory of plan stability; for I have argued that such an appeal in these kinds of cases would not do justice to the fact that our agency is temporally and causally located. Instead I have appealed to a planning agent's concern with how she will see her present decision at plan's end. It is this concern, not an appeal to a two-tier pragmatic structure, that supports a distinctive kind of in-

---

51 J. David Velleman emphasizes the significance of those evaluations of a person that "are relative to the perspective of his life as a whole" in his "Well-Being and Time," *Pacific Philosophical Quarterly* 72 (1991), 48–77, at p. 67.

52 I am not saying that at the time of follow-through one might not anticipate such later assessments – including forms of regret – concerning general character traits, or courses of action that began well before the time of follow-through. I am only saying that it is not one's anticipation, at the time of follow-through, of those later attitudes that is critical to plan stability, for those later attitudes are not focused on what is now, at the time of follow-through, in one's control.

tention stability in certain no-unanticipated-information cases, and thereby a path between resolution and sophistication.[53]

Resolution does not do full justice to the way in which our agency is located temporally and causally. Sophistication does not do full justice to the way in which our engagement in planning agency normally bestows a special significance on how we will see our now-present action at plan's end. By avoiding both extremes we arrive at a view of instrumentally rational planning agency that does justice both to the fact that we are planners and to the fact that we are temporally and causally located agents. Instrumental rationality does limit access to certain kinds of autonomous benefits, even for a planning agent. Nevertheless, there are no-unanticipated-information

---

53 I do not claim this is the only source of the cited intention stability. My concern is only to identify a major source of such stability, one that responds differently to toxin and to temptation, and one that is not grounded in a two-tier pragmatic structure. In my discussion of the toxin case in *Intention, Plans, and Practical Reason*, ch. 6, I argued, as I do here, that rationality stands in the way of follow-through. But my argument there assumed that our approach to stability in such no-new-information cases should stay roughly within the two-tier framework I had developed primarily for new-information cases in which our resource limits play a central role and in which the crucial issue is whether or not to reconsider one's prior intention. I no longer accept that assumption.

Remarks in this and the preceding paragraph in the text are intended to indicate briefly what seem to me to be some significant differences between my view here and ideas about temptation and related cases in Gauthier's "Resolute Choice and Rational Deliberation: A Critique and a Defense," *Noûs* 31 (1997), 1–25. Concerning cases of temptation, Gauthier contrasts preferences that the agent has at the time of action with "(temporal) *vanishing point* preferences that he acknowledges when choice is not imminent" (p. 20). The notion of a vanishing-point preference is in some respects similar to, but is not the same as, my notion of one's attitude at plan's end: Vanishing-point preferences are preferences, either earlier or later, when "choice is not imminent," not specifically at plan's end. Gauthier's view about cases like Ann's is "based on a comparison of the effects on an agent's overall prospects of different modes of choice" (p. 23). I have here, in contrast, eschewed such a two-tier pragmatic approach to such cases and appealed instead to the significance to a planning agent of anticipated regret or nonregret at plan's end. Finally, Gauthier appeals (p. 24) to possible regret, at the time of action, concerning an earlier decision. The regret I appeal to is regret one anticipates at the time of action that one will have later, at plan's end.

cases in which an instrumentally rational planning agent can reasonably commit herself in advance to a plan or policy and then reasonably follow through, rather than simply conform to her rankings at the time of action.

PART TWO

SHARED AGENCY

5

Shared Cooperative Activity

I. SHARED COOPERATIVE ACTIVITY: THREE FEATURES

We have a recognizable and important concept of a shared cooperative activity. This concept picks out a distinctive kind of interpersonal interaction, one that many of us see as important in our lives. You and I might sing a duet together, paint a house together, take a trip together, build something together, or run a give-and-go[1] together in a basketball game. In many such cases ours will be a shared coopera-

Ancestors of this essay were presented at colloquia at Stanford University, University of California at Davis, the March 1990 Paris Conference on Convention cosponsored by Stanford University and The Ecole Polytechnique, Davidson College, University of North Carolina–Chapel Hill, University of North Carolina–Greensboro, University of California at Berkeley, and the Rational Agency research group at the Center for the Study of Language and Information. I have benefited in particular from the suggestions and criticisms of Dorit Bar-On, David Brink, Philip Cohen, Rachel Cohon, David Copp, Charles Dresser, Fred Dretske, Jean Hampton, John Heil, Daniel Herwitz, Thomas Hill, David Israel, Martin Jones, Michael Jubien, Pierre Livet, Kirk Ludwig, Al Mele, Michael O'Rourke, John Perry, Martha Pollack, Gary Rozencrantz, Geoffrey Sayre-McCord, Debra Satz, Kwong-loi Shun, Thomas Smith, Bruce Vermazen, Bernard Williams, and the editors of the *Philosophical Review*. Work on this essay was supported in part by the Stanford University Humanities Center and by the Center for the Study of Language and Information. Support from the Center for the Study of Language and Information was made possible in part through an award from the System Development Foundation.
1 A standard offensive basketball play.

tive activity. Such shared cooperative activities can involve large numbers of participating agents and can take place within a complex institutional framework – consider the activities of a symphony orchestra following its conductor. But to keep things simple I will focus here on shared cooperative activities that involve only a pair of participating agents and are not the activities of complex institutions with structures of authority.

Shared cooperative activity (SCA) involves, of course, appropriate behaviors. If you and I successfully engage in the SCA of painting the house together then, of course, we paint the house together. But we might paint the house together without acting cooperatively. Perhaps neither of us even knows of the other's activities, or though we each know of the other's activities neither of us cares.

Given appropriate behaviors, what else is needed for ours to be a SCA? Suppose that you and I sing a duet together, and that this is a SCA. I will be trying to be responsive to your intentions and actions, knowing that you will be trying to be responsive to my intentions and actions. This mutual responsiveness will be in the pursuit of a goal we each have, namely, our singing the duet. You may have this goal for different reasons than I do; but at the least we will each have this as a goal. Finally, I will not merely stand back and allow you to sing your part of the duet. If I believe that you need my help I will provide it if I can.

This suggests that we can identify, in a rough and preliminary way, a trio of features characteristic of SCA:

(i) *Mutual responsiveness*: In SCA each participating agent attempts to be responsive to the intentions and actions of the other, knowing that the other is attempting to be similarly responsive. Each seeks to guide his behavior with an eye to the behavior of the other, knowing that the other seeks to do likewise.[2]

(ii) *Commitment to the joint activity*: In SCA the participants each have an appropriate commitment (though perhaps for differ-

2 See Thomas Schelling, *The Strategy of Conflict* (Cambridge: Harvard University Press, 1960), chap. 4.

ent reasons) to the joint activity, and their mutual responsiveness is in the pursuit of this commitment.[3]

(iii) *Commitment to mutual support*: In SCA each agent is committed to supporting the efforts of the other to play her role in the joint activity. If I believe that you need my help to find your note (or your paint brush) I am prepared to provide such help; and you are similarly prepared to support me in my role. These commitments to support each other put us in a position to perform the joint activity successfully even if we each need help in certain ways.

Using this trio of features as my guide, I want to say more precisely what SCA is. I hope thereby to lay the groundwork for an understanding of the distinctive value to us of SCA. But here I limit myself to the prior question about the nature of SCA.

One point is clear: There are cases which satisfy (i) without satisfying either (ii) or (iii). Consider two opposing soldiers in a battle. Each tries to be responsive to the intentions and actions of the other, knowing that the other is trying to be similarly responsive. Each acts on his expectations about the other, expectations based on beliefs about the other's expectations about him, and so on "in the familiar spiral of reciprocal expectations."[4] So there is cognitive interdependence. But each is being responsive in this way in the pursuit of a personal goal of survival, and neither is prepared to help the other. So there can be mutual responsiveness in the pursuit of personal goals without commitment to a joint activity and without commitment to mutual support. This said, I turn to (ii).

II. COMMITMENT TO THE JOINT ACTIVITY

In SCA each agent is appropriately committed to the joint activity. But what does this mean? What is it for me to be committed to *our*

3 Similar ideas are suggested by, for example, H. P. Grice, "Logic and Conversation," in *The Logic of Grammar*, ed. Donald Davidson and Gilbert Harman (Encino, Calif.: Dickenson, 1975), at 68, and by John Cooper, "Friendship and the Good in Aristotle," *Philosophical Review* 86 (1977): 290–315, at 305.

4 Schelling, 87.

joint activity? My initial conjecture is that this commitment typically involves, in part, an *intention in favor of the joint activity*.[5] Each agent may have such an intention for different reasons: When we paint together I may be primarily concerned with having a newly painted house, you with getting some exercise. But in SCA each agent will typically[6] have such an intention for some reason or other.[7]

We must be careful here. In analyzing SCA we will run into problems of circularity if we appeal to intentions that we *act together cooperatively*. To avoid these problems we need to distinguish joint-act-types that are *cooperatively neutral* from those that are *cooperatively loaded*. A cooperatively loaded joint-act-type – for example, trying to solve a problem together – already brings in the very idea of cooperation. In contrast, in the case of cooperatively neutral joint-act-types, joint performance of an act of that type may be cooperative, but it

---

5 Thanks to Philip Cohen for helping to persuade me of some of the virtues of this initial conjecture. I offer a general account of the commitment characteristic of intention in *Intention, Plans, and Practical Reason* (Cambridge: Harvard University Press, 1987), hereafter *Intention*.

6 Let me indicate why I say only "typically." I argue in *Intention*, chapter 8, that, while intentionally to *A* one needs to intend something, in certain cases an individual can intentionally *A* without intending *to A*. There will probably be similar complexities for cases of SCA; but here (with the exception of a brief remark in note 10) I put them to one side.

7 A number of theorists have explored, in varying ways, conjectures about the role of intentions, or other practical attitudes, in favor of a joint activity. See, for example, Wilfred Sellars, *Science and Metaphysics* (London: Routledge & Kegan Paul, 1968), 217ff.; Margaret Gilbert, *On Social Facts* (New York and London: Routledge, 1989), esp. chap. 7; Hector J. Levesque, Philip R. Cohen, and José H. T. Nunes, "On Acting Together," *Proceedings of the National Conference on Artificial Intelligence* (Menlo Park, Calif.: AAI Press/MIT Press, 1990), 94–99; John R. Searle, "Collective Intentions and Actions"; Barbara J. Grosz and Candace L. Sidner, "Plans for Discourse"; and Jerry R. Hobbs, "Artificial Intelligence and Collective Intentionality: Comments on Searle and on Grosz and Sidner." These last three papers are in *Intentions in Communication*, ed. Philip R. Cohen, Jerry Morgan, and Martha E. Pollack (Cambridge: MIT Press, 1990). Raimo Tuomela believes that "one can only intend to do something oneself in the last analysis" ("What Goals Are Joint Goals?" *Theory and Decision* 28 [1990]: 1–20, at 10) but still appeals to the idea of having a joint action as a goal. See Raimo Tuomela and Kaarlo Miller, "We-Intentions," *Philosophical Studies* 53 (1988): 367–89.

need not be. There is, for example, a clear sense in which we can go to New York together or paint the house together without our activity being cooperative. We might satisfy the behavioral conditions for such joint activities without having the attitudes essential to cooperative activity. Our analysis of SCA should appeal to intentions in favor of joint activities *characterized in cooperatively neutral ways*.

Talk of my intention that we perform a joint-act-type *J* may still seem suspect. I cannot, after all, attempt to perform your or our actions. But if this is true about attempts, isn't it also true about intentions? Isn't what one intends one's own actions? And if so, how can we make sense of an appeal to my intention that *we J*?

In response, I grant that what one attempts are one's own actions. But it is a mistake to assume that intending and attempting are subject to the same constraints on their contents. Many approaches to intention see intentional action and action done with an intention as the basic phenomena, thereby lending support to the idea that intention must be tied directly to action. This may make it plausible that the limits of what one can attempt are the limits of what one can intend. But, as I have argued elsewhere, our conception of intention also significantly involves our conception of the roles of future-directed intentions as elements of partial plans.[8] This planning conception of intention allows us to be more liberal about what can be intended than we are about what can be attempted; for references to things other than our own actions can function appropriately in our plans. I can engage in planning aimed at settling on means to our joint action: I can, for example, figure out how to support our singing the duet – perhaps by helping you find your note. And I can try to ensure that the rest of my plans are consistent with our performance of a certain joint action: I can, for example, eschew ways of singing that will

---

8 In *Intention* I argue that intentions, as elements of partial plans, pose problems for further practical reasoning, given the demand that one's plans be means–end coherent, and constrain solutions to those problems, given demands for the consistency of plans. In these ways prior partial plans provide a settled background framework for further practical reasoning. The point I go on to make in the text is that intentions in favor of joint activities can play analogous roles in structuring further reasoning.

prevent your coming in on time. In these ways the planning conception of intention supports the legitimacy of the appeal to my intention that *we J*.[9]

In our SCA, then, you and I each intend that we perform the (cooperatively neutral) joint action.[10] I now turn to cases that suggest in different ways that such intentions, while necessary, do not yet ensure the appropriate kind of commitment to the joint action.

III. MESHING SUBPLANS AND INTERDEPENDENT INTENTIONS

Suppose you and I each intend that we paint the house together. However, I intend that we paint it red all over, and you intend that we paint it blue all over. We each know this about the other, know that we each know this, and so on. And neither of us is willing to compromise. Even if as a result we end up painting the house together (some combination of red and blue), ours would not be a SCA.[11]

You and I each have subplans with respect to our house painting, and these subplans disagree. This may suggest that SCA requires agreement in the agents' subplans. But this is too strong. Suppose I intend that we paint the house with an inexpensive paint, and you intend that we paint it with a paint purchased at Cambridge Hardware. I don't care where we buy the paint, and you don't care about the expense. Still, we could proceed to paint the house with an inexpensive paint from Cambridge Hardware. Our activity could be cooperative despite differences in our subplans.

---

9 Though we can still retain a distinction between intentions *that* we *J* and intentions *to* perform some action. In "Objects of Intention" (*Philosophical Studies* 70 [1993]: 85–128), Bruce Vermazen also argues that intentions are not limited to intentions to act.

10 But recall the qualification cited in note 6. There may be cases of SCA in which the relevant intentions in favor of *J* are more qualified. For example, it can perhaps be enough in certain cases only to intend that we *J* unless *p*, for some unexpected *p*. But here I put such complexities to one side.

11 Thanks to Rachel Cohon for helping me get this example right.

In this second case, despite differences in our subplans, there is a way of our painting the house together such that none of the activities would violate either of our subplans. Let us say that our individual subplans concerning our J-ing *mesh* just in case there is some way we could J that would not violate either of our subplans but would, rather, involve the successful execution of those subplans. In the first case, then, our subplans fail to mesh; in the second case they do mesh, despite some divergence.

This suggests that in SCA each agent does not just intend that the group perform the (cooperatively neutral) joint action. Rather, each agent intends as well that the group perform this joint action in accordance with subplans (of the intentions in favor of the joint action) that mesh.

Why not just say that cooperative activity must be motivated by subplans that do *in fact* mesh? Why should we build a meshing condition into the *content* of each individual's intention? Well, suppose that you and I each intend that we paint the house together, our subplans happen so far to mesh, but neither of us is committed to maintaining this mesh. Suppose our subplans happen to agree on red. We may still ask how I would be disposed to act if you were unexpectedly to announce a preference for blue. In the absence of a commitment to mesh I would tend to be willing to bypass (rather than seek a mesh with) your subplans, so long as we still thereby paint the house together. For example, I might try to pour red paint into your paint can when you are not looking. And this would signal the absence of a cooperative attitude characteristic of SCA. If, in contrast, I intended not merely that we paint together, but that we do so in accordance with meshing subplans, then I would need instead to track this more complex goal. I would normally do this by working with you to achieve such a mesh.

Of course, even if I intend that we perform the joint action in accordance with meshing subplans I need not be willing to accept *just any* subplans that mesh. There may, for example, be colors that are, for me, simply beyond the pale.[12] What you and I will be prepared

12 Credit the example to an editor of the *Philosophical Review*; blame the pun on me.

to accept will depend in part on our relevant desires and intentions. If these diverge too much we may fail to arrive at adequate, meshing subplans and so fail in our effort at SCA.

In SCA, then, each agent intends that the group perform J in accordance with subplans that mesh. Turn now to another example. You and I each intend that we go to New York together, and this is known to both of us. However, I intend that we go together as a result of my kidnapping you and forcing you to join me. The expression of my intention, we might say, is the Mafia sense of "We're going to New York together." While I intend that we go to New York together, my intentions are clearly not cooperative in spirit. Cooperation, after all, is cooperation between intentional agents each of whom sees and treats the other as such; and in intending to coerce you in this way I intend to bypass your intentional agency. This suggests that for our J-ing to be a SCA I must intend that we J in part *because of* your intention that we J and its subplans. In this way my intention favors your participation as an intentional agent.

However, once we bring into the content of my intention the efficacy of your intentions, it is a short step to including as well the efficacy of *my own* intentions. In SCA I will see each of the cooperators, *including me*, as participating, intentional agents. If this obliges me to include the efficacy of your intention and subplans in the content of my relevant intention, then it also obliges me to include the efficacy of my own intention and subplans in this content. Otherwise there would be in the content of my intention a deep asymmetry between you and me; and I do not see what would support such an asymmetry.

These considerations, taken together, argue that in SCA each agent intends that the group perform the joint action in accordance with and because of meshing subplans of each participating agent's intention that the group so act. That is, for cooperatively neutral J, our J-ing is a SCA only if

(1)(a)(i) I intend that we J.

(1)(a)(ii) I intend that we J in accordance with and because of meshing subplans of (1)(a)(i) and (1)(b)(i).

(1)(b)(i) You intend that we J.

(1)(b)(ii) You intend that we *J* in accordance with and because of meshing subplans of (1)(a)(i) and (1)(b)(i).[13]

Some important points of clarification about the intentions cited in (1): I may intend that we *J* by way of meshing subplans even though there are as yet no specific, meshing subplans such that I intend that we *J* by way of them. You and I may not yet have filled in each of our subplans, or we may have filled them in in ways which do not yet mesh. We may be involved in negotiations about how to fill in our plans even while we have already started to *J*. What (1) requires is only that we each intend that there be meshing subplans on which we eventually act. Indeed, given my intention in favor of our achieving meshing subplans, I may still bargain with you in an effort to ensure that we *J* in a certain way. This may eventually prevent us from arriving at subplans that mesh; but it may not. If our bargaining does lead to meshing subplans our resulting *J*-ing may still be a SCA. Finally, even once our subplans have been completed in ways that mesh, (1) does not require that all the details of each agent's subplans be known to the other. According to (1) I must intend that my subplans mesh with yours whatsoever they may be. But I may neither know nor care about the details of some of your subplans. Though I need to know that you will buy the paint, I may remain ignorant about where you buy it.

Conditions (1)(a) and (1)(b), so interpreted, are central to my account of SCA. But more needs to be said. Begin by recalling the case of coercion. In this case I intended to force you into joining me on a trip to New York in a way that would bypass your intentional agency. But not all coercion works like that. Suppose I put a gun to your head and tell you that either you must decide that we will go to New York together and then act on that decision or I will pull the trigger. This is attempted coercion, and my attitude is not coopera-

13 I number the conditions in this way to make it clear how they are related to others to be introduced later. In stating (1)(a)(ii) and (1)(b)(ii) in this way I am assuming that they entail that I/you intend that we *J* in accordance with and because of (1)(a)(i) and (1)(b)(i). These conditions are to some extent in the spirit of Grice's classic discussion of meaning; but there are also very important differences. See H. P. Grice, "Meaning," *Philosophical Review* 66 (1957): 377–88.

tive, to say the least. But in this case what I intend does include the efficacy of your intention in the route from my threat to your action. To block such cases let us add the further condition

(1)(c) The intentions in (1)(a) and in (1)(b) are not coerced by the other participant.[14]

Consider now the cognitive conditions on SCA. It follows from (1)(a)(ii) and (1)(b)(ii) that we each believe the conjunction of (1)(a)(i) and (1)(b)(i). But we will want to say something stronger than this. In SCA the fact that there is this mutually uncoerced system of intentions will be in the public domain. It will be a matter of common knowledge among the participants.[15] I will know that we have these intentions, you will know that we have these intentions, I will at least be in a position to know that you know this, and so on. So we will want to add

(2) It is common knowledge between us that (1).

It is the web of intentions cited in (1) that ensures the commitments to the joint activity characteristic of SCA. In SCA, then, there is an important kind of interdependence of intention. The system of intentions characteristic of SCA must be *interlocking*; for each agent must have intentions in favor of the efficacy of the intentions of the other. In this way each agent must treat the relevant intentions of the other as *end-providing* for herself; for each intends that the relevant intentions of the other be successfully executed. And this system of intentions must also be *reflexive*; for each agent must have intentions concerning the efficacy of her own intentions.[16] SCA involves appro-

---

14 Suppose that in reaching meshing subplans you intentionally use large advantages in bargaining power to dictate the terms of our agreement. In some extreme cases this may count as coercion. If it does then condition (1)(c) on SCA will fail to be satisfied. (Here I benefited from discussion with Debra Satz.)

15 There is a large literature on the idea of common knowledge. See, for example, David Lewis, *Convention: A Philosophical Study* (Cambridge: Harvard University Press, 1969). Here I simply use it as an unanalyzed idea.

16 A number of philosophers have argued that in individual intentional action the content of the agent's intention involves a kind of self-referentiality. (See, for example, Gilbert Harman, "Practical Reasoning," *Review of Metaphysics* 29 [1976]:

priately interlocking and reflexive systems of mutually uncoerced intentions concerning the joint activity.

IV. COMMITMENT TO MUTUAL SUPPORT

Return now to feature (iii) of SCA: the commitment of each agent to support the other's attempts to play her role in the joint action. Do the attitudes cited so far ensure this feature?

To some extent they do. Suppose I intend that we sing the duet together. I am committed to pursuing means and preliminary steps I believe to be necessary for our so acting. That follows from demands of means–end rationality on my intentions. So I am committed to helping you play your role in our joint action to the extent that I believe such help to be necessary.

But what if I believe that you will not need my help? I might then intend that we sing together and still not be at all prepared to help you should you unexpectedly need it. Consider, for example, the case of the unhelpful singers: You and I are singing the duet. I fully expect you to get your notes right, and so I intend to coordinate my notes with yours so that we sing the duet. But I have no disposition at all to help you should you stumble on your notes; for I would prefer your failure to our success. Were you unexpectedly to stumble I would gleefully allow you to be embarrassed in front of the audience – as I might say, "One false note and I'll abandon you to the wolves." And you have a similar attitude: You fully expect me to get my notes right, and so you intend to sing your notes in a way that meshes with mine. But were I to stumble you would not help; for you prefer my failure to our success.[17] We each intend that we sing the duet in the

_____

431–63; and John Searle, *Intentionality* [Cambridge: Cambridge University Press, 1983].) When I intentionally raise my arm what I intend is that it go up as a result of this very intention. Or so it is claimed. My claim about the reflexivity of the intentions in SCA is close to being an analogous view about SCA. Nevertheless, my view about SCA does not by itself entail the aforementioned view, or even some close variant of it, about individual intentional action. Indeed, I suspect that SCA and individual intentional action will differ in this respect.

17 These dispositions not to help may themselves be publicly known. My point is

world as we expect it to be, and we each intend that we do so by way of meshing subplans. But we do not have commitments to support each other of the sort characteristic of SCA. If we, as unhelpful singers, do in fact sing the duet together our singing may be *jointly intentional*; but it is not a SCA.[18]

SCA involves commitments to support the other that go beyond those of the unhelpful singers. How much beyond? Some participants in a SCA may be willing to incur what would normally be seen as fairly high costs in helping the other; others may be willing to help only if the costs thereby incurred are of a sort that would normally be seen as minimal. Willingness to support the other comes in degrees. Is there a threshold beyond which feature (iii) of SCA is realized?[19] I think there is.

Suppose (a) you and I satisfy conditions (1) and (2) on SCA, as these conditions have so far been specified, and are embarked on our J-ing; (b) a problem arises for you: you continue to have the relevant intentions but you need help from me to act in ways necessary for our J-ing successfully; (c) I could successfully help you without undermining my own contribution to our J-ing; (d) there are no new reasons for me to help you in your role in our J-ing (you do not, for example, offer me some new incentive to help you); (e) this is all common knowledge. Let us say that circumstances satisfying (a)–(e) are *cooperatively relevant to our J-ing*. For our J-ing to be a SCA there must be at least some cooperatively relevant circumstance in which I would be prepared to provide the necessary help. And similarly for you.

This is a minimal requirement; and there will be cases of SCA in

---

not that there is an absence of what Levesque et al. call a "robustness against misunderstandings" ("On Acting Together," 95).

18 So John Searle's remark that "[t]he notion of . . . collective intentionality, implies the notion of *cooperation*" is too strong ("Collective Intentions and Actions," 406). Still, both jointly intentional action and SCA will involve somewhat similar webs of intentions concerning the joint activity. So if a joint-act-type were to be loaded with respect to joint intentionality but still not, strictly speaking, cooperatively loaded, we would still not want to appeal to it in specifying the intentions essential to SCA.

19 I am indebted to David Copp for helping me formulate the problem in this way.

which it is important that the participants' willingness to help goes beyond this. Still, it is a requirement with some bite. In particular, the mere presence of intentions that we *J* (by way of meshing subplans) need not by itself ensure satisfaction of this requirement. That is the lesson of the case of the unhelpful singers. Let us say that an intention is *minimally cooperatively stable* if there are cooperatively relevant circumstances in which the agent would retain that intention. In SCA the agents' relevant intentions [that is, the intentions cited in condition (1)] are minimally cooperatively stable.[20] This stability of intention ensures that there is a commitment to help in some cooperatively relevant circumstance.

I can now fully state my account of the attitudes essential to SCA.[21] Where *J* is a cooperatively neutral joint-act-type, our *J*-ing is a SCA only if

(1)(a)(i) I intend that we *J*.

(1)(a)(ii) I intend that we *J* in accordance with and because of meshing subplans of (1)(a)(i) and (1)(b)(i).

(1)(b)(i) You intend that we *J*.

(1)(b)(ii) You intend that we *J* in accordance with and because of meshing subplans of (1)(a)(i) and (1)(b)(i).

(1)(c) The intentions in (1)(a) and in (1)(b) are not coerced by the other participant.

(1)(d) The intentions in (1)(a) and (1)(b) are minimally cooperatively stable.

(2) It is common knowledge between us that (1).

---

20 I discuss a general notion of intention stability in several places. See, for example, *Intention*, and "Planning and the Stability of Intention," *Minds and Machines* 2 (1992): 1–16. In my view, while some degree of stability is characteristic of the intentions of reasonable agents, an intention may be reasonable in its stability and yet still not be minimally cooperatively stable.

21 With this account in hand we can return to the distinction between jointly intentional action and SCA and treat the former as the genus and the latter as a species of that genus. At least part of what is distinctive of SCA is its satisfaction of (1)(c) and (1)(d), and certain aspects of (1)(a)(ii) and (1)(b)(ii). (I was helped here by conversation with David Copp.)

V. MUTUAL RESPONSIVENESS AND THE CONNECTION CONDITION

If our J-ing is a SCA three things must be true: we J; we have the appropriate attitudes; and these attitudes are appropriately *connected* to our J-ing. Having given my account of the attitudes involved in SCA, I turn to the connection condition.

This brings us back to feature (i) of SCA: mutual responsiveness. Our intentions that we J by way of subplans that mesh will normally lead each of us to construct our own subplans with an eye to meshing with the other's subplans. This is mutual responsiveness of *intention*. But in SCA there will also be mutual responsiveness *in action*. Consider our SCA of singing the duet. Our intentions lead each of us to be appropriately responsive to the actions of the other: I listen closely to when and how you come in, and this helps guide my own singing; and you are similarly responsive. In SCA our relevant attitudes lead to the joint activity by way of mutual responsiveness both of intention and in action. This supports the following claim:

For cooperatively neutral J, our J-ing is a SCA if and only if
- (A) we J,
- (B) we have the attitudes specified in (1) and (2), and
- (C) (B) leads to (A) by way of mutual responsiveness (in the pursuit of our J-ing) of intention and in action.

This connection condition helps us see the difference between SCA and what I will call *prepackaged cooperation*. In prepackaged cooperation we have the attitudes specified in (1) and (2), and we work out, in advance, just what roles we each will play in our J-ing. So there is mutual responsiveness of intention. But then we each go off and play our role with no further interaction with the other: there is no mutual responsiveness in action. While our activity of prior planning may itself be a SCA, our noninteractive performance of J does not satisfy condition (C), the connection condition: It is prepackaged cooperation, not SCA. Suppose, for example, you and I lay plans for you to go to San Francisco while I go to New York.²² We might

22 Example courtesy of an editor of the *Philosophical Review*.

106

have a web of intentions concerning this joint activity, a web that satisfies (1) and (2). And our activity of prior planning may itself be a SCA. But if when we each go our separate ways there is no mutual responsiveness in action, our activity is prepackaged cooperation, not SCA.

VI. COMPETITION AND LEVELS OF MESH

Suppose you and I play a game of chess together. This will involve some cooperation. We cooperate in keeping the pieces in place, making our moves public, following rules about the movements of pieces, and so on. Yet within this cooperative framework our activity is competitive: I am not trying to mesh my specific game plan with yours; instead I am trying to thwart your game plan. A joint activity can be cooperative down to a certain level and yet competitive beyond that. And on the present account such an activity – one in which we do not intend that our subplans mesh all the way down – is not a SCA.

We can nevertheless capture the sense in which our competition takes place within a cooperative framework. You and I do not intend that our subplans mesh all the way down. But you and I do intend that our subplans mesh down to the level of the relevant rules and practices. Our chess playing is not a full-blown SCA. But it is jointly intentional, and it involves shared cooperation down to the cited level.[23]

VII. CONCLUDING REMARKS

We can tie some threads together by reviewing some of our examples. The case of the battling soldiers is one of mere mutual responsiveness in which only feature (i) is present. In the Mafia case and in the case in which we firmly disagree about the color of the paint, there are intentions in favor of the joint action. But these intentions fail, in different ways, to be appropriately interlocking. So feature (ii) is not fully present. In the case of the unhelpful singers each agent

23 John Searle makes a similar point in "Collective Intentions and Actions," 413–14.

intends that they perform the joint action by way of subplans that mesh. But these intentions are not minimally cooperatively stable. So we have features (i) and (ii), but not feature (iii). In prepackaged cooperation there is mutual responsiveness of intention, but not mutual responsiveness in action; so feature (i) is not fully present. Finally, SCA involves mutual responsiveness – of intention and in action – in the service of appropriately stable, interlocking, reflexive, and mutually noncoerced intentions in favor of the joint activity. This account of SCA is broadly individualistic in spirit; for it tries to understand what is distinctive about SCA in terms of the attitudes and actions of the individuals involved.[24] And in restricting its analysans to joint-act-types that are cooperatively neutral, it aims at a noncircular account of SCA, one that is reductive in spirit[25] and that emphasizes an important kind of interdependence of intention.

---

24 Assuming that the common knowledge condition can be understood along individualistic lines.

25 In "Collective Intentions and Actions" John Searle argues that "collective intentional behavior is a primitive phenomenon" (401) and that we should eschew "a reductive analysis of collective intentionality" (406). In *On Social Facts* Margaret Gilbert focuses on "plural subject concepts": When we cooperatively sing the duet together we constitute a "plural subject." Gilbert argues that this notion of a plural subject is not itself reducible (see, e.g., 435–36). In contrast with both Searle and Gilbert, I have argued that a useful reduction may be possible here.

6

Shared Intention

In *Choice: The Essential Element in Human Action* Alan Donagan argued for the importance of "will" to our shared understanding of intelligent action.[1] By "will" Donagan meant a complex of capacities for forming, changing, retaining, and sometimes abandoning our choices and intentions. (Choice is, for Donagan, a "determinate variety of intending.")[2] Our capacity to intend is to be distinguished both from our capacity to believe and from our capacity to be moved by desires. And Donagan thought that intentions involve what, following Austin, he called " 'as it were' plans."[3]

I am broadly in agreement with these main themes in Donagan's

Thanks to Margaret Gilbert and Raimo Tuomela, thoughtful commentators on presentations of earlier, shorter versions of this article. Thanks also to Philip Clark, Rachel Cohon, Fred Dretske, David Hilbert, Henry Richardson, and Debra Satz for their useful philosophical advice. Barbara Herman and J. David Velleman provided rich and probing comments when this article was presented at the September 1992 Memorial Conference in Honor of Alan Donagan, held at the University of Chicago. Some of the issues they raised are discussed further in my "Shared Intention and Mutual Obligation" (presented at the Pacific Division American Philosophical Association, San Francisco, March 1993). (See this volume, essay 7.) Work on this article was supported in part by the Center for the Study of Language and Information, made possible in part through an award from the System Development Foundation.

1 Alan Donagan, *Choice: The Essential Element in Human Action* (London: Routledge & Kegan Paul, 1987).

2 Ibid., p. 97.

3 Ibid., p. 96.

book, and I will pretty much take them for granted in what follows.[4] I will suppose that intention is a distinctive attitude, not to be reduced to ordinary desires and beliefs; that intentions are central to our shared understanding of ourselves as intelligent agents; and that "the study of intention" is in part the "study of planning."[5] My hope is that these common elements in our views about intention can serve as a basis for reflection on the phenomenon of shared intention.

I

That we do sometimes have intentions that are in an important sense shared seems clear. We commonly report or express such shared intentions by speaking of what *we* intend or of what *we* are going to do or are doing. Speaking for you and myself I might say that we intend to paint the house together, to sing a duet together; and I might say that we are going to New York together. In each case I report or express a shared intention.

Sometimes we speak of the intentions of structured social groups: The Philosophy Department, for example, intends to strengthen its undergraduate program. But some shared intentions are not embedded in such institutional structures. These will be my main concern here: I will focus on cases of shared intention that involve only a pair of agents and do not depend on such institutional structures and authority relations. Supposing, for example, that you and I have a shared intention to paint the house together, I want to know in what that shared intention consists.[6]

On the one hand, it is clearly not enough for a shared intention to

---

4 I developed ideas that are in some respects similar to Donagan's themes in my *Intention, Plans, and Practical Reason* (Cambridge, Mass.: Harvard University Press, 1987). Of course, there are various differences in our views. Donagan discusses one of these – concerning the consistency demands to which intentions are subject – in *Choice*, pp. 98–105. My detailed treatment of choice differs in certain ways from Donagan's (see *Intention, Plans, and Practical Reason*, chap. 10). And there are other differences as well. But these differences are not relevant here.

5 Donagan, *Choice*, p. 95.

6 There is a recent literature in artificial intelligence that focuses on similar issues. See, e.g., Philip R. Cohen and Hector J. Levesque, "Teamwork," *Noûs* 25 (1991): 487–512; Barbara J. Grosz and Candace L. Sidner, "Plans for Discourse"; and Jerry

110

paint the house together that each intends to paint the house. Such coincident intentions do not even ensure that each knows of the other's intention or that each is appropriately committed to the joint activity itself. On the other hand, a shared intention is not an attitude in the mind of some superagent consisting literally of some fusion of the two agents. There is no single mind which is the fusion of your mind and mine.

Now, one way in which you and I may arrive at a shared intention is to make an appropriate, explicit promise to each other. But such promises do not ensure a shared intention, for one or both parties may be insincere and have no intention to fulfill the promise. Nor are explicit promises necessary for shared intentions. Consider Hume's example of two people in a row boat who row together "tho' they have never given promises to each other."[7] Such rowers may well have a shared intention to row the boat together.

To understand shared intention, then, we should not appeal to an attitude in the mind of some superagent; nor should we assume that shared intentions are always grounded in prior promises. My conjecture is that we should, instead, understand shared intention, in the basic case, as a state of affairs consisting primarily of appropriate attitudes of each individual participant and their interrelations.[8]

Hobbs, "Artificial Intelligence and Collective Intentionality: Comments on Searle and on Grosz and Sidner." The latter two essays are in *Intentions in Communication*, ed. Philip R. Cohen, Jerry Morgan, and Martha E. Pollack (Cambridge, Mass.: MIT Press, 1990), pp. 417–44 and pp. 445–59, respectively.

My discussion here picks up a number of threads and uses ideas from my "Shared Cooperative Activity," *The Philosophical Review* 101 (1992): 327–41 [this volume, essay 5]. In that essay my concern was with a certain kind of shared activity; in the present essay my concern is with a certain kind of shared attitude. I seek a unified treatment of both.

7 David Hume, *A Treatise of Human Nature*, ed. L. A. Selby-Bigge (Oxford: Oxford University Press), p. 490. See David Lewis's remarks about this example in his *Convention: A Philosophical Study* (Cambridge, Mass.: Harvard University Press, 1969), p. 44, e.g.

8 Let me explain why I say only "primarily." I claim below that shared intentions involve "common knowledge." I do not try here to say what common knowledge is. But it may be that it involves some external situation in the environment of the agents that functions as what Lewis calls a *"basis* for common knowledge" (p. 56).

How do we determine in what this complex of attitudes consists? Begin with a related query: What do shared intentions do, what jobs do they have in our lives? I think we can identify three main answers to this query.

First, our shared intention to paint together will help coordinate my activities with yours (and yours with mine) in ways that track the goal of our painting the house. Someone will scrape before, not after, the new paint is applied by someone. Second, our shared intention will coordinate our actions in part by ensuring that my planning about my role in the house-painting is coordinated with your relevant planning, and vice versa. If I plan to get the paint but not the brushes I will likely check whether you plan to get the brushes. Third, our shared intention will tend to provide a background framework that structures relevant bargaining. Though we share the intention to paint together we might have conflicting preferences about who scrapes and who paints, or about what color paint to use. Such conflicts call for bargaining in some form – not bargaining about whether to paint together but, rather, bargaining about how we are to paint together.

Our shared intention, then, performs at least three interrelated jobs: It helps coordinate our intentional actions; it helps coordinate our planning; and it can structure relevant bargaining. And it does all this in ways that track the goal of our painting the house together. Thus does our shared intention help to organize and to unify our intentional agency in ways to some extent analogous to the ways in which the intentions of an individual organize and unify her individual agency over time. An account of what shared intention is should explain how it does all this.

So what we want to know is this: Are there attitudes of each of the individual agents – attitudes that have appropriate contents and are interrelated in appropriate ways – such that the complex consisting of such attitudes would, if functioning properly, do the jobs of shared intention? Can we describe an appropriate complex from whose proper functioning would emerge the coordinated action and planning, and the relevant framework for bargaining, characteristic of shared intention? If so, we would have reason to identify shared intention with this complex.

II

Such an approach to shared intention will need to draw on an understanding of the intentions of individuals, with special attention to the roles of such intentions in coordination. Here I briefly sketch an approach to such matters that I have developed elsewhere.[9]

Suppose I intend now to practice the tenor part tomorrow at noon. If all goes well my activity between now and then will include all necessary preliminary steps – for example, getting the music if I don't already have it – and it won't include activity incompatible with my practicing then – for example, screaming too much at an athletic event the night before. And when tomorrow noon arrives I will be in a position to practice; I will not be, say, attending a movie. This normally happens, if it does happen, because of my intention. My intention to practice my part tomorrow coordinates my activity between now and then in a way that supports my practicing at noon.

How does my intention play this coordinating role? In part, by shaping my planning between now and later. My intention to practice is an element of a partial plan. As time goes by I need to fill in this plan appropriately; otherwise it will suffer from means–end incoherence. So my intention poses relatively specific problems of means and preliminary steps for my planning. I am faced, for example, with a problem about how to get a copy of the tenor part by noon. In contrast, my plan poses no special problem about how to get a copy of The Iliad, even if I would much like one. Further, my intention constrains my plans in ways necessary to ensure that my plans remain internally consistent and consistent with my beliefs: For example, it precludes going to a movie tomorrow at noon. In these ways my intention helps ensure that my activities between now and tomorrow are coordinated with each other in ways that support my practicing then.

For all this to work my intention will need to have a further property. Prior intentions are revocable. If things change in relevant ways it may behoove me to change my plan. Still, prior intentions

---

9 See my *Intention, Plans, and Practical Reason*.

will need to have a certain stability.[10] If we were constantly reconsidering our prior plans they would be of little use. The nonreconsideration of one's prior intentions will typically be the default.

Intentions, then, are normally stable elements of partial plans. These plans are subject to demands for coherence and consistency, demands which help structure further planning. Such planning is not the only mechanism that coordinates an individual's purposive activity over time. A tiger hunting her prey may exhibit wonderfully coordinated activity without being capable of such planning. But for creatures like us – as Donagan says, "creatures . . . of will" – planning is an important coordinating mechanism.[11]

III

I need now to discuss two more preliminary issues. First: my strategy is to see our shared intention to J as consisting primarily of attitudes of each of us and their interrelations. At least some of these attitudes will specifically concern our joint action of J-ing; after all, our shared intention to J supports coordination specifically in the pursuit of our J-ing. But much talk of joint action already builds in the very idea of shared intention. For us to try to solve a problem together, for example, we need an appropriate shared intention. We would risk criticizable circularity if our analysis of shared intention itself appealed to joint-act-types that involved the very idea of shared intention.[12] So we will want to limit our analysans to joint-act-types that are, as I will say, neutral with respect to shared intention. For example, we will want to use a notion of painting the house together that does not itself require that the agents have a shared intention.[13] I assume that we will have available appropriate conceptions of joint activity that

10 See my discussion in *Intention, Plans, and Practical Reason*, and in "Planning and the Stability of Intention," *Minds and Machines* 2 (1992): 1–16.
11 The quote from Donagan is from *Choice*, p. 137.
12 Donagan discusses an analogous problem for individual intentional action in *Choice*, pp. 87–88. See also this volume, essay 5, pp. 96–7.
13 Think of a case in which we paint it during the same time period but we are each ignorant of the other's activity.

are neutral with respect to shared intention; or anyway, my discussion is limited to such cases.

A second problem: the attitudes of the individual participants that are constitutive of a shared intention will include intentions of those participants. But what I intend to do is to perform actions of my own: I cannot intend to perform the joint action J. So how will the conception of the joint action get into the intentions of the individuals?

Distinguish two strategies. First, we can appeal to my intention to play my part in our J-ing, where this entails that our J-ing, while not something I strictly speaking intend, is something I want.[14] Second, we can try to exploit the fact that we speak not only of intentions *to*, but also of intentions *that* – for example, my intention that Scott clean up his room. Accordingly, we can speak of my intention that we J.[15]

Consider the second strategy. The idea here is not to introduce some fundamentally new and distinctive attitude. The attitude we are appealing to is intention – an attitude already needed in an account of individual intelligent agency. But we are allowing this attitude to include in its content the joint activity – our J-ing.[16] Such appeals to my intention that we J will seem reasonably natural given an emphasis on the roles of intentions in plans. This is because my conception of our J-ing can function in my plans in ways similar to my conception of my own A-ing: In each case I face problems of means and preliminary steps; and in each case I need to constrain the rest of my plans

14 An appeal to my intention to play my part in our J-ing is similar to the approach of Raimo Tuomela and Kaarlo Miller to what they call "we-intention" (see "We-Intentions," *Philosophical Studies* 53 [1988]: 367–89, esp. pp. 375–76).

15 A strategy similar to one once urged on me by Philip Cohen. In "Objects of Intention," *Philosophical Studies* 70 (1993): 85–128, Bruce Vermazen defends appeals to intentions that are not intentions to act.

16 This contrasts with John Searle's conception of "we-intending" in his "Collective Intentions and Actions," in Cohen, Morgan, and Pollack, eds., pp. 401–15. A we-intention, for Searle, is a distinctive attitude of an individual – an irreducible addition to the kinds of attitudes of which we are capable. On the tack I am taking, my intention that we J and my intention to play my part in our J-ing are both intentions – they are both instances of the same attitude; but they are intentions that differ in their contents.

in the light of demands for consistency. And susceptibility to these demands for coherence and consistency is a characteristic sign of intention.

It might be objected that talk of an intention that we *J* conflicts with the plausible idea that one must see what one intends as to some extent within one's influence or control. That is why I can intend to raise my arm but not that the sun shine tomorrow. But, in fact, this need be no objection to the second strategy; for that strategy can build an appropriate influence condition into its understanding of my intending that we *J*. It can say, roughly, that for me to intend that we *J* I need to see your playing your role in our *J*-ing as in some way affected by me.

So the second strategy coheres with the planning conception of intention and can acknowledge a plausible influence condition. In what follows I will pursue this second strategy: My account of our shared intention to *J* will appeal to your and my intention that we *J*. I will not try to settle the question of exactly what version of the influence condition we should accept, for none of my main points depends on this issue. Nor will I try to argue that the first strategy must fail. My claim here is only that the second strategy is fruitful.

IV

I want to say what it is for us to intend something primarily in terms of (a) intentions and other attitudes of each and (b) the relations of these attitudes to each other.[17] This account should explain how it is

---

17 Note that my target is *our* shared intention. My direct target is not what Tuomela calls a "we-intention"; for a we-intention is an intention of an individual that concerns a group's activity (see Raimo Tuomela, "We Will Do It: An Analysis of Group-Intentions," *Philosophy and Phenomenological Research* 51 [1991]: 249–77). Nor is my target what John Searle calls a "collective intention" in his "Collective Intentions and Actions." A collective intention, as Searle understands it, is an intention of an individual concerning a collective's activity. Indeed, both Tuomela and Searle want to allow that there can be a we-intention/collective intention even if there is in fact only one individual – one who falsely believes others are involved (see Searle, "Collective Intentions and Actions," pp. 406–7; and Tuo-

that shared intentions support the goal-directed coordination of shared activity, in part by way of coordinated planning and relevant bargaining. Limiting myself to joint-act-types that are neutral with respect to shared intention, I proceed by considering a series of views.

View 1: We intend to *J* if and only if I intend that we *J* and you intend that we *J*.

View 1 does ensure that the participants in a shared intention to *J* each are, in a way, committed to their *J*-ing. But View 1 is nevertheless too weak. After all, each of us can intend that we *J* without even knowing of the other's intention that we *J*.[18] Yet at least that much cognitive linkage is involved in shared intention. Indeed, it seems reasonable to suppose that in shared intention the fact that each has the relevant attitudes is itself out in the open, is public. This suggests that we turn to:

View 2: We intend to *J* if and only if
  1. I intend that we *J* and you intend that we *J*, and
  3.[19] 1 is common knowledge[20] between us.[21]

Now consider an example: You and I each intend that we go to New York together; and this is common knowledge. However, I intend that we go together as a result of my kidnapping you, throw-

---

mela, "We Will Do It," p. 254). In contrast, it takes at least two not only to tango but even for there to be a shared intention to tango.

18 This is true even if, to intend that we *J*, I must believe that your relevant activity depends on mine.

19 This numbering will help keep matters clearer as we proceed.

20 There is a large literature on common knowledge. See, e.g., Lewis. I use here an unanalyzed notion of common knowledge.

21 View 2 is in the spirit of Raimo Tuomela's analysis of "intentional joint goal" (see his "What Are Goals and Joint Goals?" *Theory and Decision* 28 [1990]: 1–20, esp. p. 10). View 2 is also close to what Margaret Gilbert calls a "strong shared personal goal analysis" of the psychological background of what she calls "acting together" (see "Walking Together: A Paradigmatic Social Phenomenon," *Midwest Studies* 15 [1990]: 1–14, esp. p. 3). Gilbert rejects such an analysis: She argues that it does not guarantee appropriate obligations and entitlements. My reasons for rejecting View 2 are quite different. I turn to Gilbert's concerns later.

ing you in my car, and thereby forcing you to join me. The expression of my intention, as we might say, is the Mafia sense of "we're going to New York together." In intending to coerce you in this manner I intend to bypass your intentional agency. And that seems to rule out a shared intention to go to New York: My intention will surely not support coordinated planning about how we are going to get to New York. Granted, if I succeed in what I intend, our activity will in a way be unified: We will indeed go together to New York. But since the way our activity is tied together bypasses your relevant intentions, this is not the kind of unified agency characteristic of shared intention.[22]

This suggests that in shared intention I not only intend that we *J*; I also intend that we *J* in part because of your relevant intention. I intend that our performance of the joint activity be in part explained by your intention that we perform the joint activity; I intend that you participate as an intentional agent in a joint activity that, as I know, you too intend. However, once we require that the content of an intention of mine include the efficacy of your intention, it seems we should also require that this content include the efficacy of my corresponding intention. In a case of shared intention I see you as a participating, intentional agent. This requires, we have said, that I intend that your intention in favor of the joint activity be effective. But I also see myself as a participating, intentional agent. So there is reason also to require that I intend that my own intention in favor of the joint activity be effective. Why would what I intend include a requirement that your intention that we *J* be effective, and yet not include an analogous requirement concerning my own intention that we *J*?

These considerations, when taken together, argue for:

View 3: We intend to *J* if and only if
    1. (a) I intend that we *J* and (b) you intend that we *J*

22 This example, and the one to follow after View 3, are also discussed in my "Shared Cooperative Activity." [See this volume, essay 5, especially pp. 99–101, where I have more to say in defense of conditions to be added in Views 3 and 4, and pp. 101–2, where I have more to say about the kind of coercion involved in the Mafia example.]

2. I intend that we *J* because of 1(a) and 1(b); you intend that we *J* because of 1(a) and 1(b)
3. 1 and 2 are common knowledge between us.

In shared intention the constitutive intentions of the individuals are interlocking, for each agent has an intention in favor of the efficacy of an intention of the other. And the intentions of each involve a kind of reflexivity, for each has an intention concerning the efficacy of an intention of her own.

Now, Donagan has argued that the choice characteristic of individual intentional action is a choice that one act in a way explained by that very choice: "The choices that explain actions are explanatorily self-referential."[23] The idea that shared intention involves reflexive intentions of the individuals is in a way similar in spirit to this claim of Donagan's. Nevertheless, my claim about shared intention is compatible with the rejection of the need for self-referentiality in the case of individual intentional action. In a case of shared intention each agent sees herself as one of a pair of participants. Given that she intends that the relevant intention of the other be effective, and given that she recognizes that she and the other each have an intention in favor of the joint activity, there is pressure on her also to intend that *her* intention be effective. But this pressure arises from the social context of the shared intention and need not be present in the case of individual, nonshared intentional activity. So there is room for the conjecture that it is only when we get to shared intention that each agent is obliged to include in what she intends a reference to the role of her own intentions.

To return to the main thread, note that View 3 does not require that you and I either have or aim at having a shared conception of

23 Donagan, *Choice*, p. 88. Others who have defended similar views about the self-referential causes of intentional action include Gilbert Harman, "Practical Reasoning," *Review of Metaphysics* 29 (1976): 431–63, and *Change in View* (Cambridge, Mass.: MIT Press, 1986); John Searle, *Intentionality* (Cambridge: Cambridge University Press, 1983); and J. David Velleman, *Practical Reflection* (Princeton, N.J.: Princeton University Press, 1989). For a trenchant critique of such views, see Alfred Mele, "Are Intentions Self-Referential?" *Philosophical Studies* 52 (1987): 309–29.

how we are to *J*. Suppose you and I each intend that we paint the house together in part because of each of our intentions. However, I intend that we paint it red all over; you intend that we paint it blue all over. All this is common knowledge; and neither of us is prepared to compromise.[24] On View 3 we have a shared intention to paint the house. But this seems wrong, for neither of us is committed to the interpersonal coordination of our relevant subplans.

Granted, for me to intend that we paint the house, despite my knowledge of our differences, I need to think there is some real possibility that we will nevertheless paint it. But perhaps I think this because I think I can trick you about the color of the paint in your can. We might then satisfy 1–3 of View 3; and yet we would still not have a shared intention. For our intention to be shared neither of us can intend that the other's relevant subplans be subverted. A shared intention should function to unify our *intentional* agency at least to this extent; otherwise it would not support appropriately coordinated planning.

So we need to go beyond View 3. But we also need to be careful not to go too far. First, it would be too strong to require that the subplans of our intentions in 1a and 1b completely match, for there can be features of your subplan that I do not even know or care about, and vice versa. Perhaps your subplan includes painting in over-alls or buying the brushes at a certain store. While I need to know you will show up with the brushes, I may well neither know nor care how you are dressed or where you get the brushes. So our subplans may well not completely match. Still, it seems that we will each want them in the end to *mesh*: Our individual subplans concerning our *J*-ing *mesh* just in case there is some way we could *J* that would not violate either of our subplans but would, rather, involve the successful execution of those subplans. If I intend that we paint solely with red paint and you intend that we paint solely with blue, our subplans do not mesh. But if you intend to get the paint at Greg's Hardware, and I simply do not know or care about where you get the paint, then our subplans, while they do not completely match, may still mesh. And it is meshing subplans that are our concern in shared intention.

24 Rachel Cohon helped me get this example into shape.

There is a second way in which we must be careful not to go too far. For you and I to have a shared intention to J we need not *already* have arrived at subplans that mesh. Much of our relevant planning may occur after we have arrived at our shared intention. All that is plausibly required is that we each intend that we J by way of meshing subplans. This leads us to:

View 4: We intend to J if and only if
1. (a) I intend that we J and (b) you intend that we J.
2. I intend that we J in accordance with and because of 1a, 1b, and meshing subplans of 1a and 1b; you intend that we J in accordance with and because of 1a, 1b, and meshing subplans of 1a and 1b.
3. 1 and 2 are common knowledge between us.

On View 4, then, I need neither know nor seek to know of all your subplans for us to have a shared intention; nor need we already have arrived at complete, meshing subplans. What is required is that each of us *intends* that we J by way of meshing subplans. Perhaps you and I have not yet filled in our subplans. Or perhaps we have filled in each of our subplans, they do not yet mesh, but we each intend to seek revisions that allow them to mesh. We may even have conflicting preferences concerning subplans and be involved in negotiations about how to fill in our plans. We may be involved in such negotiations even while we have already begun to J.

It is worth reflecting on this last point. Our shared intention can serve as a relatively fixed background against which relevant bargaining can take place. Suppose you and I jointly intend to paint the house together but we have yet to agree on the colors or on the division of roles. Given our conflicting preferences we may engage in various forms of bargaining. Difficulties in such bargaining may, of course, lead either of us to reconsider the intention that we paint together. But so long as we continue so to intend, our bargaining will concern not whether to paint together but how. Our bargaining will be framed by our shared intention.

Recognition of such potential bargaining raises a question. Suppose that you and I satisfy conditions 1–3 of View 4 with respect to our going to New York together but that there are large differences between us in relevant bargaining power. Perhaps it is a very important matter for you but only a welcome break from work for me. Suppose I plan to use this difference to bargain hard for meshing subplans that are very much to my liking. Perhaps I plan to put a lot of pressure on you to pay for both tickets. According to View 4 we could still have a shared intention. Is that an acceptable result?

I believe that it is; though, of course, too much stubbornness might result in the dissolution of our shared intention. Granted, at some point the exploitation of large differences in bargaining power becomes coercive. When it does our activity of going to New York together (if that is what we manage to do) will not be a fully cooperative activity. But it may still be one that is jointly intentional; and we may still have a shared intention so to act.[25] There still may be appropriate kinds of coordination in our planning and action.

A virtue of View 4 is that it allows for shared intention even when the agents have different reasons for participating. We can intend to sing the duet together even though my reason is the love of the music and yours is, instead, the chance to impress the audience.

View 4 does have a drawback: It does not yet provide for a shared intention to play a competitive game together. You and I might have a shared intention to play chess together and yet neither of us intend that our subplans mesh all the way down. After all, I intend to try to scuttle your plans for checkmating me. I think such cases will force modest modifications in View 4; but I will not try to get this straight here. Instead, I want to explore further whether, cases of competitive games to one side, View 4 provides for appropriate explanations of the coordinated planning and action, and associated bargaining, characteristic of shared intention.

V

Begin by reflecting on three basic points. First, shared intention, as I understand it, is not an attitude in any mind. It is not an attitude in

---

25 For suggestions of other conditions on cooperative activity that are not ensured by the successful execution of a shared intention, see my "Shared Cooperative Activity."

the mind of some fused agent, for there is no such mind; and it is not an attitude in the mind or minds of either or both participants. Rather, it is a state of affairs that consists primarily in attitudes (none of which are themselves the shared intention) of the participants and interrelations between those attitudes.

Second, to say in what shared intention consists I have sought to combine two main elements: (1) a general treatment of the intentions of individuals and (2) an account of the special contents of the intentions of the individual participants in a shared intention. Intentions of individuals are normally stable elements in larger, partial plans of those individuals. These plans are subject to demands for means–end coherence and consistency. Because of these demands, intentions tend to pose problems for further practical reasoning and to constrain solutions to those problems. Given these features of the intentions of individuals, and given the special contents identified in View 4, I want to explain how that in which a shared intention consists supports coordinated planning and action, and appropriate bargaining, in pursuit of the joint activity.

Shared intention consists primarily of a web of attitudes of the individual participants. These attitudes of the individuals are subject to various rational pressures. In particular, the intentions of the participants are subject to demands for consistency and coherence. The specific impact of these demands will depend, of course, on the contents of these intentions. And in shared intention the relevant intentions of the individual participants have the special contents we have been discussing. So – and this is the third point – what we want to show is that intentions of individuals with these special contents should lead to planning, bargaining, and action of those individuals which, taken together, constitute appropriately coordinated planning and unified shared activity. The unified action and coordinated planning characteristic of shared intention is to be explained primarily by appeal to the functioning of the attitudes which are constituents of the shared intention.

Let us see how steps in the direction of View 4 contribute to such an explanation. Begin with View 2. Condition 1 of View 2 requires that each intends that we J. So the demand for means–end coherence of the plans of each ensures rational pressure on each participant to pursue means to the joint J-ing. It also follows, given the demand for consistency of each agent's plans, that there is rational pressure on each to eschew courses of action believed by her to be incompatible with the joint J-ing.

So far so good. But what we learn from the Mafia case is that this does not ensure that there is rational pressure on each participant to aim at coordination with the other's successful execution of *her* intention. Yet the pursuit of coordination with the other's successful execution of her relevant intention is essential to the kind of coordinated planning characteristic of shared intention.

This brings us to View 3. The conditions of View 3 ensure rational pressure on each participant to seek means not only to the joint J-ing but also to the joint J-ing by way of the other's intention. Now, I frequently form my intentions in the light of my expectations about your intentions and actions, including expectations about how my intentions will influence yours. Since my expectations about how my intentions will influence yours may depend on my expectations about how you expect my intentions to be influenced by yours, this can get quite complex. But in this, as Schelling says, "spiral of reciprocal expectations," we still each see the other's intentions merely as data for our deliberations, albeit as data that are potentially affected by our own decisions.[26] In contrast, agents who satisfy the conditions cited in View 3 do not see each other's relevant intention merely as a datum, for each intends that the joint activity go in part by way of the efficacy of the other's intention. Each is rationally committed to pursuing means, and eschewing obstacles, to the complex goal of their J-ing by way of the other agent's relevant intention. Each aims at the efficacy of the intention of the other.

In requiring that the participants' intentions interlock in this way, View 3 gives up on the idea, implicit in View 2, that the crucial linkage between the attitudes of those who share an intention is merely cognitive.[27] Appropriate common knowledge, or the like, is

26 Thomas Schelling, *The Strategy of Conflict* (Cambridge, Mass.: Harvard University Press, 1960), p. 87.

27 Gilbert in "Walking Together," and Searle in "Collective Intentions" also reject related ideas, though for different reasons.

not a sufficient link for shared intention. Each agent needs also to embrace as her own end the efficacy of the other's relevant intention.

However, the conditions of View 3 still do not ensure that each agent aims at there being meshing subplans. The conditions of View 3 do ensure that each agent seeks a consistent individual plan in support of a joint J-ing in which each agent's intention that they J is efficacious. But these conditions do not ensure that each agent intends that the subplans of both, taken together, be jointly consistent: That is the lesson of the painting case. But shared intention should bring with it rational pressure in the direction of subplans of both participants that are, taken together, jointly consistent. By requiring that the participants intend that they J by way of meshing subplans, View 4 ensures such rational pressure.

Finally, View 4 makes it clear why shared intentions will sometimes frame relevant bargaining. On View 4 each agent aims at a performance of the joint J-ing that goes by way of each participant's relevant intention and its meshing subplans. So even if the participants have differing preferences about how they are to J, neither participant will be in a position to pursue such preferences in ways that bypass the other's intentions/subplans. This makes it likely that in such cases the demand on each agent that her plans be means–end coherent will lead to rational pressure in the direction of bargaining that is framed by the shared intention.

Suppose, then, that the intentions of individual participants have the contents and interrelations cited in View 4; and suppose that these intentions – like intentions generally – are subject to demands for consistency and means–end coherence. These rational pressures on these intentions of those individuals will issue in pressure in the direction of coordinated planning and action, and appropriate bargaining, directed at the joint action of J-ing. And that is what I wanted to show.

VI

Margaret Gilbert has argued that in an important sense of "acting together" each participant has associated nonconditional obligations to act and nonconditional entitlements to rebuke the other for failures to act.[28] On View 4, if you and I have a shared intention to *J* then you ought to perform your role *if* you continue to intend that we *J*. But View 4 by itself seems to offer no guarantee that by virtue of our having a shared intention you have a nonconditional obligation to perform. Does this suggest that something is missing in View 4?

Recall that intentions are subject to a demand for stability. One reason for this is that the reconsideration of an intention already formed can itself have significant costs; a second is that an agent who too easily reconsiders her prior intentions will be a less reliable partner in social coordination. This latter, social pressure toward stability is particularly relevant to the stability of intentions constitutive of a shared intention. So our approach to shared intention can account for rational pressure on a participating agent not too easily to abandon her relevant intentions.

Note further that if each agent's relevant intentions are fairly stable it will normally be reasonable for each to rely on the other to stick with the joint project. The stability of the constituent intentions thereby supports each in planning on the contributions of the other, just as we would want in coordinated planning.

When I too easily abandon my intention that we take a walk together I am, then, being unreasonable. But it does not follow that in abandoning my intention I am violating a nonconditional obligation to you, a nonconditional obligation grounded in our shared intention. To be sure, shared intentions are frequently accompanied by such obligations. In arriving at a shared intention we frequently make promises or reach agreements which generate corresponding nonconditional obligations. Further, once we begin executing a shared intention implicit promises frequently arise – promises that generate nonconditional obligations. Still, such a promise or agreement does not seem to be, strictly speaking, necessary for a shared intention.

Imagine two singers who each highly value their duet-singing but nevertheless have a clear understanding between them that neither is making any binding promise to or agreement with the other concern-

28 For example, pp. 5–6 of "Walking Together." This summarizes aspects of her much longer discussion in *On Social Facts* (London: Routledge, 1989).

ing their singing. Each publicly states that she reserves the right to change her mind. These two could still share an intention to sing a duet together.[29] They could still engage in coordinated planning aimed at their singing the duet and in which each relies on the participation of the other. Granted, the normal case of shared intention will not be like this. In a normal case there will likely be some promise or agreement; and that will further contribute to the confidence of each that she can plan on the participation of the other. Nevertheless, such a promise or agreement does not seem essential to shared intention. And when there is no such promise or agreement, or some other obligation-generating process, the shared intention may not impose a nonconditional obligation to stick with the joint action.

Consider two different responses to this. First, one might try to insist that the mere satisfaction of the conditions of View 4, in the absence of some further obligation-generating agreement, does not ensure shared intention.[30] So our singers do not in fact have a shared intention.

At this point perhaps the dispute is merely verbal and we should simply speak of shared intention in a weaker and in a stronger sense. The weaker sense is captured, pretty much, by View 4. The stronger sense involves yet a further condition, that there be a binding agreement.[31] I have argued that shared intention in the supposed weaker

29 Lewis makes a similar point (p. 34).
30 This is roughly in the spirit of some of Gilbert's remarks as commentator on an earlier and shorter version of this article at the Central Division of the American Philosophical Association (APA), Louisville, Ky. (April 1992). (Gilbert put the point in terms of a special notion of "joint commitment," indicating that "it may be reasonable enough to think of [joint commitment] as an 'implicit agreement'.") This was also Raimo Tuomela's tack in his replies as commentator on an earlier shorter version of this article (presented at the meetings of the Society for Philosophy and Psychology, Montreal, June 1992).
31 In her comments at the Central Division of the APA, Gilbert suggested (as Paul Weirich brought out in the discussion period) that such a binding agreement, and the resulting obligations and entitlements, would itself be sufficient for a shared intention. But that seems to me wrong, since binding agreements do not guarantee intentions on the part of the individual agents to act accordingly. That is why I understand the stronger sense of shared intention, if such there be, to include the

sense supports coordinated planning and action, and relevant bargaining, aimed at the joint activity and that it is typically but not necessarily accompanied by relevant nonconditional obligations. That seems to me a reason to see the phenomenon captured by View 4 as at the heart of the matter. At the least we have seen that there is an important kind of shared intention that does not essentially involve such obligations. Such shared intention is primarily a psychological – rather than primarily a normative – phenomenon. The step to nonconditional obligations and entitlements is a step beyond this more basic phenomenon.

Consider a second response to my defense of View 4. One might urge that a shared intention in the sense of View 4 could only come about by way of a process of a sort that generates corresponding nonconditional obligations. Perhaps the process is not, strictly speaking, one of agreement or the exchange of promises; it may just be a more general kind of mutual assurance. But this process will nevertheless be sufficient to support corresponding obligations.

My reply to this is twofold. First, the main claim – that shared intention must *always* come about by way of an obligation-generating process – does not seem to me very plausible: The case of the cautious singers who disavow obligation seems a fairly clear counterexample.[32] But, second, even if I were wrong about this, this need not be an objection to View 4. We could still allow that View 4 says what shared intention *is*, while noting that the creation of a shared intention brings with it certain normative consequences. We could still agree with View 4 that shared intention consists primarily of a web of individual psychological states and their interrelations. It would just

conditions cited in View 4 as well as a further condition specifying an appropriate normative relation between the participants.

32 I believe that certain cases of coerced shared intention would also provide counterexamples to this overly general claim. Other potential counterexamples may come from cases of shared intention in which the common knowledge is grounded in the background knowledge of the participants and is not the result of assurances each gives the other (a point J. David Velleman helped me see – though he did this while trying to convince me that such cases posed problems for View 4). I discuss these matters further in "Shared Intention and Mutual Obligation," this volume, essay 7.

turn out that the creation of this psychological web has normative consequences.

VII

This approach to shared intention is broadly individualistic in spirit.[33] Granted, much recent work in the philosophy of mind has argued that our ordinary ways of specifying the contents of the attitudes draw on features outside of the individual whose attitudes are in question. Such external features may include the causal context of the use of names or natural kind terms,[34] as well as relevant linguistic practices of the community in which the individual is located.[35] The individualism of my approach to shared intention can grant these insights about what determines the content of an individual's attitudes. The claim is not that we can specify these contents in ways that do not appeal to elements outside the individual whose attitudes are in question. The claim, rather, is that shared intention consists primarily of attitudes of individuals and their interrelations. The coordinated planning and action, and framework for bargaining, characteristic of shared intention emerge from the proper functioning of these attitudes of the individual participants.

33 Assuming that the common knowledge condition can be understood along individualistic lines.
34 Hilary Putnam, "The Meaning of 'Meaning'," in his *Mind, Language and Reality* (Cambridge: Cambridge University Press, 1975), vol. 2.
35 Tyler Burge, "Individualism and the Mental," *Midwest Studies in Philosophy* 4 (1979): 73–121.

7

Shared Intention and Mutual Obligation

I

Our intentions are sometimes shared. You and I might intend to sing a duet together, to paint the house together, to play basketball together, to have a conversation together. Such shared intentions help to organize and to unify our intentional agency in important ways. Further, as Margaret Gilbert has emphasized, in many cases in which

This is a shortened and revised version of "Shared Intention and Mutual Obligation," presented at the Cerisy Conference (June 1993) on "Limits of Rationality and Collective Knowledge." The original essay appeared as a working paper in *Cahiers d'epistmologie*, Université du Québec à Montréal, 1993, and then (in French translation) in *Les limites de la rationalité: I. Rationalité, éthique et cognition*, Jean-Pierre Dupuy and Pierre Livet, eds. (Paris: Éditions La Découverte, 1997), pp. 246–266. The present essay is taken primarily from part 2 of the earlier version and has been revised in part in response to comments from Thomas Scanlon. Yet earlier versions of this essay were presented at Ohio State University, University of California at San Diego, the University of Utah, and at the 1993 Meetings of the Pacific Division of the American Philosophical Association. I owe special thanks to Alain Boyer, Margaret Gilbert, Barbara Herman, Raimo Tuomela, and J. David Velleman, each of whom has thoughtfully commented on relevant essays of mine. My research was supported in part by the Center for the Study of Language and Information. Final revisions of this shortened version were completed while I was a Fellow at the Center for Advanced Study in Behavioral Sciences. I am grateful for financial support provided by The Andrew W. Mellon Foundation.

you and I have such a shared intention we see each other as in some ways obligated to each other to play our respective roles.[1]

In "Shared Intention" I sketched an account of the nature of shared intentions of small groups, in the absence of authority relations.[2] With respect to a group consisting of you and me, and concerning joint activity J, my proposal was as follows:

> *Shared Intention Thesis* (*SI thesis*): We intend to J if and only if
> (1) (a) I intend that we J and (b) you intend that we J.
> (2) I intend that we J in accordance with and because of (1)(a), (1)(b), and meshing subplans of (1)(a) and (1)(b); you intend that we J in accordance with and because of (1)(a), (1)(b), and meshing subplans of (1)(a) and (1)(b).
> (3) (1) and (2) are common knowledge between us.[3]

I argued that such a complex of interlocking intentions of the individuals would play the basic roles characteristic of shared intention, namely, coordinate the intentional conduct and planning of each of us, and structure relevant bargaining between us, in ways that track the goal of our J-ing. My argument for this claim made no explicit appeal to obligations and entitlements that may be generated by such an interlocking web of intentions.[4] This raises the question, briefly considered at the end of "Shared Intention," whether the SI thesis fails to do justice to the relation between shared intention and mutual obligation. In the present essay I return to this question.

---

1 See Margaret Gilbert, *On Social Facts* (Princeton: Princeton University Press, 1989), esp. chap. VII, and "Walking Together: A Paradigmatic Social Phenomenon" *Midwest Studies* 15 (1990): 1–14. A related idea can be found in Paul Grice's discussion of "cooperative transactions" in his "Logic and Conversation" in *Studies in the Way of Words* (Cambridge: Harvard University Press, 1989): 22–40. See esp. p. 29, item 3.
2 "Shared Intention," *Ethics* (October, 1993) [this volume, essay 6]. I further develop and refine aspects of this account (aspects not directly germane to the present discussion) in my "I Intend that We J," in Raimo Tuomela and Ghita Holmstrom-Hintikka, eds., *Contemporary Action Theory* vol. II (Dordrecht: Kluwer – Synthese Library Series, 1997): 49–63 [this volume, essay 8].
3 "Shared Intention," p. 106 [this volume, p. 121]. I there termed this "View 4."
4 See "Shared Intention," pp. 107–11 [this volume, pp. 122–6].

II

A shared intention does typically bring with it associated obligations to play one's own role and entitlements that one's partner play her role. Typically, when you and I intend to sing the duet together you have some sort of entitlement to my playing my role, and I have some sort of associated obligation to you, and vice versa. If we share this intention then I am typically not completely free simply to opt out without your consent or some special justification.

One might see such a web of mutual entitlements and obligations as essential to and partly constitutive of a shared intention.[5] My own view is that this is too strong a connection between shared intention and mutual obligation. My alternative is to embed my account of shared intention in an understanding both of the normal processes that typically issue in shared intention, and of the normative background of such processes. I believe that the normal etiology of a shared intention does bring with it relevant obligations and entitlements when the shared activity is itself permissible.[6] But I also believe that this etiology is not essential to shared intention itself.

Let me begin by sketching some reasons for being wary of too tight a connection between shared intention and obligation. Consider two cases:

CASE 1. Suppose that I tell you that unless you join with me in a shared intention to sing the duet I am going to blow up your house. I thereby coerce you into satisfying your side of conditions (1)–(3) of the SI thesis.[7] So, according to the SI thesis, you and I could thereby come to have the cited shared intention. But given that your partici-

---

5 This is in the spirit of Gilbert's work. See references in note 1.

6 I doubt that a shared intention, for example, to engage in "ethnic cleansing" would bring with it a web of obligations and entitlements. That is why I confine my attention to cases in which the shared activity is itself permissible. Judith Thomson discusses related cases in her *The Realm of Rights* (Cambridge: Harvard University Press, 1990), pp. 313–16.

7 This coercion goes through your intentional agency; so it should be contrasted with the coercion in the Mafia case discussed in "Shared Intention," pp. 103–4 [this volume, pp. 117–18].

pation in this shared intention is coerced in this way, it seems to me that in this case I have no entitlement to your playing your part.[8]

One reaction to Case 1 might be to see it as a counterexample to the SI thesis, one that shows the need to add a further noncoercion condition on shared intention. But I think this would be an overreaction. I grant that such coercion should affect our judgment about whether we act *cooperatively* if we go ahead and sing together: in such a case our so acting would not count as a cooperative activity. Nevertheless, the complex state we are in by way of the coercion will tend to play the roles cited as characteristic of shared intention. That being so, I think we should say, with the SI thesis, that Case 1 is a case of shared intention. Such a shared intention may well issue in shared intentional activity that is not shared cooperative activity.

CASE 2. Suppose you and I each announce our intention in favor of our duet singing, given that the other has the relevant intentions. Indeed, we announce intentions of just the sorts required by the SI thesis. And you and I each expect our announcement to lead the other justifiably to the corresponding belief. But each of us adds to our announcement the qualification: "It is very likely that I will continue so to intend. But I reserve the right to change my mind at will and I recognize that you do too. Neither of us is obligated to the other to continue so to intend."[9] According to the SI thesis, this explicit disavowal of an obligation need not block the shared intention. Each of us may have the appropriate intentions and be confident, given our knowledge of the other, that she too will in fact continue so to intend. But it does seem that the exchange of such disavowals can sometimes block mutual obligation.[10] If, in the present case, you do change your mind midstream you could plausibly point

---

8 I do not say that coercion always blocks obligation, only that it can and that it plausibly does in the present case. In her discussion of a similar case Judith Thomson insists that I have no "claim" on you to perform. See her *The Realm of Rights*, pp. 310–11.

9 I discussed such a case at the end of "Shared Intention."

10 Which is not to say that such a disavowal will always block an obligation that would otherwise be incurred.

to your prior disavowal as allowing you to drop out without the need for my consent. So, again, we seem to have shared intention without mutual obligation.

Cases 1 and 2 suggest that shared intention need not ensure mutual obligation.[11] Nevertheless, it still seems that many times a shared intention does bring with it obligations to perform, and entitlements to the other's performance. We need to understand the basis for such mutual obligations.

III

One might note that once the participants begin to carry out their shared intention they are likely to exchange relevant benefits. By scraping the wall you intend to paint I provide a benefit of sorts to you. And perhaps – though I will not try to sort this out here – the provision of such a benefit grounds an obligation to reciprocate. Nevertheless, this approach does not seem likely to uncover the most basic connections between shared intention and mutual obligation; for there can be shared intentions that are never in fact carried out.

A more fruitful approach is to look at the normal etiology of shared intention. Now, we cannot suppose that this normal etiology must include an exchange of promises.[12] Hume's two rowers, who successfully row the boat together, may have a shared intention to row together "tho' they have never given promises to each other."[13] But even Hume's rowers probably tried to influence each other's relevant expectations in a context in which each wanted to know

---

11 I do not mean to suggest that Cases 1 and 2 exhaust the cases in which there is shared intention, a kind of mutual assurance, and yet not relevant obligations. For example, as Tom Reed suggested in conversation, certain kinds of deception about one's reasons for favoring the shared activity may also block relevant obligations.

12 As I indicated in "Shared Intention" (note 31), I also do not think such an exchange of promises would be sufficient for shared intention; for one or both of the parties may be insincere and have no intention to fulfill the promise.

13 *A Treatise of Human Nature*, ed. by Selby-Bigge (Oxford: Oxford University Press), p. 490. A complication is that Hume's rowers are actually engaged in shared activity, so some sort of obligation of reciprocation may be engaged.

about the other's relevant behavior. Such purposive creation of relevant expectations seems a plausible candidate for a feature that is both common to a wide range of etiologies of shared intentions and a potential basis for relevant obligations and entitlements.

My conjecture, then, is that the typical etiology of yours and my shared intention involves the intentional, purposive creation by me of expectations on your part about what I will do, and vice versa. When you and I have a shared intention to sing the duet it is likely that I will have purposively led you to expect that I will participate if you do; that you will have purposively led me to an analogous expectation; and that each of us wants such grounds for such expectations. Such purposive creation of expectations, in such a context, normally grounds an obligation to act as one has indicated. And that, roughly, is the general feature of the normal etiology of a shared intention that grounds a web of mutual obligations and entitlements.

IV

To develop this conjecture it will be useful to turn to an important essay of Thomas Scanlon.[14] Scanlon's main claim is that the basic grounds for an obligation to keep one's promise reside, not in the existence of a special social practice, but rather in a more general principle concerning obligations generated by "explicit and intentional expectation-creation" (205). Scanlon does not say that making a promise is merely intentionally creating an expectation that one will act in a certain way. His view, rather, is that "the wrong of breaking a promise . . . [is an] instance[s] of a more general family of wrongs which are concerned . . . with what we owe to other people when we have led them to form expectations about our future conduct" (200).

I will not try here to assess this general claim about the nature of the obligation to keep one's promises. Instead, I will simply focus on

14 "Promises and Practices," *Philosophy and Public Affairs* 19 (1990): 199–226. Parenthetical page references in the text are to this essay. Judith Thomson's *The Realm of Rights* chap. 12, develops an account that is similar in spirit to Scanlon's, though there are interesting differences. I am much indebted to both these discussions.

a central component of Scanlon's account of "what we owe to other people when we have led them to form expectations about our future conduct," namely, what Scanlon calls a "principle of fidelity." I think this principle is on its face plausible; and I want to see whether some such principle can help shed light on the relation between shared intention and mutual obligation.

Here is Scanlon's "principle of fidelity":

> *Principle F*: If (1) A voluntarily and intentionally leads B to expect that A will do x (unless B consents to A's not doing x); (2) A knows that B wants to be assured of this; (3) A acts with the aim of providing this assurance, and has good reason to believe that he or she has done so; (4) B knows that A has the beliefs and intentions just described; (5) A intends for B to know this, and knows that B does know it; and (6) B knows that A has this knowledge and intent; then, in the absence of some special justification, A must do x unless B consents to x's not being done.[15]

Part of Scanlon's argument for this principle appeals to what he calls "the value of assurance" – the value, as he also puts it, of having a certain matter settled.[16] I too would want to emphasize this value. One ground for it is that a planning agent needs to be able to plan on certain future events, needs to be able to treat certain future events as settled or as a matter which she herself can settle.[17] This is especially true for planning agents in a social world. The fact that we are planning agents in a social world would, then, be an important premise in an argument for something like Principle F.

But here my concern is not to assess Scanlon's argument for Principle F, but only to see whether some such principle, if defensible,

15 "Promise and Practices," p. 208. The appeal to a possible "special justification" is intended to allow, for example, for the nonbinding nature of deceptive expectation creation in certain games. See p. 202 n. 4.

16 P. 206. However, to have a matter settled one need not have been assured by someone.

17 Scanlon notes (p. 208) that the value of assurance also goes beyond its value for planning; and I think he is right here as well.

could contribute to our understanding of shared intention and its relation to mutual obligation. And it does seem that Principle F points to a ground of obligation that is plausibly present in a wide range of cases of shared intention. The core of this ground of obligation is a voluntary action aimed at providing the other with a certain kind of desired assurance.[18] Granted, it may be that Principle F does not identify all the relevant sources of mutual obligation present in various cases of shared intention. This is a point to which I will return below. For now, however, I will take it as a plausible working hypothesis that something along the lines of Principle F captures what is at the heart of the idea that there is a close connection between shared intention and mutual obligation.

Let us consider Cases 1 and 2 in light of Principle F. Note first that condition (1) of Principle F requires that the relevant action be voluntary. This means that coerced assurance will not satisfy that condition. So Principle F can allow that in Case 1 the coerced participant has no obligation to the coercer to play his part.[19]

Consider now Case 2. Again, Principle F seems to allow that the exchange of disavowals blocks associated obligations; for such a disavowal seems to ensure that the agent does not act with the aim of providing the relevant assurance, and so does not satisfy condition (3) of principle F.[20] If I indicate that I reserve the right to change my mind at will, I thereby indicate that, though I am trying to lead you

18 I understand – and I take Scanlon to understand – assurance to be, roughly, the intentional effort to lead someone to expect a certain act or event. It is not part of the very concept of "A assures B that he (i.e., A) will do x" that A gives B some *entitlement* to A's doing x. Such an entitlement, if such there be, will follow only given some further normative principle, like Principle F.

19 Scanlon remarks that "a promise may not bind if it was obtained through coercion or through deceit" (p. 215). But he also indicates that he thinks that sometimes a coerced promise can obligate (p. 224, note 19). All that we need to say here, though, is that at least in Case 1 there is no obligation induced by the coerced assurance, and that that is compatible with Principle F.

20 Note that the aim in condition (3) of Principle F takes its content from the expectation described in condition (1): It is to lead "B to expect that A will do x (unless B consents to A's not doing x)." My remarks from here to the end of this paragraph benefited from comments from Scanlon on the earlier version of this essay.

to expect that I will sing my part, I am *not* trying to lead you to expect that I will sing my part unless you consent to my not singing. In my disavowal I indicate that my singing or not will not be dependent on the absence or presence of such consent on your part. That is why Scanlon says that "the conditions of . . . principle [F] specify that no such warning has been given"(209).[21]

Principle F, then, seems to explain why, on the one hand, shared intention is normally accompanied by mutual obligation and yet, on the other hand, why in Case 2, as in Case 1, shared intention and mutual obligation can come apart. This supports the idea that shared intention consists, at least roughly, in what the SI thesis says it consists in: a public interlocking web of intentions of the individuals. The relation of shared intention to mutual obligation is then to be determined by identifying relevant principles of obligation – for example, Principle F – that are, perhaps quite typically, engaged in cases of shared intention, though we need also to allow for cases, like Cases 1 and 2, in which there is no mutual obligation.

V

Return now to a basic feature of Principle F: Its duty of fidelity is triggered by appropriate, purposive expectation creation. In Cases 1 and 2 there are actions of purposive expectation creation, but these do not (or so I have claimed) generate relevant obligations given the presence of coercion or of associated disavowals. We now need to ask whether such actions of purposive expectation creation can even be entirely absent from the etiology of a shared intention. If so then there may be a further way in which shared intention may fail to involve mutual obligation.

Now, the SI thesis does allow for cases of shared intention in

---

21 See also Scanlon's remark in note 9, p. 211. In a paper to which Scanlon indicates he is responding, Joseph Raz sketches an example similar to Case 2. See Joseph Raz, "Voluntary Obligations and Normative Powers," *Proceedings of the Aristotelian Society* (suppl. vol.) (1972): 79–102, at p. 99. Michael Robins also discusses a similar case in his *Promising, Intending and Moral Autonomy* (Cambridge: Cambridge University Press, 1984), p. 8.

which neither participant aims in her action to lead the other to have the relevant expectations. Granted, it must be common knowledge that each has the relevant intentions; and such common knowledge will frequently be the result of purposive acts of expectation creation. But such common knowledge might, on occasion, derive from other sources. Perhaps you and I are not in direct contact with each other but through past experiences we know much about each other's values, beliefs, and patterns of action, know that we each know, and so on. Or perhaps a mutual acquaintance serves as a two-way conduit of relevant information. Or perhaps the social setting makes it clear what each intends – as when you and I arrive at a public basketball court and simply begin, without bothering to assure each other of our intentions, to take turns shooting. In such cases there might be common knowledge of each other's intentions of a sort that, on the SI thesis, is characteristic of shared intention.[22] Yet in such cases – I will say that each of them is a version of *Case 3* – Principle F would not be engaged; for though each participant has the requisite knowledge, this is not because he or she has been purposively assured by the other.

One might see this as a challenge to the SI thesis:[23] If you and I can have a shared intention without trying to indicate to each other that we each have the relevant intentions, then the notion of shared intention has become unacceptably weak. Or so it might be claimed. I think, however, that such a reaction would throw the baby out with the bath-water. Acts of assurance are not needed for there to be a complex that plays the central roles of shared intention: the support of coordinated planning and action, and the provision of a relevant framework for bargaining, all in the pursuit of the shared activity. Granted, acts of assurance will normally (though not always) be part of the etiology of a shared intention, and issue in associated obligations and entitlements. And it is important that such obligations can also help contribute to the stability of the relevant intentions, thereby

22 Both Barbara Herman and J. David Velleman made this point in comments on my "Shared Intention" presented at the Conference in Honor of Alan Donagan, University of Chicago, September 1993.
23 As did J. David Velleman in his comments on "Shared Intention."

making it easier for each to plan on the other's actions. But such obligations are not essential for shared intentions to play their characteristic roles.

Granted, it may well be that versions of Case 3, while they do not fall under Principle F, do fall under other principles that specify normative demands on the parties. After all, as noted earlier, it may well be that Principle F is only one of several principles of duty or obligation that may be relevant in cases of shared intention. Scanlon, for example, explores principles of "due care" and of "loss prevention" that may be engaged in some versions of Case 3.[24] So we cannot yet conclude that in Case 3 we have shared intention without any mutual obligation. We can only conclude that in Case 3 we have shared intention without mutual obligations of the sort that are grounded in Principle F – mutual obligations of the sort that are, I have suggested, typical of normal cases of shared intention.

Nevertheless, this discussion of Case 3, taken together with our discussion of Cases 1 and 2, helps reinforce my basic strategy for defending the SI thesis in the face of concerns about the relation between shared intention and mutual obligation. The strategy is first to describe a social-psychological web of interlocking attitudes that plays the roles definitive of shared intention. We then go on to ask about further normative consequences of that web.[25] The SI thesis aims to accomplish the former task, thereby saying what shared intention is.[26] We then proceed with the latter inquiry by asking which principles of duty and obligation are engaged by which cases of shared intention.

VI

Shared intention consists in a public web of attitudes of individuals, a web that helps support the coordinated organization of the planning and activity of each as part of the shared, intentional activity of both.

---

24 Though these principles ascribe duties that are not themselves obligations to play one's part in the shared activity. See pp. 203–4.
25 See "Shared Intention," p. 112 [this volume, pp. 128–9].
26 Though see "I Intend that We J," p. 50 [this volume, p. 144], for a complexity.

The normal etiology of such a web has normative consequences; and Scanlon's Principle F goes some way toward helping us say what some of those normative consequencs are. Other principles of obligation may also be engaged in certain cases. But we need not see the associated normative consequences as themselves constitutive of shared intention.

8

I Intend That We *J*

I

In several recent papers I have sketched a general approach to phenomena of shared agency that do not involve relations of authority (Bratman, 1992; 1993). I focused, in particular, on what I called shared intention, shared intentional activity, and shared cooperative activity. The basic idea was that at the heart of these phenomena is shared intention – a shared intention, for example, to paint the house together. Shared intentional activity, in the basic case, is activity suitably explainable by a shared intention and associated forms of mutual responsiveness. Shared cooperative activity requires, further, the absence of certain kinds of coercion, and commitments to mutual support in the pursuit of the joint activity.[1]

What are shared intentions? My strategy here was two-pronged. I tried to specify roles distinctive of shared intention: roles such that it would be plausible to identify shared intention with what plays those roles. I argued, in particular, that our shared intention to *J* plays three interrelated roles: It supports coordination of our intentional activities in the pursuit of *J*, it supports associated coordination of our planning,

Thanks to Annette Baier, Margaret Gilbert, Elijah Millgram, Vance Ricks, Frederick Stoutland, and J. David Velleman for helpful comments.
1 John Searle, in contrast, does not distinguish between shared intentional and shared cooperative activity (see Searle, 1990, p. 406).

and it structures relevant bargaining (Bratman, 1993, p. 99 [this volume, p. 112]). I then argued that a certain kind of public, interlocking web of intentions of each of us would play those roles. This supported my conjecture that shared intention could be identified with that web of intentions of the individuals.

Shared intentions are intentions of the group. But I argued that what they consist in is a public, interlocking web of the intentions of the individuals.[2] At the heart of the theory, then, is the story of the nature of the interlocking web of intentions that, I claimed, would play the roles characteristic of shared intention. Just what are the relevant intentions of the individuals, and how are they interrelated when there is shared intention – when *we* intend that we *J*?

My answer was that when you and I together intend to *J* we each intend that we *J*,[3] and we each intend that we *J* in accordance with and because of meshing subplans of each of our intentions that we *J*. Such intentions are interlocking in the sense that we each intend both that our *J*-ing proceed by way of each person's relevant intentions and that these intentions appropriately mesh. I also supposed that this interlocking web of intentions would be out in the open, a matter of common knowledge.[4]

Let me now note two main concerns about this proposal. First, my argument for the identification was incomplete. We can see this by noting a parallel between my argument and David Lewis's classic formulation of an argument for mind–body identities (Lewis, 1972). Lewis argued that our concept of mental state M is associated with a complex, causal, functional role R in the sense that our concept of M is the concept of the state that plays R. We discover that physical state B is the state that plays R – at least in our world. We conclude that M is B. Or so Lewis argued. Similarly, my argument was that shared

---

2 David Copp takes a similar approach to social preference in Copp (1995, pp. 150–151).

3 As Philip Cohen once suggested in conversation.

4 For this overall view see Bratman (1993, esp. p. 106) [this volume, p. 121]. It may be that an appeal to common *knowledge* is a bit too strong, since it brings in demands for justification or reliability of belief that may be too strong. But these are not matters we need go into here.

intention is the state that plays the indicated trio of roles. The cited web of individual intentions plays those roles. So shared intention is that web.

The problem with this argument is that one might wonder whether there might not be *other* ways in which these roles could be realized. Might there not be other combinations of individual attitudes and public acts and conditions, combinations that even in our world would function together in ways that realized the roles of shared intention? To continue the analogy with functionalist arguments in the philosophy of mind, the concern is that, for all that I have said, shared intention might be multiply realizable (Putnam, 1967).

I think that at most what I was in a position to conclude in my earlier papers was that the indicated web of interlocking intentions was one important case of shared intention. To reach a stronger conclusion I would have needed to show that there is no other way in which these roles would be played; and it is not clear that is true. Once we grant this point, however, we can distinguish two lines of response, analogous to two common responses to concerns about multiple realizability.[5] On the one hand, we might try seeing our shared intention as a higher-order functional state of our two-person system, and see the cited web of individual intentions as one "realization" of that functional state. On the other hand, we might try to see complexes that play the roles of shared intention as themselves species of shared intention. On this latter approach the cited web of interlocking intentions really is one important kind of shared intention – though there may also be other kinds.

I will not try to argue here for one or another of these responses. I think much of the spirit of my proposal can be saved either way. Instead, I want to focus on a second major concern about my view, a concern that would remain no matter how we responded to issues of multiple realizability.

My approach to shared intention makes essential use of the idea that an individual agent can have an intention that a group, of which

---

5 Putnam (1967) is associated with the first way, Lewis (1980) with the second.

he is a part, perform a certain joint activity: It makes use of the idea that *I* might intend that *we J*. This idea is not yet that of shared intention; so there need be no straightforward circularity in the account. Shared intention is an intention of the group.[6] You and I together may have a shared intention to dance a tango. *I* cannot by myself have a shared intention to dance a tango, though I can intend to dance one with you. On my proposal I can also have an intention that *we* dance the tango; and it is such an intention on my part, together with an analogous intention on your part, which is central to *our* shared intention to dance the tango.

It is at this point, however, that a problem seems to arise. In what sense can I intend *our* activity? This idea is assumed in my treatment of shared intention, but may seem problematic. What one normally intends, it will be said, are one's own actions: It is not clear in what sense I can intend *our* action. Indeed, it might be thought that my use of this idea begs many of the hard questions that arise in trying to make sense of the very idea of a shared intention.

Versions of this objection have been developed, in slightly different ways, in recent papers by Annette Baier, Frederick Stoutland, and J. David Velleman.[7] I think that these criticisms are important. I also think that they are answerable and that our answer can deepen our understanding of the relation between an agent's intentions and her predictions of the intentions and actions of other agents.

---

6 So it should be distinguished from what Raimo Tuomela (1991, 1995) calls a "we-intention" and what Searle (1990) calls a "collective intention." In both these latter cases the cited intentions are not shared intentions but, rather, intentions of the individual concerning a group activity. (I made this point in Bratman, 1993.) Since then I have learned that a similar point concerning Tuomela's approach was made earlier in Belzer (1986).) As Vance Ricks has emphasized in conversation, in his 1990 paper Searle does not try to tell us how various "collective" intentions need to be interrelated for there to be shared intention.

7 Baier (1997b), Stoutland (1997) and Velleman (1997). A similar worry was once also expressed in discussion with Daniel Farrell. It is also suggested by Raimo Tuomela's remark that "one can only intend to do something oneself in the last analysis" (1990, p. 10).

II

As I have indicated, we might see our shared intention as a higher-order functional state of our two-person system and see the cited web of interlocking intentions as a realization of that functional state. Or we might instead see such a web of your and my intentions as constituting one species of shared intention. I want to leave both options open. But to keep the discussion manageable, I will use the second approach to frame my response to the Baier–Stoutland–Velleman objection. The view I will work with, then, is that the cited web of interlocking intentions of the individuals constitutes one important kind of shared intention. When I speak of shared intention it is this kind of shared intention that will be my target. The Baier–Stoutland–Velleman challenge is that my characterization of this kind of shared intention involves an incoherence. I believe that my response to this challenge does not depend on the decision to see the web as constituting a kind of shared intention, rather than as realizing a higher-order functional state which is the shared intention. We will, though, have reason at the end to return to issues about the multiple realizability of shared intention.

There is one more preliminary issue I need to note, one that has been pursued recently by Christopher Kutz (Kutz, 1996, pp. 75–78). Many times our conception of a joint activity builds in the idea of shared intentionality. The very idea of, say, dancing a tango together may seem already to bring in the idea that our activity is a shared intentional activity. So understood, this idea of our joint activity would not be "neutral with respect to shared intention."[8] On my approach, our shared intention to dance a tango together involves my intention that we dance the tango together. The content of this intention seems already to bring in the idea of shared intentional activity. But I wanted to explain shared intentionality by appeal to the idea of shared intention. So I worried that we were threatened by an unacceptable circularity.

---

8 Bratman (1993, p. 101 [this volume, p. 114]). In Bratman, 1992, I made a similar point about conceptions of joint activity that presuppose that it is cooperative.

Worries along such lines are not new to the theory of action. Suppose we try to understand individual intentional action as action explainable in the right way by the agent's beliefs, desires, and intentions. I raise my arm intentionally, we might try saying, when I raise it because of my appropriate attitudes. Must those attitudes include an intention to raise it intentionally? That would seem to court an unacceptable circularity. A natural strategy here is to eschew appeal to attitudes that include in their content the very idea of intentional action. Instead, we limit ourselves to contents that, at most, involve a concept of action that leaves it open whether the action is intentional.[9]

I suggested a similar strategy with respect to shared intentionality. Our shared intention involves my intention that we J. But we try to understand J, as it appears in the content of my intention, in a way that leaves it open whether our J-ing is a case of shared intentionality.

Granted, in both the individual and the shared case people many times think directly in terms of activities that are intentional – individually or jointly. If I intend to vote against the motion, what I intend is probably best understood as including the idea that my vote is intentional. And if you and I intend to get married, or to have a conversation, what each of us intends is a jointly intentional activity of our getting married, or conversing. Still, it seems that if individual intentional activity is, at bottom, activity explainable by appropriate attitudes, we should be able to identify some basic cases which avoid this circularity. We can then understand other cases in ways that build on our understanding of these basic cases.

Similarly in the case of shared intentionality. We seek basic cases in which each participant intends a joint activity understood in a way that is neutral with respect to shared intentionality. We might appeal, for example, to a notion of painting the house together which leaves it open whether this activity exhibits shared intentionality. (It might fail to exhibit shared intentionality if, for example, we each painted in ignorance of the other person's activity.) We then try to understand those cases in which the agent's conception of the shared activ-

9 For a version of this issue see Donagan (1987, pp. 87–88).

ity explicitly supposes it is a shared intentional activity, in a way that builds on our understanding of these basic cases.[10] There will be hard issues about how exactly to go from basic cases to cases more like that of our shared intention to marry, or to have a conversation – just as there are analogous issues about the individual case. For present purposes, however, I put those issues aside in order to concentrate on the challenge posed by Baier, Stoutland, and Velleman.

III

The objection is that an appeal to my intention that *we J* is illicit, even if *J* is neutral with respect to shared intentionality. It is illicit, or so it is alleged, for it appeals to intentions that violate a basic condition on being an intention.

What condition? There are, I think, important features of intention that pose no special problem for my intention that we *J*. Our *J*-ing may serve as an end for my planning and my actions. I may constrain my plans so as not to settle on options incompatible, given my beliefs, with our *J*-ing. I may see myself as faced with a problem about how, given the end of our *J*-ing, this is to be achieved. Our *J*-ing may, that is, serve as an end in my plans, constrain those plans, and pose problems of means and preliminary steps for those plans. That in these ways my attitude toward our *J*-ing can play roles characteristic of intention lends support to the idea that I really can intend that we *J*.[11] So what exactly is the problem?

The answers given are similar in spirit, but subtly different in formulation. Stoutland writes:

an intention necessarily includes a reference to the one who has the intention. An agent can intend only to do something *herself*. (Stoutland, 1997, p. 55)

We may call this the *own action* (*OA*) condition. The OA condition rules out my intending that we paint the house, for such an intention

---

10 This is, I believe, in the spirit of Kutz's discussion, from which I have benefited.
11 I argue that such roles are characteristic of intention in Bratman (1987), where I develop what I call a planning theory of intention.

would be in favor of an action whose agent is not simply the person who has the intention. So the OA condition clearly challenges my approach to shared intention.

Now, Baier too had suggested the OA condition in a 1970 paper:

The proper objects of intending . . . seem limited to my actions (not the sun's) and to things I can do. (Baier, 1970, p. 649)

In her recent discussion, however, she reformulates this as the condition "that one cannot intend what one does not take oneself to control" (Baier, 1997b, p. 25). This is a subtly different condition, for it allows that I can intend, say, our painting the house so long as I suppose I "control" not only my actions but your relevant actions. (Perhaps I have some sort of psychological ascendancy over you.) Let us call this the *control* (*C*) condition. This C condition, while differing from the OA condition, still poses a serious challenge to my approach. In a normal case of shared intention we each recognize the other as an agent in control of her or his own actions. So it is not clear how in such cases my supposed intention that we *J* will satisfy this control condition.

Velleman's challenge is in a similar vein. "Your intentions," he avers, "are the attitudes that resolve deliberative questions, thereby settling issues that are up to you" (Velleman, 1997, p. 32). I may only intend what I think my so intending settles. Call this the *settle* (*S*) condition.

How exactly is the S condition supposed to challenge my intention that we *J*? Not merely because what I intend in such a case is our action. Indeed, Velleman explicitly *rejects* the OA condition:

There is nothing problematic about first-person-plural intentions in themselves. One person can decide or plan the behavior of a group for example, if he holds authority or control over the behavior of people other than himself. (Velleman, 1997, p. 34)

The problem arises in those standard cases in which "[w]hat we are going to do is supposed to be determined by you and me jointly" (p. 34). In such a case how can I intend that we *J*, consistent with the S condition? For me to intend that we *J* I must – according to the S condition – see my intention as settling whether we *J*. But that seems incompatible with seeing you as also intending that we *J* and so as also having an intention that settles whether we *J*:

how can I frame the intention that "we" are going to act, if I simultaneously regard the matter as being partly up to you? And how can I continue to regard the matter as partly up to you, if I have already decided that we really are going to act? The model seems to require the exercise of more discretion than there is to go around. (Velleman, 1997, p. 35)

Now it seems to me that Velleman is right, for the reason he gives, that the main objection to my intending that we *J* is not to be found in the OA condition. It is to be found, instead, in the C and/or the S condition – in conditions that link what is intended to what one sees as under one's own control or as settled by one's intention. So let us reflect on these conditions.

IV

Recall Anscombe's example of the person – call him Abe – who moves the pump handle, thereby pumping water into the house (Anscombe, 1963). We may suppose that he intends to pump water into the house and that this is compatible with the C and S conditions: Abe believes both that his intention settles whether he will pump water into the house, and that he is in control of whether he will pump water into the house.

What happens, however, if Abe knows that his success in pumping the water into the house depends on the acts of other agents? Does that fact by itself baffle intention?

Suppose some other agent is maintaining the system which Abe uses. Suppose, for example, that Barbara's job is to keep pushing a certain pump handle so that the water pressure will stay sufficiently high in the system. Fully expecting Barbara to continue doing her job, Abe moves his pump, intending thereby to pump water into the house. Abe knows that he controls his pumping water into the house only given the background condition that Barbara continue with her job. But that presumably does not baffle Abe's intention. Indeed, Baier herself suggests a similar point when she qualifies her control condition by noting that "individual control is never total, never absolutely independent of what others are doing" (Baier, 1997b, p. 25).

Barbara's activity is part of a normal background of Abe's activity, a background that does not depend on whether or not Abe acts. But sometimes needed contributions to one's successful activity are themselves dependent on one's initiation of that activity.

Begin by considering a conditional contributor that is not itself an agent. Suppose the water system leaves the water at a low pressure, but has a mechanism that monitors activity on the lines. When it detects relevant activity – for example, the movement of a pump handle – it triggers a valve that raises the water pressure. All this is done mechanically, without the direct intervention of any other agent.

It seems clear that Abe may know that this is how the system works and still intend to pump the water into the house. But what happens if the monitoring mechanism is another person? Suppose that Bill monitors the system and turns a valve that increases water pressure whenever he detects someone trying to pump water. Abe knows that Bill plays this role. Abe believes that his control of whether he will pump water into the house depends, in part, on Bill's turning his valve at the appropriate time. Abe also believes that Bill will turn his valve when the time comes, for Bill monitors Abe's pumping and responds accordingly.

Abe believes that if he intends to pump water into the house he will. But he knows that this is in part because of Bill's actions. Will this awareness of Bill's role baffle Abe's intention to pump water into the house? I think that, just as in the case in which this role is played by a mechanism that is not itself an intentional agent, the answer should be no. So long as Bill's contribution is known by Abe to be reliable, Abe can form an intention whose success requires Bill's contribution. This continues to be so even if Bill's contribution (in contrast with Barbara's) is itself dependent on Abe's action.

Baier may, perhaps, think otherwise. After noting that the control needed for intention is "never total" she goes on to say that "we can construe control to mean control given normal background absence of human sabotage of our efforts."[12] Abe has control given that Bill monitors and acts in the indicated ways. If Bill were to fall asleep on the job Abe would not control his pumping water into the house. Now it does not seem that the "normal . . . absence of human sabotage of our efforts" precludes Bill's falling asleep at the job. So perhaps Baier would insist that Abe really does not have the kind of control needed for him to intend to pump water into the house. If so, however, I think Baier would be appealing to an overly strong and controversial necessary condition on intention. It seems to me that no straightforward, noncontroversial condition should preclude Abe from intending to pump water into the house in the case in which Bill must also play his role.

Bill tracks pump movements. But we can also imagine a system in which what is tracked is the intention to pump. One way to detect such an intention would be to detect a pump movement in appropriate circumstances. But there can be other ways as well, including communication. Suppose Charlie is the monitor and will raise the water pressure as soon as he supposes that Abe intends to pump water. Charlie's intervention is conditional on Abe's intention, however detected. In such a case, I think, Abe can still intend to pump water into the house. That his control goes by way of Charlie's rather than Bill's mediation does not seem to matter.

These examples suggest that plausible C or S conditions on intention should allow that control can be mediated by another agent and that this mediation can itself be conditional on that very intention. I may intend X while believing that my control over X would proceed by way of a process that involves other agents responding to my intention. I need only see my intention as settling whether or not X given what will happen, and what others will do, if I do so intend. Plausible C or S conditions should allow for such, as I will say, *other-agent conditional mediation.*[13]

---

12 (Baier, 1997b, p. 25). In her Carus Lectures (1997a, Lecture II), however, Baier emphasizes that in our intentional activity we frequently trust others to play their roles. This would seem to support the idea that Abe may intend to pump water, given that he trusts Bill to play his role.

13 This conclusion seems to me broadly in the spirit of Joel Feinberg's critical discus-

V

Once we allow for other-agent conditional mediation, what happens to the objection to my intending that we *J* ?

Suppose we have the following structure of intention and knowledge:[14]

(1a) I intend that we paint.

(1b) You intend that we paint.

(2) My intention is known to you, and yours is known to me.

(3a) The persistence of (1a) depends on my continued knowledge of (1b): if I did not know that (1b) I would not intend that we paint.

(3b) The persistence of (1b) depends on your continued knowledge of (1a): If you did not know that (1a) you would not intend that we paint.

(4) We will paint if but only if (1a) and (1b).

(5) (1)–(4) are common knowledge between us.

In this situation I can infer that we will paint if, but only if, I intend that we paint. I can also infer that this role of my intention goes in part through your relevant intention and action: My intention supports your intention (in the sense of (3b)) and your intention helps support our painting. And you can draw an analogous inference concerning the role of your intention that we paint. We each can infer, that is, that we each have control over our painting that is other-agent conditionally mediated. So it seems that even given plausible versions of the C and S conditions on intention, we can each have in such a situation the kind of intention concerning the joint activity that is required by my account of shared intention.

---

sion of a proposal of H. L. A. Hart and A. M. Honere that Feinberg labels the "voluntary intervention principle" (Feinberg, 1970) For another discussion of related issues see Postema (1995, pp. 58–60).

14 I ignore here the idea that in shared intention we each intend that the activity proceed by way of meshing subplans of each of our intentions. This idea is central to my overall view, but can be safely put to one side in a discussion of the Baier–Stoutland–Velleman objection.

Is this enough to block the challenge based on the appeal to C and S conditions? Not yet; for it is not yet clear how we can newly arrive at such a structure of intentions.

Return to Abe and Charlie. Charlie intends to raise the water pressure once he detects Abe's intention to pump. Charlie's intention is present prior to and independently of Abe's intention. This allows Abe to treat it as part of the background in deciding whether to pump: Abe can recognize that given Charlie's intention, Abe would pump water into the house if he intended to. In the case of our painting the house together, in contrast, each of our intentions that we paint depends on our knowledge of the other person's intention that we paint: (1a) depends on my knowledge of (1b); and (1b) depends on your knowledge of (1a). So it may seem that I cannot have the intention that we paint until after you do; yet you cannot have the intention that we paint until after I do. If we somehow arrive at the structure described in conditions (1)–(5), there is a way in which each agent's intention in favor of the shared activity satisfies a C or S condition that allows for other-agent conditional mediation. But it may seem mysterious how we could ever get into this position.

In the Abe and Charlie case Abe knows Charlie's intention is already fixed, so he (Abe) can just go ahead and decide to pump water. He can just go ahead and settle the matter of his pumping water. In contrast, if we have not yet arrived at a shared intention to paint, I know that your intention that we paint is not already fixed. So, as Velleman would say, since your later formation of this intention is required for success, it seems that I cannot simply settle the matter of whether we paint. So, given the S condition on intention, I cannot intend that we paint. Or so it is alleged.

VI

Recall Abe, only now suppose the other agent is Diane. Suppose that Diane does not yet intend to raise the pressure once Abe intends to pump. But Diane is a kind soul and has access to the pressure valve. Recognizing this, Abe might be justifiably confident that if Diane knew that Abe intended to pump water Diane would decide to turn the pressure valve. And he might be confident that if he intended to pump Diane would know it.

Given this confidence, can Abe decide to pump water? Can he, in the relevant sense, "settle" the matter of whether the water is pumped? I think that he can, given that he is in a position to predict that Diane will respond appropriately. Does this mean that Diane is under Abe's control in some unusual way? I think not. For Abe to decide to pump water he must be able to predict that Diane will respond appropriately; but this need not mean that Abe has Diane under his control in some unusual sense. I can predict that if I ask you for the time you will tell me the time; so I can intend to get the time from you. This is not an unusual form of control of your action, but just the ordinary predictability of ordinary agents.

Suppose now that the issue of whether we paint together is one that is obviously salient to both of us. I know you are not yet settled on this course of action because you are not yet confident of my attitude. But I know that you would settle on this course of action if only you were confident about my appropriate attitude. I infer that if you knew that I intended that we paint, then you would intend that we paint, and we would then go on to paint together. Given this prediction, I form the intention that we paint and make it known to you; and then, as I predicted and as a result, you too form the intention that we paint.

How might this happen? Well, I might just report: "I intend that we paint on the assumption that you will thereby be led as well to an intention that we paint." Or I might simply start painting, given that I expect that you will see this and thereby, knowing me fairly well, recognize my intention that we paint and so arrive as well at such an intention and just jump in. Or the process may involve the sort of exchange that Velleman, building on work of Margaret Gilbert, describes. I might say "I'll paint if you will" and you might respond "Then I will."[15] Other scenarios are no doubt possible. Granted, it

---

15 Velleman's discussion of such an exchange is a major part of his positive proposal about shared intention, a proposal I will not try to discuss here. (Velleman's proposal is, roughly, that the concatenation of the two statements in an appropriate

may seem that in at least some of these scenarios my intention is only a conditional intention; and on the Gilbert–Velleman story it may seem that all that *I* (as opposed to *we*) intend, strictly speaking, is my own activity. I will come back to these concerns in a moment. But first let us see how the basic story I have sketched tries to be responsive to the C and S conditions.

Given this story, can we say that in forming the intention that we paint I settle the matter, though only in a way that goes through your forming the intention that we paint? Or does the fact that I know that success requires your later decision and action mean that, strictly speaking, I do not settle the matter? Well, Abe settles the matter of pumping the water into the house, even though he knows his success depends on Diane's recognition of his intention and her supporting action. Granted, he settles this matter only given his predictions about Diane; but he is in a position reliably to make those predictions, so he is in a position to settle the matter in a sense plausibly required for intention. But if Abe settles the matter in such a case, it seems to me that I can settle the matter of our painting so long as I am in a position reliably to make the appropriate predictions. I do not settle the matter in a sense that precludes that the route to success involves further voluntary activity on the part of another agent. But we have seen that in that sense of "settling the matter" the S condition on intention is unacceptably strong.

When I decide that we paint together, I suppose that my intention that we paint will lead you so to intend as well. Does this mean that, strictly speaking, *you* don't get to settle the matter of our painting or, at least, I don't see you as settling this matter? Well, you remain a free agent; it really is a decision that is up to you and without which

---

context is itself the shared intention: These statements "combine to form a joint statement saying, in effect, that they will jointly prompt" the joint activity. They "add up to . . . a single token intention that is literally shared between us" (p. 47).) Both Gilbert and Velleman (following Gilbert) emphasize forms of mutual dependence between the constituents of a shared intention. In this respect what I say here is very much in the spirit of their work, though we disagree about what those constituents are and I do not see such mutual dependence as in general necessary for me to intend that we *J*. Gilbert's views can be found in Gilbert (1989 and 1990).

we really will not paint. I predict that, in part as a result of my intention, you will so decide; but that does not mean that you do not decide. I can predict what I know to be your free decision. I can predict that you will freely, in response to my intention, intend that we paint, and so settle the matter of our painting together. That is why I can now intend that we paint.

In this story my situation is like Abe's in the case of Diane, while yours is like Abe's in the case of Charlie. I need to predict that you will form an intention you do not yet have, in response to my intention, just as Abe needs to predict that Diane will form an intention she does not yet have in response to Abe's intention. When you later come to intend that we paint, you can recognize that I already so intend and form your intention in the light of that recognition, just as Abe can form his intention in the light of his recognition of Charlie's intention to raise the water pressure once he detects Abe's intention. So there is a kind of temporal asymmetry. But that does not mean that, in the end, we do not each intend the same thing: that we paint. There seems, then, to be a natural way in which you and I each might arrive at intentions that we J as part of a web of intentions in which, on the theory, a shared intention to J consists.

Recall Velleman's query:

How can I frame the intention that "we" are going to act, if I simultaneously regard the matter as being partly up to you? And how can I continue to regard the matter as partly up to you, if I have already decided that we really are going to act? (1997, p. 35)

The answer is, first, that I can "frame" the intention that we J in part on the assumption that you will, as a result, come also so to intend. While I confidently predict you will come so to intend, I also recognize that you remain a free agent and this decision is really up to you, just as I can recognize that your decision to tell me the time, in response to my query, is up to you but fully predictable. Second, even after I have formed the intention that we J, in part because I predict you will concur, I can recognize that you still need to concur: It is just that I am fully confident that you will. Third, and finally, once we arrive at a structure of intentions that satisfies (1)–(5) we can each see the matter as partly up to each of us.

VII

We need, however, to return to the concern that in the story I have told my intention is really only a conditional intention. The worry is that even given this story, it is not true that we each intend that we J, contrary to my account of shared intention.

There is a weak and a strong version of this concern. The weak concern is that my intention is really only a conditional intention that we J *if* you come to intend that we J. The strong concern is that my intention is really only a conditional intention to play my part if you play yours.

Begin with the weak concern. It is granted that initially I intend that we paint *on the assumption that* you will come also so to intend. The worry is that this is really only a conditional intention that we paint if you so intend.

Now, there is in general a difference between intending X on the assumption that p, and conditionally intending X if p. In many cases, one's confident prediction that p is enough to make the intention nonconditional (with respect to p) even though one intends on the assumption that p (and so would change one's mind if one discovered that not-p). I intend to garden today, in part because the forecast is for good weather. I am confident that the weather will be good, but if it turns out bad I will change what I intend. I intend to garden on the assumption of good weather; but it seems that given my confidence about the weather I need not merely conditionally intend to garden if the weather is good.

Can we simply reply, then, that I might intend that we J on the assumption that you will as a result come to intend that we J, and yet, being confident that you will as a result come so to intend, intend (nonconditionally) that we J (rather than merely intend that we J *if* you so intend)? Well, can Abe intend (nonconditionally) to pump water into the house while knowing that his success depends on Diane's recognition of his intention and her supporting activity? Or is Abe, at least at first, limited to a conditional intention? I am inclined to think that Abe can have the nonconditional intention in this case so long as he can reasonably predict that Diane will respond accordingly. So I am inclined to think that I might simply intend, right from the start, that we J – though this is on the assumption that you will, as a result, intend that we J.

But suppose this is rejected and it is insisted that I only intend that we J if (and only if) you come to intend that we J. You will, we may assume, know that. So you know that if you do form the intention that we J and I know that, then I will (nonconditionally) intend that we J. Your case, at this point, is like Abe's when he needs support from Charlie. Abe knows that Charlie (in contrast with Diane) already conditionally intends to raise the water pressure if he (Abe) intends to pump water. So Abe can just go ahead and intend to pump water; or so I have argued. Similarly, you can just go ahead and intend that we J. And once you do, and I know it, that is what I too will intend – just as you expect.

This seems to me an adequate response to the weak concern. What about the strong concern? The concern is that all that I conditionally intend is to play my part: I do not intend our joint activity, J, even conditionally. Yet we share the intention to J; and that seems to challenge my account of shared intention.

The occasion for this concern was our reflection on the sort of scenario emphasized by Gilbert and Velleman: a scenario in which, in an appropriate context, I say "I'll paint if you will," you respond "Then I will," and we are thereby led to a shared intention to paint. Each utterance, taken by itself, seems to express only an intention to perform one's own individual act, not an intention that we act. So perhaps neither of us really has the intention that *we* act, though we do have the shared intention that we act.

A preliminary point is that even if we each are thereby expressing only intentions to perform acts of our own, it does not follow that we do not each thereby come to have an intention that we act. Perhaps once I hear you (as in the old song[16]) say you will, I arrive at the intention that we paint, on the assumption that, knowing this, so will you. We come thereby to realize a structure partly described by conditions (1)–(5).

In any case, it is not clear how the objection is supposed to work. Suppose that in the Gilbert–Velleman scenario there really does

16 "Lonely Teardrops."

emerge something which plays the roles of shared intention. And suppose that in this scenario we really do not each intend the joint activity. Then the most we can conclude is that this is another kind of shared intention or, to put it the other way, another way of realizing the higher-order state of our having a shared intention. By itself the Gilbert–Velleman scenario does not preclude cases in which the agents do intend the joint activity. To do that, what is needed is an argument that an appeal to a single agent's intention that the group *J* involves an incoherence. But we are still without such an argument.

To be sure, and as I granted earlier, we are also so far without an argument that for there to be shared intention there *must* be, on the part of each participant, an intention in favor of the shared activity. For all that I have argued here there may be scenarios of the Gilbert–Velleman sort in which neither agent, strictly speaking, intends the shared activity and yet there is a kind of shared intention. However, my concern here has not been to defend the necessity of my conditions for shared intention, but only to defend the coherence of those conditions as at least constituting an important kind of shared intention. The Baier–Stoutland–Velleman objection is that these conditions, in involving my intention that we *J*, are incoherent. It is to this objection that I have tried to respond.

REFERENCES

Anscombe, E. 1963. *Intention*. Ithaca: Cornell University Press.

Baier, A. 1970. "Act and Intent." *The Journal of Philosophy* 67, pp. 648–58.

— 1997a. *The Common Mind*. The Paul Carus Lectures, Presented at the 1995 Eastern Division Meetings of the American Philosophical Association. Chicago: Open Court.

— 1997b. "Doing Things with Others: The Mental Commons" in Alanen, L., Heinämaa, S., and Wallgren T., eds., *Commonality and Particularity in Ethics*, New York: St. Martin's Press, Inc.

Belzer, M. 1986. "Intentional Social Action and We-Intentions." *Analyse & Kritik* 8, pp. 86–95.

Bratman, M. E. 1987. *Intention, Plans, and Practical Reason*. Cambridge, Mass.: Harvard University Press.

— 1992. "Shared Cooperative Activity." *The Philosophical Review* 101, pp. 327–41. [This volume, essay 5.]

— 1993. "Shared Intention." *Ethics* 104, pp. 97–113. [This volume, essay 6.]

Copp, D. 1995. *Morality, Normativity, and Society*. New York: Oxford University Press.

Donagan, A. 1987. *Choice: The Essential Element in Human Action*. London: Routledge & Kegan Paul.

Feinberg, J. 1970. "Causing Voluntary Actions" in Feinberg, J., ed., *Doing and Deserving*. Princeton: Princeton University Press, pp. 152–86.

Gilbert, M. 1989. *On Social Facts*. Princeton: Princeton University Press. (Originally published by Routledge.)

— 1990. "Walking Together: A Paradigmatic Social Phenomenon." *Midwest Studies* 15, pp. 1–14.

Kutz, C. 1996. *Complicity: Collective Action in Ethics and Law*, Ph.D. Dissertation, University of California at Berkeley.

Lewis, D. 1972. "Psychophysical and Theoretical Identifications." *Australasian Journal of Philosophy* 50, pp. 249–58.

— 1980. "Mad Pain and Martian Pain" in Block, N., ed., *Readings in Philosophy of Psychology*, vol. 1. Cambridge, Mass.: Harvard University Press, pp. 216–22.

Postema, G. 1995. "Morality in the First-Person Plural." *Law and Philosophy* 14, pp. 35–64.

Putnam, H. 1967. "Psychological Predicates" in Capitan, W. H., and Merrill, D. D., eds., *Art, Mind, and Religion*. Pittsburgh: University of Pittsburgh Press, pp. 37–48.

Searle, J. 1990. "Collective Intentions and Actions" in Cohen P., et al., eds., *Intentions in Communication*. Cambridge, Mass.: MIT Press, pp. 401–15.

Stoutland, F. 1997. "Why Are Philosophers of Action so Anti-Social?" in Alanen, L., Heinämaa, S., and Wallgren T., eds., *Commonality and Particularity in Ethics*, New York: St. Martin's Press, Inc.

Tuomela, R. 1990. "What Are Goals and Joint Goals?" *Theory and Decision* 28, pp. 1–20.

— 1991. "We Will Do It: An Analysis of Group-Intentions." *Philosophy and Phenomenological Research* 51, pp. 249–77.

— 1995. *The Importance of Us: A Philosophical Study of Basic Social Notions*. Stanford: Stanford University Press.

Velleman, J. D. 1997. "How To Share an Intention." *Philosophy and Phenomenological Research* 57, pp. 29–50.

161

PART THREE

RESPONSIBILITY AND IDENTIFICATION

9

Responsibility and Planning

I

We see ourselves as both responsible agents and planning agents. How are these two kinds of agency related?

Begin with planning agency. We frequently settle in advance on prior, partial plans for future action. We then proceed to fill in these plans in a timely manner, and to execute them when the time comes. Such planning plays an important organizing role in our lives, both individual and social.[1] It helps us organize our own activities over time, and it helps us organize our own activities with the activities of others.

We typically see present actions as elements in planned activities that extend over time. Frequently, it is only when seen in this light that our present activities make the right kind of sense to us. You will not understand why I am now typing this sentence unless you see this action as embedded in a larger planned activity, one that includes elements both past and (I hope!) future.

An earlier version of this essay was presented at the 1995 Georgia State University Conference on Freedom and Responsibility, and at Washington State University in September, 1995. The present version has benefited greatly from discussions on each occasion. Special thanks for useful questions and discussions along the way go to B. Ackerman, J. Fischer, E. Gampel, A. Mele, S. Rieber, H. Silverstein, and G. Yaffe.

1 See my *Intention, Plans, and Practical Reason* (Cambridge, MA: Harvard University Press, 1987), in which I develop what I call a planning theory of intention.

We also see many of our actions as shaped by intentions and plans that are in an important sense shared. When you and I are talking with each other our activity is normally seen by each of us as embedded in a shared activity of having a conversation, or trying to solve a problem, or trying to arrange a lunch meeting, or. . . . There is a sense in which *we* intend this shared activity – a sense in which we have a *shared* intention that structures our planning and action. This is a main way in which our planning agency supports interpersonal organization and coordination.

We also see ourselves as responsible agents. We see ourselves as responsible for certain actions and upshots not merely in the sense in which the crack in the radiator may be causally responsible for the failure of the engine. As Susan Wolf has emphasized, we see ourselves as responsible agents in a deeper sense than this.[2] One way to begin to get at this sense is to note that we suppose we are, normally, appropriate targets for moral praise and blame; for resentment and gratitude; for pride, guilt, and shame; for admiration, respect and hurt feelings. We don't think that all purposive agents are responsible agents in this sense. I do not resent or blame – or anyway, do not think it appropriate to resent or blame – the cat for eating my pet parakeet, or my one-year-old for spilling the milk. I recognize these as, alas, cases of purposive agency, but of purposive agency that is not culpable or an appropriate target of resentment. We do not see such agents as deeply responsible.

Deeply responsible agency can, on reflection, seem threatened by causation or determinism in a way in which planning agency seems not to be. The contemporary literature is rich with various forms of compatibilism and incompatibilism concerning responsibility and causation and/or determinism. In what follows, however, I avoid tackling these debates head-on. My primary question concerns, instead, the relation between planning agency and deeply responsible agency. I take it as given, for present purposes, that we are both planning agents and deeply responsible agents. In both respects our agency goes beyond simple purposive agency. I want to know how

2 S. Wolf, *Freedom within Reason* (New York: Oxford University Press, 1990), pp. 5, 41.

these two distinctive aspects of our agency are related. The answers I sketch lean heavily on central ideas in Peter Strawson's classic discussion, in "Freedom and Resentment,"[3] of the relation between responsible agency, interpersonal relationships, and attitudes like resentment and gratitude – as Strawson calls them, "reactive attitudes." My answers, like Strawson's discussion, are broadly in the spirit of compatibilist views of responsible agency; but my answers do not by themselves constitute a defense of compatibilism.

II

Before proceeding I need to clarify my question. Many philosophers have explored hierarchical models of motivation as a possible key to accounts of free and responsible agency.[4] Such models emphasize higher-level critical assessment of lower-level desires and the like – for example, a second-order desire concerning one's first-order desire to go to the corner tavern.

I have no quarrel with the idea that such higher-level critical reflection is a distinctive aspect of our agency. But note that hierarchical relations between desires of different orders differ from relations of embedding between intentions and larger plans of action. Consider, for example, the relation of my intention to go to the corner tavern to my larger plan of action – one that includes, say, having a conversation with my friends, having a drink, playing darts, and one that sees aspects of my planned activity as embedded in shared intentional activities with my friends. This does not yet bring in directly the sort of higher-order forms of critical assessment on which hierarchical theories like Harry Frankfurt's focus.[5] Instead, it locates my activity

---

3 First published in 1962 and reprinted in G. Watson (ed.), *Free Will* (Oxford: Oxford University Press, 1992), pp. 59–80. Page references will be to this volume.

4 See e.g. H. Frankfurt, "Freedom of the Will and the Concept of a Person," *Journal of Philosophy* 68 (1971), pp. 5–20; W. Neely, "Freedom and Desire," *The Philosophical Review* 83 (1974), pp. 32–54; K. Lehrer, "Freedom, Preference and Autonomy," *The Journal of Ethics* 1(1) (1997), pp. 3–25.

5 There is a complexity here. A number of philosophers suppose that an intention to *A* is an intention that that very intention to *A* lead to one's *A*-ing. G. Harman, in "Desired Desires" [in R. G. Frey and C. W. Morris (eds.), *Value, Welfare and*

167

of going to the tavern within a larger, planned activity, one that is, so to speak, spread out over time and across agents.

There can be confusion here because plans also typically have a structure that we can naturally describe as hierarchical. Intended ends embed intended means, for example. But the hierarchical relations here are between ways of acting, or between means and ends, not between desires of different orders. While I grant the significance of Frankfurt-type higher-order critical reflection, my main concern is instead with hierarchical planning and its relation to responsible agency.[6]

III

At first glance it may seem that planning agency and responsible agency are not very closely related at all.

A person who suffers an extreme form of addiction to a certain drug might still engage in complex planning about how to get it. She might even share a plan with another for getting the drug. Yet if this addiction is sufficiently powerful and one she would very much want not to have, she may well not be a fully responsible agent in this area of her life. So planning agency does not ensure responsible agency.

Morality (Cambridge: Cambridge University Press, 1993)], has pointed out that if we see intention as self-referential in this way, then any intention involves a second-order attitude. I will not try here to assess the significance of this challenge to hierarchical accounts of responsible agency.

6 Theories that are hierarchical in Frankfurt's sense do not, of course, preclude the introduction of embeddings of intentions within larger plans. Indeed, in a more recent essay Frankfurt has argued, in response to concerns about identification and a threatened regress of higher-order desires, for the importance of certain kinds of coordinating decisions. He writes: "A person who makes a decision concerning what to do . . . adopts a rule for coordinating his activities to facilitate his eventual implementation of the decision . . . a function of decision is to integrate the person both dynamically and statically. Dynamically, insofar as it provides . . . for coherence and unity of purpose over time . . ." ["Identification and Wholeheartedness" in F. Schoeman (ed.), *Responsibility, Character, and the Emotions* (Cambridge: Cambridge University Press, 1987), pp. 27–45, p. 43]. A "rule for coordinating his activities" is, I take it, a kind of partial plan for action. Frankfurt is, it seems, adding plans and planning to his theory.

Nor, it seems, does responsible agency insure planning agency. In a moment of pique I slap you. I do this intentionally but spontaneously. My slapping you is not explicitly embedded by me into a larger plan of mine. In slapping you I do not exercise any special capacities for planning. Yet you would no doubt resent me, and I should feel guilty and ashamed. This was not, after all, a nervous tic, or an epileptic seizure. If I had just as spontaneously hit you with a baseball bat I would no doubt be liable to criminal sanctions.

One can, then, be responsible for non-planned acts, and not responsible for planned acts. Nevertheless, it seems to me that these two distinctive aspects of our agency are significantly related. That, anyway, is a conjecture I will be exploring.

IV

There are two kinds of relations we might discover. First, we might discover that the fact that a specific action is a display of planning agency can reasonably affect our judgment of the agent's culpability for that specific action. Second, we might discover that being a planning agent is connected to being a responsible agent in a general sense – it is connected to being an agent who is at least potentially accountable for particular actions.[7] Let us begin with the first possibility.

Suppose I slap you not simply out of sudden anger, but as part of a larger plan for forcing you to give me your wallet. My intention to slap you is explicitly embedded in this larger plan. When it comes time to assess my degree of culpability for my action this seems a relevant fact. It is not the only relevant fact. If I need your wallet to buy a drug my overpowering addiction to which is my motivation in the first place, that is relevant as well. Nor is such an embedding

7 Versions of this distinction can be found in G. Watson's distinction [in his "Responsibility and the Limits of Evil" in F. Schoeman (ed.), *Responsibility, Character, and the Emotions* (Cambridge: Cambridge University Press, 1987), pp. 256–286] between excusing and exempting conditions, and J. Wallace's distinction [in his *Responsibility and the Moral Sentiments* (Cambridge, MA: Harvard University Press, 1994)] between blameworthiness conditions and accountability conditions. This distinction plays an important role in P. Strawson's "Freedom and Resentment," a paper to which I turn below.

necessary for a significant degree of culpability. Acting out of sudden anger is very different from being in the throes of an epileptic seizure. Still, the relation of my present-directed intention to my larger plans also seems relevant to my degree of culpability.

Consider three general ways in which plan-embedding may influence culpability. First, it might provide a *broader target of assessment*. Sometimes this amounts to an aggravating condition: The fact that my slapping you was part of a plan to rob you works this way. Sometimes this can be a mitigating, or even exculpating condition. This might be so if I slap a friend as part of a plan to get him to focus on the foolhardiness of what he is about to do.

Second, such an embedding might constitute or indicate a *deeper level of commitment* to the action. The fact that my intention to slap you is embedded in a larger plan means that the action is not isolated from, but to some extent integrated into, my larger plans and projects. It is to some extent integrated into the larger plans I have at the time of action. And it will also tend to be to some extent integrated into my ongoing, planned activities. This is because the plans of planning agents will normally have a certain stability, persist through time, and structure later conduct.

Consider, for example, the concern with premeditation in the criminal law of homicide. Premeditation is frequently seen as an aggravating condition, as a condition relevant to the degree of culpability and to susceptibility to capital punishment.[8] But what exactly is premeditation? The term "premeditation" suggests a concern only with forethought. But why should it matter whether the agent merely thought about the action in advance? After all, she might earlier have thought about the action only to dismiss it. But one form of forethought does seem especially relevant to the aggravation of culpability, namely: preplanning. If one thinks about the action in advance as part of one's planning how to do it, or of planning on one's doing it, and then one goes on intentionally to act as planned, one is commit-

---

8 There is a lively debate here, and the Model Penal Code has rejected the test of "premeditation and deliberation" as necessary for first-degree murder. For useful discussion see J. Kaplan and R. Weisberg, *Criminal Law: Cases and Materials*, second edition (Boston: Little, Brown and Co., 1991), pp. 335–347.

ted to the action in a way that seems relevant to one's degree of culpability.

Third, plan-embedding can sometimes support a relevant *link* between the present target of blame or praise and the agent at the time of action. Suppose I slap you on Monday. On Tuesday I continue to have the larger plan to get money by stealing in such ways. Though my slapping you on Monday is now in the past, I continue to have the larger plan within which that slapping was embedded. So I will normally continue to have a kind of identification with and commitment to that action.[9]

Cases of conspiracy may provide an interpersonal analogue of such a linking role. Suppose you and I conspire to rob a bank. This normally involves having a shared intention to (try to) rob it, and constructing shared plans concerning how. Such shared intentions and plans may make us each in some way responsible for the shared activity that ensues, and not just each individually responsible for our specific contribution to that activity.

The fact that an intended action is embedded in a larger plan can, then, play one or more of these roles in reasonably affecting our judgment of culpability for particular actions.

V

We can deepen the discussion by turning, as promised, to Strawson's efforts, in "Freedom and Resentment," to understand responsible agency in terms of the "reactive attitudes." Strawson sees as central to our conception of responsibility "participant reactive attitudes"[10] like resentment, gratitude, hurt feelings, and certain kinds of anger. These are, he says, "natural human reactions to the good or ill will or indifference of others towards us, as displayed in *their* attitudes and actions."[11] Such reactive attitudes "belong to involvement or partici-

---

9 I take this to be a modest and defensible version of an idea that Hume overstates in his *A Treatise Concerning Human Nature*, edited by L.A. Selby-Bigge (Oxford: Oxford University Press, 1888) Bk. II, Part III, Sec. II. Wallace criticizes Hume's version in Wallace, pp. 122–123.

10 Strawson, p. 67.

11 Strawson, p. 67.

pation with others in interpersonal human relationships."[12] Moral indignation and disapprobation are "sympathetic or vicarious or impersonal or disinterested or generalized analogues"[13] of such participant reactive attitudes. Feelings of guilt and remorse are "self-reactive attitudes."[14] These three types of reactive attitude are "humanly connected":[15] For us they come as a package deal.[16] All involve a "demand for the manifestation of a reasonable degree of goodwill or regard."[17] All contrast with an "objective attitude" toward someone, an attitude that sees him or her as a complex system whose behavior is to be predicted, shaped, guarded against, even graded, but who is not seen as a potential participant in relations of love, friendship, collegiality, rivalry and the like.[18] To hold a person responsible for certain of her actions is to include her and those actions among the targets of one's web of reactive attitudes. As Gary Watson has put it, "to regard oneself or another as responsible just is the proneness to react to them in these kinds of ways under certain conditions."[19]

The strategy, then, is to understand being responsible in terms of regarding or holding responsible, and then understand holding responsible in terms of the reactive attitudes. Primary among these attitudes are the participant reactive attitudes. These attitudes are understood as central to our "involvement or participation with others in inter-personal human relationships."[20] In this way Strawson tries to understand responsible agency in terms of attitudes and interpersonal relations that would be a part of a naturalistic social psychology.

---

12 Strawson, p. 66.

13 Strawson, p. 70.

14 Strawson, p. 71.

15 Strawson, p. 72.

16 Wallace, p. 35, notes some odd aspects of this way of characterizing the different kinds of reactive attitudes, but we do not need to sort out these details here.

17 Strawson, p. 71.

18 Contrary to a suggestion of D. Dennett, an objective attitude need not see another as a nonintentional system. I can try to predict and control the behavior of someone by way of predicting and controlling his or her relevant intentional states [see his "Mechanism and Responsibility" in G. Watson (ed.), *Free Will* (Oxford: Oxford University Press, 1992), pp. 150–173, esp. p. 158].

19 Watson, "Responsibility," p. 257.

20 Strawson, p. 66.

Both participant and moral reactive attitudes are reactions to "the qualities of others' wills."[21] Standard excuses of ignorance, accident, or external compulsion work, when they do work, by showing that the quality of the agent's will does not merit resentment, indignation, or the like. If you didn't know (and couldn't reasonably be expected to know) that my gouty toes were sticking out from under the table – or if you were pushed by another, or are in the throes of an epileptic seizure – then I will not (or anyway, should not) resent you or blame you when you step on my toes, though I will no doubt wish you hadn't. I will not, or should not, resent you because your action did not display ill will.

This suggests a broadly Strawsonian connection between plan-embedding and culpability for a specific action. Such embeddings can constitute or indicate important facts about the quality of an agent's will. In a case of preplanning, for example, the fact of embedding indicates that the agent had an extended period of time during which to consider, and perhaps to reconsider, the action; and so the action is more clearly a reflection of stable attitudes.[22] In a case in which one's present plans continue to endorse and build on one's earlier intended act, or the intended act of a co-conspirator, one's "will" continues to endorse the action.

This is an extension, but I think a natural extension, of Strawson's use of the notion of the quality of an agent's will. Strawson argued that conditions like ignorance and lack of control excuse, when they do excuse, because they indicate that the relevant action does not display ill will. The present point is that embeddings in larger plans sometimes reasonably shape judgments of culpability for a particular action because such embeddings can indicate or constitute important aspects of the quality of the agent's will.

VI

We not only make judgments of culpability or praiseworthiness concerning specific actions; we also see some agents as, and some as not,

---

21 Strawson, p. 70.
22 As C. Ginet emphasized in conversation.

responsible agents in general. How are such judgments of responsible agency affected by the presence or absence of capacities for planning agency?

Here, again, I think we can make progress by reflecting on Strawson's essay. Strawson notes that there are cases in which an action manifests a quality of will that would normally support negative reactive attitudes, yet the agent is an "inappropriate object of that kind of demand for goodwill or regard."[23] Strawson thinks, for example, that certain kinds of extreme immaturity or mental illness "invite us to suspend our ordinary reactive attitudes towards the agent."[24] A young child might knowingly step on my toes, might do this out of a kind of ill will, and yet not be a fully appropriate target of resentment or indignation. Some form of "objective" attitude is called for instead, though one compatible with some forms of love and affection. Extreme immaturity, like certain kinds of mental illness, is an exempting condition. Such conditions contrast with conditions that excuse particular actions without challenging the status of the agent as in general a target of reactive attitudes.[25]

Strawson suggests that when we respond to an exempting condition by adopting an objective attitude, "our adoption of the objective attitude is a consequence of our viewing the agent as *incapacitated* in some or all respects for ordinary inter-personal relationships."[26] I think that this idea can help us understand the relation between responsibility and planning. But, as both Jonathan Bennett and Thomas

---

23 Strawson, p. 65.

24 Strawson, p. 65.

25 The terminology of "excuses" and "exemptions" follows Watson, "Responsibility."

26 Strawson, p. 69. Strawson's examples of such incapacities include "the fact that his picture of reality is pure fantasy, . . . or . . . that his behavior is, in part, an unrealistic acting out of unconscious purposes" (p. 69). In this quoted passage Strawson is explaining a reason for taking the objective attitude rather than a *personal* reactive attitude. As I read Strawson, though, he has a similar conception of why we take the objective attitude rather than *im*personal reactive attitudes. See his discussion on p. 73. For a useful discussion of related issues about criminal insanity see M. Moore, *Law and Psychiatry: Rethinking the Relationship* (Cambridge: Cambridge University Press, 1984), Chap. 6.

Scanlon have emphasized, Strawson's discussion of this idea is incomplete: Strawson does not tell us in a general way what are to count as ordinary interpersonal relationships and exactly why they are precluded by the conditions we treat as exempting conditions.[27] Strawson asks us to

think of the many different kinds of relationship which we can have with other people – as sharers of a common interest; as members of the same family; as colleagues; as friends; as lovers; as chance parties to an enormous range of transactions and encounters.[28]

But this is, so far, just a list; and not an unproblematic one at that since a member of my family might be extremely young or insane.

One might at this point be skeptical about the strategy of focusing on so-called ordinary interpersonal relationships. Jay Wallace expresses such skepticism as follows:

What matters for accountability, is not merely one's capacity for ordinary or normal interpersonal relationships, since immoral but culpable behavior may disqualify one from these; it is, rather, one's suitability for a certain kind of moral relationship. . . . a relationship defined by the successful exchange of moral criticism and justification.[29]

But even if "immoral but culpable behavior may disqualify one from" ordinary interpersonal relationships, it does not follow that such behavior indicates an *incapacity* for such relationships. Being disqualified

27 Scanlon, for example, writes: "One needs to know more about what these relationships are, about why moral reactive attitudes depend on them, and about how these relationships are undermined or ruled out by factors such as insanity" ["The Significance of Choice" in S. M. McMurrin (ed.), *Tanner Lectures on Human Values*, Vol. VIII (Salt Lake City, UT: University of Utah Press, 1988), pp. 149–216, p. 165]. (See also Scanlon's remarks on p. 163.) Bennett says we are not told why the psychiatrist–patient relationship – in which an objective attitude is common on the part of the psychiatrist – is not an "ordinary" relationship ["Accountability" in Z. van Straaten (ed.), *Philosophical Subjects* (Oxford: Clarendon Press, 1980), pp. 14–47, p. 35]. For this case, though, Strawson might say that what is special about this relationship is that each agrees that the therapist is to take primarily an objective attitude toward the patient within the context of the therapy.

28 Strawson, p. 63.

29 Wallace, p. 164.

from certain relationships is not, after all, the same as being incapacitated for those relationships. Loss of a driver's license does not entail loss of the ability to drive a car. Strawson's suggestion is not that being disqualified for ordinary interpersonal relations exempts; the suggestion is, rather, only that an incapacity to participate in such relationships exempts.

In contrast with Wallace, I want to pursue Strawson's suggestion that we focus on ordinary interpersonal relationships. My aim is not to provide a full response to all significant questions about the use of this idea in a theory of responsible agency. My more limited aim is, rather, to see to what extent this idea might help us achieve a deeper understanding of the relationship between responsible agency and planning agency.[30]

VII

Begin with a preliminary issue. Bennett notes that I might resent your action even if you are a stranger with whom I have no previous, significant interpersonal relation.[31] Strawson would agree, since he explicitly cites relationships of "chance parties to an enormous range of transactions and encounters."[32] So what exactly is supposed to be the relation between the reactive attitudes and interpersonal relations? Bennett's proposal is that what should be emphasized "is not the

---

30 Other recent work influenced by Strawson's essay has tended, like Wallace's, to focus on specifically moral relationships. G. Watson (in Watson, "Responsibility") has argued that to be a responsible agent one must be capable of entering into certain relations of moral communication. T. Scanlon has highlighted interrelations of "possible participants in a system of co-deliberation. Moral praise and blame can thus be rendered inapplicable by abnormalities which make this kind of participation impossible" (Scanlon, p. 167). In contrast, I want to explore some implications of Strawson's original focus on the garden-variety category of "ordinary" relationships. I will argue that among the capacities normally needed fully to participate in such relationships are certain planning capacities. Of course, it might also turn out that capacities for planning agency are also normally needed fully to participate in the specifically moral relationships highlighted by Scanlon, Wallace, and Watson (there are hints of such an idea in Scanlon, p. 174).

31 Bennett, p. 42.

32 Strawson, p. 63.

relations *within which* reactive attitudes arise, but rather the relations *towards which* they point."[33] "[R]eactive attitudes," Bennett suggests, "essentially embody or point towards or prepare for interpersonal relations."[34] The reactive attitudes are, in part, responses to someone as at least a potential participant in ordinary interpersonal relationships. In many cases these attitudes arise within a prior relationship. But one can also blame or resent a stranger or a hermit.

This returns us to the question of how to characterize such ordinary interpersonal relationships. One basic observation is that ordinary interpersonal relationships will normally obtain not merely *at* a time but *over* time.[35] I am a friend, colleague, rival, lover, consultant, joint investigator, co-conspirator, discussant with a person over a period of time. For this to work our relevant activities need to be sufficiently organized over time, and the relevant activities of each of us will normally need to be somewhat predictable to the other. Organization and predictability of activities over time is a background condition for many kinds of ongoing interpersonal relationships and activities. Further, many activities characteristic of ordinary interpersonal relationships will be shared and will involve relevant shared intentions – to have a conversation, to try to solve a problem, to compete in a certain game, to rob a bank. Such shared intentions will help support the interpersonal organization typical of shared activities. Finally, all these interactions will be replete with communication, both linguistic and otherwise. This may include, but will not normally be limited to, communication of specifically moral demands.[36]

Intrapersonal and interpersonal organization of activity, shared intention, communication – these are central features of an enormous range of ordinary interpersonal relationships, from friendships to conspiracies. And now the important point to note is that all of these features normally involve planning agency. Planning is a main source

---

33 Bennett, p. 43.

34 Bennett, p. 44.

35 My appreciation of this point has been deepened by discussions with B. Ackerman.

36 As noted, Watson, "Responsibility," sees specifically moral communication as central to responsible agency.

of support of the coherent organization of our activities over time. Planning makes us more predictable both to others and to ourselves. Only planning agents can participate in the kinds of shared intentions and plans typical of a wide range of shared activities. Finally, communication generally involves distinctive kinds of intentions and plans to influence each other's attitudes, as well as the recognition of what these intentions and plans are. That was Paul Grice's basic insight.[37]

These last two points are related.[38] Having a conversation, engaging in dialogue, trying to communicate with each other are paradigmatic cases of shared intentional activity. And shared intentional activities will normally involve forms of communication.

VIII

Let us take stock. I have drawn on a pair of theses from Strawson:

> (1) Responsible agency can be understood at least in part in terms of the web of reactive attitudes.
> (2) The reactive attitudes are, in part, responses to someone as a potential participant in ordinary interpersonal relationships.

Reflection on the very idea of ordinary interpersonal relationships then led me to a connection between planning agency and responsible agency. We can capture this purported connection in two further theses:

> (3) Ordinary interpersonal relationships normally involve agents
>> (a) whose activities are appropriately unified and organized over time,
>> (b) who sometimes participate in relevant shared intentions and shared intentional activities, and
>> (c) who communicate with each other.

37 See his "Meaning," first published in 1957 and reprinted in his *Studies in the Way of Words* (Cambridge, MA: Harvard University Press, 1989), pp. 213–223.
38 As Grice would emphasize. See his discussion of "the Cooperative Principle" in his "Logic and Conversation" in his *Studies*, pp. 22–40, pp. 26–30.

(4) Planning agency is normally involved in and needed for (3)(a)–(3)(c).

Responsible agency, then, normally draws on planning capacities. And now we need to reflect further on what those capacities are.

Begin with individual planning agency. An individual planning agent needs to be able to conceive of her agency as extending both into the future and backwards, into the past. She needs to be able to see herself as an agent whose present conduct is part of larger planned activity of hers, activity that has begun earlier and will – or, anyway, may well – continue in the future. She needs, in short, to be able to take herself seriously as a planning agent with a history and a future.

Return now to forms of shared agency. Here we need to ask what it is for you and me to share an intention. I have argued elsewhere[39] that this involves, *inter alia*, roughly the following conditions: First, we each recognize the other as a participant in the shared intention, a participant whose intentions in favor of the shared activity are partly constitutive of the shared intention. Second, we each intend that the other person's relevant intentions be effective in our joint activity. Third, we each intend that we each fill in and execute each of our individual plans for participating in the joint activity in ways that mesh with and do not thwart each other.

Suppose, for example, that you and I share an intention to rob the bank together. We each see each other as an intentional participant. We each see each other as having intentions whose contents include our robbing the bank as well as, at least potentially, more detailed specifications of his or her own role in that joint activity. We each intend that these intentions of each of us be effective in the joint activity; and we each intend that we each fill in our bank-robbing plans in ways that can mesh into a coherent joint plan.

---

39 See my "Shared Cooperative Activity," *The Philosophical Review* 101 (1992), pp. 327–41, and my "Shared Intention," *Ethics* 104 (1993), pp. 97–113 [essays 5 and 6 in this volume]. To be more precise, I think there is a network of interrelated concepts here: shared intention, shared intentional activity, and shared cooperative activity. Here I draw only on some general features of my proposed account of this network.

This means that shared intentions involve capacities for subtle forms of interpersonal responsiveness. To participate with you in a shared intention I need to be able to recognize you as an intentional agent who has appropriate intentions; I need to be able to include in what I intend the effectiveness of your intentions; and I need to be able to fill in my own plans in ways that are responsive to and mesh with your plans. I need in these ways to take seriously *your* status as a planning agent. We take such complex social capacities for granted when we participate in shared intentions and engage in shared intentional activities.

So we can now supplement theses (1)–(4) with one further thesis:

(5) Planning agency of a sort normally involved in (3)(a)–(3)(c) draws on abilities to conceive of one's own agency as extended over time, and on capacities for complex forms of mutual responsiveness with other planning agents.

Taken together, theses (1)–(5) articulate important connections between responsible and planning agency, and highlight capacities central to our planning agency.

Let me add one further observation. One might worry that Strawson's focus on ordinary interpersonal relationships runs the risk of mistakenly treating as essential to responsibility idiosyncratic forms of interaction that happen to be common in our culture.[40] Theses (3)–(5) aim at a level of generality that can help defuse this worry. We may grant that there will be a great deal of variation across societies and cultures in the details of particular forms of interaction, and still recognize forms of intrapersonal and interpersonal organization of action, shared intention, and communication as deep commonalities. Strawson remarks that "in the absence of *any* forms of these [reactive] attitudes it is doubtful whether we should have anything that *we* could find intelligible as a system of human relationships."[41] The same goes, I think, for forms of organization of action, shared intention, and

---

40 J. M. Fischer articulates a version of this concern in his *The Metaphysics of Free Will* (Cambridge, MA: Blackwell, 1994), pp. 212–213. Strawson acknowledges and briefly responds to such a concern in Strawson, p. 80.

41 Strawson, p. 80.

communication. And it is these very general features that make plan-ning agency especially salient.

IX

Can planning incapacities to some extent exempt? Suppose that I know you have some basic incapacity for planning agency. It is not just that you are disinclined to exercise such capacities: You really do not have one or more of the relevant capacities. Perhaps you have no capacity for planning at all, even for planning that concerns solely your own activities. Perhaps you are unable seriously to consider the projection of your own agency into the future – to see yourself as an agent who persists over time and who can later continue her plans and projects. Perhaps you suffer from some severe disorder of mem-ory, a disorder that undermines serious planning. Or perhaps, though you are an individual planner, you do not have the capacities of social responsiveness needed for sharing in intentions, plans, and intentional activities. This may involve an inability even to recognize others as planning agents at all. Or it may involve instead an inability to aim at the effectiveness of another person's agency, or to aim at a mesh with her agency. How would or should my recognition of such incapaci-ties shape my reactive responses to you? If you were the agent of some harm to me, would or should my recognition of such planning incapacities to some extent temper my resentment, indignation, and the like?

Such incapacities do not preclude ill will. But the same point can be made about extreme immaturity, or forms of insanity; and we have supposed that extreme immaturity or insanity can exempt even in the presence of ill will. The kinds of planning incapacities just noted do not seem necessarily associated with insanity or extreme immaturity, as normally understood. Our question is whether, even so, such plan-ning incapacities can to some extent exempt.

Our Strawsonian approach suggests an argument in support of an affirmative answer. In recognizing such incapacities I recognize a basic inability to participate in a wide range of social relations toward which the reactive attitudes "point." In light of this recognition it will sometimes be reasonable for me to see you less as a potential participant in such relationships and more as a complex system whose behavior it behooves me to predict and, perhaps, influence – a complex system to be, as Strawson says, "managed, or handled or cured or trained."[42] It will, that is, sometimes be reasonable for me to take a more "objective attitude."

A useful example is Jimmy, the "lost mariner" in Oliver Sacks's essay by that title.[43] Jimmy suffers from "an extreme and extraordinary loss of recent memory – so that whatever was said or shown or down [sic] to him was apt to be forgotten in a few seconds' time."[44] Jimmy's extreme amnesia does not preclude ill will. If, in a moment of pique, he were intentionally to hit Sacks (though Sacks suggests that Jimmy is not that kind of guy), I suppose Sacks would have been to some extent angry and resentful. But I also suppose that these reactions would have been much tempered by the recognition that the hitting could not be part of a sustained larger plan or project. Our discussion helps provide a rationale for this inclination to take a more "objective" stance toward Jimmy.

This rationale points toward commonalities between Jimmy's case and cases involving other kinds of planning incapacities – for example, incapacities to project one's own agency into the future, or for forms of interpersonal responsiveness. Granted, extreme memory incapacities like Jimmy's are so disruptive of normal functioning that they might tend to exempt independently of their impact specifically on planning.[45] But it is still important to see that they tend to exempt because of their impact on, among other things, planning. In that way we arrive at a unified treatment of the significance to responsibility of a range of different incapacities, all of which undermine planning agency.

42 Strawson, p. 66.
43 O. Sacks, *The Man Who Mistook His Wife for a Hat* (New York: Summit Books, 1985), pp. 22–41. Thanks to K. Machina for reminding me of Sacks's work and pointing out its relevance to my discussion.
44 Sacks, p. 25.
45 A point noted by G. Yaffe.

X

When we reflect on capacities distinctive of responsible agency it is natural to focus on two major categories. First, there are very general capacities for considering and responding to reasons for action. John Martin Fischer, for example, suggests "that the difference between morally responsible agents and those who are not consists in the 'reasons-responsiveness' of the agents."[46] But one might worry that such a general capacity by itself does not insure the ability to understand and respond to specifically moral demands.[47] One might then, for this reason, turn to specifically moral capacities.[48]

My concerns focus, in contrast, on the territory that lies between these two approaches. I believe it is important to consider capacities that, while not specifically moral, nevertheless go beyond a general

---

46 Fischer, *The Metaphysics of Free Will*, p. 163.

47 Wallace criticizes Fischer along these lines, claiming that a psychopath might satisfy the reasons-responsiveness condition (Wallace, p. 189). Fischer discusses a similar case in his "Responsiveness and Moral Responsibility" in F. Schoeman (ed.), *Responsibility, Character, and the Emotions* (Cambridge: Cambridge University Press, 1987), pp. 81–106, p. 90, note 11, and again in his *The Metaphysics of Free Will*, p. 243, note 8.

48 As do (in different ways) Scanlon, Watson, "Responsibility," and Wallace. S. Wolf offers a related view in her "Sanity and the Metaphysics of Responsibility" in F. Schoeman (ed.), *Responsibility, Character, and the Emotions* (Cambridge: Cambridge University Press, 1987), pp. 46–62, and in her *Freedom within Reason* (New York: Oxford University Press, 1990). Let me note here an important complexity in Scanlon's view. Scanlon focuses on the moral relationship of participation in a system of co-deliberation. He sees the capacity to enter into such a relationship as having both a "specifically moral component" and a "nonmoral component" (Scanlon, p. 174). He calls the nonmoral component "the capacity for critically reflective, rational self-governance." Scanlon goes on to note a connection between this general capacity and a "kind of coherence over time. Conclusions reached at one time will be seen as relevant to critical reflection at later times unless specifically overruled" (Scanlon, p. 174). This may suggest a potential connection with planning capacities, and so perhaps a point of agreement between Scanlon and me. But whereas Scanlon arrives, perhaps, at a concern with planning by way of reflection on participation in a system of co-deliberation, I have arrived at it by way of a consideration of basic aspects of (as Strawson says) ordinary interpersonal relationships.

capacity to respond to reasons for action. In this respect my approach is similar to approaches by Frankfurt and others which focus on forms of higher-order critical reflection. Such higher-order reflection is not specifically moral, but does seem to go beyond a general capacity to respond to reasons for action. Where I differ from such approaches is in my further emphasis on planning capacities, as capacities central to our search for organization and coordination over time and with each other.[49]

Recall Jimmy. He may perhaps be able at a particular time to form higher-order desires concerning his motivation at that time. What Jimmy is, tragically, missing is connection with his own history rather than present critical reflection on his present motivation. This basic incapacity substantially limits Jimmy's participation in many ordinary interpersonal relationships, in part by undermining his planning agency.

Consider a final objection: Granted that ordinary interpersonal relationships as we know them in fact draw on our planning capacities. But perhaps other kinds of creatures could achieve needed social organization and communication without the need for planning. Perhaps other mechanisms could do the work.

Of course, some alternative mechanisms of coordination will not involve forms of deeply responsible agency. Ant colonies achieve complex organization, but not by way of actions of individually responsible agents. But it also may be conceivable, for all that I have said, that there are responsible agents who are very different from us and, in particular, are not planning agents. My claim is only that we – ordinary adult human agents in a broadly modern social world – are responsible agents in part in virtue of our planning agency.

49 Frankfurt has also noted the importance of such organization and coordination. See above, footnote 6.

10

Identification, Decision, and Treating as a Reason

I. FRANKFURT'S CHALLENGE

In his 1991 presidential address to the American Philosophical Association, Harry Frankfurt describes the "notion of identification . . . [as] fundamental to any philosophy of mind and of action."[1] This is a striking claim. Standard philosophies of action tend to be rather minimalist. Some are extremely minimalist and include only belief, desire, and action. Others introduce distinctive forms of valuation. Yet others insist further on the need to include, at a basic level, intentions and plans, and the decisions which are their normal source.[2] Frank-

I would like to thank Nomy Arpaly, Larry Beyer, Sarah Buss, Rachel Cohon, John Fischer, Alfred Mele, Elijah Millgram, Jennifer Rosner, Timothy Schroeder, J. David Velleman, and Gideon Yaffe for their helpful comments.

1 Harry Frankfurt, "The Faintest Passion," *Proceedings and Addresses of the American Philosophical Association* 66 (1992): 5–16; the quotation appears on 12. For earlier remarks in a similar spirit see his "Three Concepts of Free Action," in Harry Frankfurt, *The Importance of What We Care About* (Cambridge: Cambridge University Press, 1987), 47–57, esp. 54.

2 The desire–belief model remains the standard model of intentional agency in many areas of philosophy. See, e.g., Fred Dretske, *Explaining Behavior: Reasons in a World of Causes* (Cambridge, Mass.: Bradford Books/MIT Press, 1988). Gary Watson has emphasized the need to introduce forms of evaluation not reducible to desire. See his "Free Agency," *Journal of Philosophy* 72 (1975): 205–20. My own view is a version of the last view, one that emphasizes the distinctiveness and importance of intention. To decide is to form an intention in a standard way. See Michael E. Bratman, *Intention, Plans, and Practical Reason* (Cambridge, Mass.: Harvard Univer-

furt's effort to focus our attention on "identification" poses a twofold challenge: We need to know what identification is, and we need to know if recognizing this phenomenon requires yet a further, fundamental addition to our model of our agency.

Frankfurt emphasizes that an agent may sometimes see her motivation as "external" even though it is in one straightforward sense hers. This may be the attitude a drug addict takes toward her overwhelming desire for the drug, or a person takes toward his "jealously spiteful desire to injure" an acquaintance, or someone takes toward a "spasm of emotion" that "just came over" him.[3] Seeing one's motivation as external may frequently involve characteristic feelings of estrangement, though Frankfurt does not seem to see these as essential.[4] In contrast, one may sometimes on reflection "identify" with one's motivation; one sees it as grounding action that is, in a sense that needs to be clarified, fully one's own. This is what the person in the second example might do when he eschews the desire to injure and instead identifies with, and acts on, a desire to benefit. Such identification seems to involve at least some sort of (perhaps inchoate) reflective consideration of one's motivation and some sort of (again, perhaps inchoate) endorsement in light of that reflection. In identifying with one's desire, Frankfurt says, "a person is active with respect to" that desire and he "takes responsibility" for ensuing action.[5]

How can we best make systematic sense of such talk of identification? Frankfurt has tried to do this on several different occasions, as

---

sity Press, 1987). See also Gilbert Harman, *Change in View* (Cambridge, Mass.: MIT Press, 1986) and Hector-Neri Castañeda, *Thinking and Doing* (Dordrecht: Reidel, 1975).

3 The first example is from Harry Frankfurt, "Freedom of the Will and the Concept of a Person," *Journal of Philosophy* 68 (1971); reprinted in *The Importance of What We Care About*, 11–25. The last two examples are from Frankfurt, "Identification and Externality," in Amelie Rorty, ed., *The Identities of Persons* (Berkeley: University of California Press, 1977); reprinted in *The Importance of What We Care About*, 58–68 (the examples are on 67 and 63, respectively). Page references will be to *The Importance of What We Care About*.

4 See Frankfurt, "Identification and Externality," 63. In "Alienation and Externality" (manuscript), Timothy Schroeder and Nomy Arpaly emphasize the significance of such feelings for an account of externality.

5 Frankfurt, "Three Concepts of Free Action," 54.

have some of his commentators and critics. I want to reflect on this debate and sketch a proposal that is to some extent in the spirit of Frankfurt's view in the 1987 paper, "Identification and Wholeheartedness,"[6] a view that Frankfurt rejects in his presidential address.

A preliminary caveat: One might try to see identification as a key to a compatibilist view of moral responsibility, but I will not focus here on these broader issues. My primary concern here will simply be to provide a coherent characterization of the phenomena that are the target of such talk of identification. It is possible that this is a mistake. Perhaps there is no single phenomenon of identification but instead a variety of complexly interrelated phenomena whose main commonality lies in their connection to judgments of responsibility and the like. But I want to see if we can, instead, describe – without independent appeal to judgments of responsibility – a fairly unified phenomenon that is plausibly seen as the target of such talk of identification. My conjecture is that we can do this and that what is central are phenomena of deciding to treat, and of treating, certain of one's desires as reason-giving in one's practical reasoning and planning.

II. HIERARCHIES OF DESIRE AND VALUATIONAL SYSTEMS

Let us begin at the beginning. In his 1971 paper, "Freedom of the Will and the Concept of a Person," Frankfurt used the idea of desires of higher orders to sketch an account of the "structure of a person's will."[7] Frankfurt focused on cases in which an agent had conflicting "first-order" desires concerning what to do – whether or not to take a certain drug, for example. If the agent were appropriately reflective (and not a "wanton"), she might consider which of these desires she wants to control her conduct. She might thereby arrive at a second-order desire – in Frankfurt's terminology, a second-order "volition" –

---

6 Frankfurt, "Identification and Wholeheartedness," in Ferdinand David Schoeman, ed., *Responsibility, Character, and the Emotions: New Essays in Moral Psychology* (New York: Cambridge University Press, 1987); reprinted in *The Importance of What We Care About*, 159–76. Page references will be to the latter volume.

7 Frankfurt, "Freedom of the Will and the Concept of a Person," 12.

that a certain first-order desire control her conduct and in that sense be her "will."

The agent might also experience conflict at the second-order level and might need to reflect at a yet higher level. However, at some level – perhaps simply at the second-order level, perhaps at a higher level – the agent might arrive at a relevant and uncontested highest-order volition. Frankfurt suggests that in at least some such cases the "person identifies himself *decisively* with one of his first-order desires."[8] If, despite such an identification with a given first-order desire, the agent is moved to action by a conflicting first-order desire, that effective first-order desire may count as a "force other than his own"[9] – and this is how Frankfurt describes the case of the "unwilling addict."

Now, in this original paper there is a tension between two competing views. One view is that identification with a first-order desire can be reduced to the state of affairs in which one's relevant highest-order volition favors one's being moved by that desire. The second, weaker view is that identification with a first-order desire involves such a highest-order volition in its favor but is not simply reducible to such a highest-order volition.

The first, reductive view seems wrong, however. As Gary Watson has put it: "[H]igher-order volitions are just, after all, desires, and nothing about their level gives them any special authority with respect to externality."[10] Perhaps I have a desire to make an aggressive public statement, as well as a desire not to. Perhaps I also have a second-order desire that my first-order desire not to make the statement be my will, but perhaps my reflection has not gone beyond that. It still may be an open question for me whether to see my second-order volition as an overly deferential and fearful "hang up." The mere fact that it is second-order does not suffice to ensure that through it I identify with the desire not to make the aggressive public statement.

---

8 Ibid., 21.
9 Ibid., 18.
10 Gary Watson, "Free Action and Free Will," *Mind* 96 (1987): 145–72; the quotation appears on 149.

This suggests that we try taking the second tack: Identification involves an associated highest-order volition, but it also involves something else. But now we are without a suitably complete account of the nature of identification.

Watson made these points in his 1975 paper, "Free Agency."[11] His view there was that we could not analyze identification in terms of orders of desire but that we could get at the relevant phenomena instead by appeal to a distinction between the agent's motivational and valuational systems. An addict might be moved to act on a desire for a drug even though her valuational system favors rejecting that course of action; in such a case she acts on motivation with which she does not identify. Similar remarks could be made concerning the person who is overwhelmed by a sudden passion. The conjecture, then, was that the motivational–valuational distinction could do the work that the distinction between orders of desires failed to do: tell us what we are talking about when we say that a person is moved by a desire with which she does (or does not) identify. Roughly, one identifies with one's desire to *A*, and so (if that desire moves one to *A*) with one's *A*-ing, when *A* is favored by one's valuational system.[12]

Watson, however, gives up on this view in his 1987 paper, "Free Action and Free Will."[13] The problem he sees is that it seems possible to embrace – to identify with – a course of action that one does not think to be best, or to matter most, or to be what one cares about

---

11 Watson, "Free Agency," 217–19.

12 In his later paper, "Free Action and Free Will," Watson tries to avoid an overly "rationalistic" flavor of this model by replacing talk of valuing with talk of caring about something. Susan Wolf has proposed a similar, friendly amendment, appealing to talk about "things which *matter* to a person in some positive way." See her *Freedom within Reason* (New York: Oxford University Press, 1990), 31. (Wolf goes on to criticize the use of this approach in defense of a form of compatibilism.) And there are aspects of Frankfurt's discussion in his later "The Importance of What We Care About" (in *The Importance of What We Care About*, 80–94) that have a similar structure. But these friendly amendments do not by themselves protect the view from the concerns to be noted, concerns about what Watson calls "perverse" cases.

13 "Free Action and Free Will," 149–50.

most deeply. As Watson says, "it may not be thought best, but is fun, or thrilling; one loves doing it. . . ."[14] I am fully aware, let us suppose, that drinking beer with my friends tonight will undermine my efforts in an important interview tomorrow, but I nevertheless plump for the fun of social drinking. I am not compelled. The act is fully my own. But this is not an act favored by my evaluational system. Watson continues:

Call such cases, if you like, perverse cases. . . . There is no estrangement here. One's will is fully behind what one does. Of course, a person's evaluational system might be defined just in terms of what that person does, without regret, when it comes right down to it, but that would be to give up on the explanation of identification by evaluation.[15]

I think that Watson is right here. Identification is not reducible, in a straightforward way, either to hierarchies of desires or to features of the agent's evaluations of actions. So what, then, is identification?

III. DECISIONS ABOUT DESIRES

We have noted that some models of intentional agency include in a basic way decisions and the intentions in which they normally issue. Perhaps we can understand identification in terms of these further conceptual resources. Indeed, that is what Frankfurt suggests in a 1987 paper, "Identification and Wholeheartedness."[16]

As early as his 1977 paper, "Identification and Externality," Frankfurt gave up the effort to reduce identification to hierarchies of desire.[17] He there describes a case in which "by making a particular kind of decision . . . the relation of the person to his passions is established." He goes on to remark that "decisions, unlike desires or attitudes, do not seem to be susceptible both to internality and to exter-

14 Watson, "Free Action and Free Will," 150.
15 Ibid.
16 "Identification and Wholeheartedness," 167–76.
17 Frankfurt, "Identification and Externality," 66.

nality."[18] In the 1987 paper, Frankfurt develops this suggestion by sketching an account of identification in terms of decision:

[I]t is characteristically by a decision . . . that a sequence of desires or preferences of increasingly higher orders is terminated. When the decision is made without reservation, the commitment it entails is decisive. . . . The decision determines what the person really wants by making the desire on which he decided fully his own.[19]

One "really wants" to A – one identifies with one's desire to A – when one's relevant highest-order desire favors A and one has decided in favor of that desire and its associated lower-order desires.

What is decision? Frankfurt does not provide a systematic answer, but he does offer a story about its normal roles in our agency. We are faced with two kinds of conflicts of desires.[20] Some conflicts call simply for ordering desires in terms of importance: An example might be a conflict between a desire to make more money and a desire for more leisure time. Other conflicts call instead for rejecting a desire as "an outlaw"[21] – as in the example of a "jealously spiteful desire to injure." In each case we can make a decision, but in the former case the decision's role is one of "integration," in the latter case it is one of "segregation." In either case, a function of decision is to promote both a unified system of motivation and a coordinated pattern of actions over time: "a function of decision is to integrate the person both dynamically and statically."[22]

Decisions, as understood by Frankfurt, always concern, at least in

18 Ibid., 68 and 68n.
19 Frankfurt, "Identification and Wholeheartedness," 66–67.
20 See ibid.; see also Frankfurt, "Identification and Externality," 66–67.
21 Frankfurt, "Identification and Wholeheartedness," 170.
22 Ibid., 175. I have argued in a similar spirit for the importance of similar roles for intentions and plans – the normal upshots and, so to speak, traces of decisions. By articulating the roles of intentions in coordinating plans we go a long way toward saying what intention – and so, decision – is. (See my *Intention, Plans, and Practical Reason.*) We also arrive at a model of a policy as an intention that is suitably general. (See my "Intention and Personal Policies," *Philosophical Perspectives* 3 [1989]: 443–69.) I discuss related matters in my "Responsibility and Planning," *The Journal of Ethics* 1 (1997): 27–43 [this volume, essay 9, esp. pp. 167–68].

part, desires of the agent. I do not simply decide not to take the drug. I decide in favor of my desire not to take it, and thereby identify with that desire and so with that action. If I simply opt for a course of action, Frankfurt wants to say that I make a choice but do not, strictly speaking, make a decision.[23]

I think that we do sometimes talk about making a decision simply to act in a certain way, but the important point is not about terminology. The important point is the substantive claim that identification involves decisions that concern in part our desires. While we cannot understand identification solely in terms of hierarchies of desire, we also cannot do without a kind of decision that "essentially involves reflexivity."[24]

Suppose I see the conflict between my desire for money and my desire for leisure time as calling for ordering and integration. And suppose that this time I decide in favor of leisure time. I do not thereby treat the desire for money as "external": that is the point of the distinction between this kind of conflict and the kind that calls for "segregation." But my decision is to pursue leisure time, not to pursue money. So how can the model account for the idea that I still may "identify" with both of these conflicting desires?

The answer, I take it, is that my decision is complex: It is a decision both to order these desires in this way on this occasion and to pursue leisure time on this occasion. Though it is a decision that favors one of the conflicting options, it nevertheless treats both desires as desires that are my own. I may identify with a desire even if, on the present occasion, this desire is not favored by my relevant highest-order volition: In the case at hand, after all, my highest-order volition is that my desire to pursue leisure time be my will.

In trying to provide a conceptual framework adequate to the phenomenon of identification we have moved from hierarchies of desire and valuational systems to decisions about our desires. And we have been led to a more complex relation between identification and highest-order volition. I think these are moves in the right direction,

23 See Frankfurt, "Identification and Wholeheartedness," 172.
24 Ibid., 176. Contrast this with Watson's emphasis on first-order evaluations of actions in his "Free Agency," 219.

though a full story would need to say more about what decisions are.[25] But now we need to consider a challenge to the idea that identification is a kind of decision about our desires.

IV. UNWITTING DECISIONS AND REFLECTIVE SATISFACTION

J. David Velleman has argued that an appeal to decision will not work, for there can be "unwitting" decisions with which the agent does not identify.[26] Velleman describes a case in which comments of a friend provoke me to raise my voice in anger. On later reflection I realize that earlier "grievances had crystallized in my mind . . . into a resolution to sever our friendship." But this earlier decision was unwitting, and I did not, at the time of action identify with it. At that time, "it was my resentment speaking, not I."[27]

The unwitting decision to which Velleman alludes is first-order: It is a decision to sever the friendship. Frankfurt might insist that it is merely a choice and so does not challenge his point about decisions. But Velleman's case could be developed so as to involve an unwitting decision in favor of executing the desire to break off the friendship. The challenge remains to Frankfurt's suggestion that "decisions . . . do not seem to be susceptible both to internality and to externality."

Indeed, in his presidential address Frankfurt gives up this effort to see identification as a kind of decision. His reason there seems similar in spirit to the reason suggested by Velleman's example. Concerning any mental act or occurrence, even a decision, one can raise the question of whether or not the agent identifies with it. So identification cannot consist simply in some actual mental act or occurrence.[28] So Frankfurt seeks a different approach.

25 As I indicate in note 22, I think that the planning theory of intention can help us do this by seeing intentions as normal products of decisions, and by then providing a plausible account of the nature of intention.
26 See J. David Velleman, "What Happens When Someone Acts?" *Mind* 101 (1992): 461–81.
27 Ibid., 464–65.
28 This is suggested by Frankfurt's comments in "The Faintest Passion," 13. It was

"Identification," Frankfurt now says, "is constituted neatly by an endorsing higher-order desire with which the person is satisfied."[29] To be satisfied with a higher-order desire one need not take some further attitude toward it. If some further attitude were needed, there would be a threat of a regress; for we could ask about that further attitude whether or not the agent identified with it. It is enough for satisfaction if one is content, in an appropriate way, with that desire:

Being genuinely satisfied is not a matter, then, of choosing to leave things as they are or of making some judgment or decision concerning the desirability of change. It is a matter of simply *having no interest in* making changes. What it requires is that psychic elements of certain kinds *do not occur*. . . . [This] absence must nonetheless be reflective. In other words, the fact that the person is not moved to change things must derive from his understanding and evaluation of how things are with him. Thus, the essential non-occurrence is neither deliberatively contrived nor wantonly unselfconscious.[30]

Reflective satisfaction, while reflective, is nevertheless a "nonoccurrence." Such a reflective nonoccurrence is to do the work that decision was to do on the (now rejected) 1987 view.

Suppose I am reflecting on a higher-order desire and wondering whether to challenge it. So far I have reached no decision to challenge it, but that is because my reflections so far are incomplete and inconclusive. My reflections have as yet reached no conclusion. I am not (yet) moved to "change things," and this derives from my "understanding and evaluation [so far] of how things are" with me. Yet I do not (yet) identify with that desire: its standing remains a genuinely open question for me. Granted, I also have not (yet) come to see this desire as an "outlaw," but the mere absence of such a rejection of my desire is not yet enough for identification. Identification seems to require that I somehow settle the question of the status of my desire. To settle that question, my reflections need to reach closure – they need to reach a conclusion. But that seems to mean that my reflec-

---

anticipated, but not applied to decisions, in "Identification and Externality," 65–66.

29 Frankfurt, "The Faintest Passion," 14.

30 Ibid., 13–14.

tions need to reach some sort of decision about whether to challenge that higher-order desire or to "leave things as they are": The mere absence of motivation to "change things" seems not to suffice.

Is that right? Is a decision really needed for identification? Suppose I discover that I am not moved to change things and then simply stop there and "leave things as they are." Why would that not suffice for identification? The answer is that one may leave things as they are because of some sort of enervation or exhaustion or depression or the like. If in such a case one has not actually decided to leave things as they are, one has not, I think, identified with how things are with one.

This is not completely to reject Frankfurt's strategy in the presidential address. While decision may be needed for identification, it may not be all that is needed. Perhaps what is needed is, in part, a decision with which one is "satisfied." I will argue below for such a view.

V. DECISIONS TO TREAT AS REASON-GIVING

If identification involves a decision, what kind of decision is it?

We cannot simply say that identification with a desire to A is a decision to act on that desire. There are two main reasons why. Return first to the drug addict. Suppose that faced with a powerful desire for the drug he grudgingly decides to go ahead and take it. He might even go ahead and reason grudgingly about preliminary steps and/or relevant means to the end of his getting the drug. Yet he might still see his desire for the drug as an "outlaw," as external; he might still not identify with that desire. So a decision to act on one's desire to A does not ensure identification with that desire.

Second, recall Frankfurt's distinction between two kinds of conflict of desire: conflicts that call for ordering the desires, and conflicts that call instead for rejecting a desire outright. Suppose I see a conflict as calling for ordering and integration and proceed to make a decision. To return to an earlier example: I decide this time to pursue more leisure time rather than more money. I can still treat my desire for money as my own: the mere fact that on this occasion I have decided in favor of leisure time does not ensure that I do not identify with the desire on the losing side. So identification with a desire to A does not require a decision to act on that desire.

Perhaps we have misidentified what it is that one decides when one identifies with one's desire to A. To identify with the losing desire for more money one need not decide to pursue more money. But identification may still involve a kind of decision about that desire.

What kind of decision? T. M. Scanlon emphasizes that in practical reasoning we sometimes "select among considerations to be taken into account in deciding what to do."[31] Scanlon gives an example of a person who needs to decide whether, in playing tennis, she will "play to win." This is, he suggests, a decision about whether to count the promotion of victory as a reason in reasoning about whether, say, to charge the net.

Suppose a tennis player normally desires to win but decides not to treat the promotion of victory as a reason for action when she is playing against her young son.[32] This is not yet to treat her desire for victory as, in Frankfurt's terms, an "outlaw." After all, our tennis player only decides not to treat her desire for victory as reason-giving in certain special circumstances. But suppose, in contrast, that she comes to despair about her extreme competitiveness and decides she

---

31 See Scanlon's *What We Owe to Each Other* (Cambridge, Mass.: Harvard University Press, forthcoming), ch. 1. Rachel Cohon has introduced a somewhat similar idea in her "Internalism about Reasons for Action," *Pacific Philosophical Quarterly* 74 (1993): 265–88. Cohon supposes that rational agents have "standards of practical rationality" which specify "what is a reason and what isn't" (274–75). Cohon explicitly notes that "an agent's standards might not count some of his desires as providing any reasons at all" (275). Allan Gibbard also discusses "norms that say to treat R as weighing in favor of doing X" in his *Wise Choices, Apt Feelings* (Cambridge: Harvard University Press, 1990) at 163. Neither Cohon nor Gibbard nor Scanlon, to my knowledge, consider the relation between their ideas about decisions or standards or norms about reasons for action and questions about the nature of identification in the sense that Frankfurt and his critics are after. What I am trying to do here is to draw on ideas to some extent in the spirit of such work in a way that sheds light on identification.

32 Such a decision would function as what Joseph Raz calls an "exclusionary reason." See his *Practical Reason and Norms* (London: Hutchinson, 1975; reprint, Princeton, N.J.: Princeton University Press, 1990), 35–48.

will no longer treat her desire for victory as reason-giving in any circumstances: She will no longer treat it as setting an end for her practical reasoning and action. At this point she seems to be treating that desire as "external."[33] This is the kind of decision an agent might reach concerning (to recall some of Frankfurt's examples) a "jealously spiteful desire to injure" someone or a "spasm of emotion."[34]

If this is what it is to treat a desire as external, what is it to identify with a desire? We might try saying that I identify with my desire to *A* just in case I so desire and do not treat it as external – I do not, that is, decide not to treat it as a reason in any circumstance. But, as I remarked in discussing Frankfurt's presidential address, such a mere nonoccurrence of a decision is compatible with an agent's seeing the desire's status as genuinely open, and is thus compatible with an agent's not (yet) identifying with the desire.

This suggests that to identify with a desire to *A* one needs actually to decide to treat that desire as reason-giving in one's practical reasoning and planning concerning some relevant circumstances. In requiring such a decision, and not merely the nonoccurrence of a decision not to treat the desire as a reason in any circumstance, we allow for cases that lie between identifying with a desire and treating it as external, namely, cases in which one reaches neither kind of decision. Identification so-conceived requires an actual (though, perhaps, inchoate) endorsement, not merely the absence of explicit rejection.

This leaves open the possibility that I identify with a desire even though, in a circumstance in which I treat it as reason-giving, I do not decide to act on it; for I might decide to treat a desire as reason-giving and still also decide not to act on this reason this time. This

---

33 This may be one way of interpreting Frankfurt's remark that the agent, in a case of conflict that calls for "segregation," "places the rejected desire outside the scope of his preferences, so that it is not a candidate for satisfaction at all" (Frankfurt, "Identification and Externality," 67; see also "Identification and Wholeheartedness," 170). Frankfurt, though, does not here explicitly invoke ideas of seeing or treating one's desire as a *reason*; so he may not welcome such an interpretation.

34 This kind of decision may involve characteristic feelings of estrangement of a sort emphasized in Schroeder and Arpaly, op. cit. I do not see that such feelings are necessary, though. In any case, my concern here is rather with the role of such a decision in one's reasoning and action.

may happen concerning my desire for money in the face of conflict with my desire for more leisure time.

But what does it mean to treat a desire as reason-giving? Is it, in short, to identify with that desire? Are we moving in a circle?

What is needed for our purposes here is a modest understanding of what it is to treat a desire as reason-giving, one that allows us to avoid unacceptable circularity in our story about identification. One way to try to do this is to appeal to the idea that I treat my desire as reason-giving in the relevant sense when I treat it as end-setting – where to treat it as end-setting is, in part, to treat it as potentially justifying, at least to some extent, my performance of relevant means and/or relevant preliminary steps. This is, at best, only part of the story. A desire in favor of a side constraint on action, for example, might be reason-giving without being end-setting.[35] But let us limit our attention here to the basic case of an end-setting desire. If this proves useful in understanding identification, we can return later to address further complexities.

The suggestion so far, then, is that to identify with a desire to A one needs to decide to treat that desire as reason-giving in at least some of one's relevant practical reasoning and planning. One treats one's desire as reason-giving when one treats it as setting an end that can to some extent justify means and/or preliminary steps. This is not to say that one treats one's desire as reason-giving only if one decides so to treat it. In many cases we simply and unreflectively treat our desires in this way without some further decision so to treat them. The suggestion so far is only that the special phenomenon of identifying with one's desire involves a decision to treat that desire as a reason.

VI. BEING SATISFIED WITH A DECISION TO TREAT AS REASON-GIVING

Return to our grudging addict. Suppose that in response to his powerful desire for the drug, he gives in and decides to take the drug.

---

35 See Robert Nozick, *Anarchy, State, and Utopia* (New York: Basic Books, 1974), 29–33.

Having reached this decision he proceeds to reason concerning means and preliminary steps to the end of taking the drug. Does that mean that he is treating his desire for the drug as reason-giving? If so, might he not have decided to treat it in this way?

There seem to be two different cases. Sometimes the addict's reasoning treats his desire for the drug as a kind of threat of future pain and the like. Sarah Buss describes such a case:

Since the addict is confident that his desire for drugs will soon so overpower him as to prevent him from acting intentionally, and since the struggle to remain drug-free is extremely painful, he decides to cease resisting his desire, and to take the steps necessary for satisfying it.[36]

In such a case the addict is trying to respond to his desire for drugs in the way one might try to respond to one's feeling that one will sneeze violently unless one takes certain steps. To respond in this way is not to treat that desire as reason-giving in the relevant sense. So the approach we are taking promises to explain the sense in which such an addict does not identify with his desire for the drug. The problem is that there also seem to be cases in which the addict grudgingly treats his desire as end-setting and reasons about means and preliminary steps toward that end. In such reasoning he is treating his desire for the drug as reason-giving in our modest sense. Yet it seems that he may still not identify with this desire.

A reply might be to challenge the idea that there can be cases of the second sort of addictive action, cases in which one really does treat the addiction-based desire for the drug as reason-giving and yet does not identify with it.[37] In a related spirit, one might try saying

36 Sarah Buss, "Autonomy Reconsidered," in Peter A. French, Theodore E. Uehling, Jr., and Howard K. Wettstein, eds., *Midwest Studies in Philosophy XIX: Philosophical Naturalism* (Notre Dame, Ind.: University of Notre Dame Press, 1994), 95–121; the quotation appears on 101. (Nomy Arpaly and Timothy Schroeder present a somewhat similar picture of the unwilling addict in their "Praise, Blame, and the Whole Self," *Philosophical Studies* [forthcoming].)

37 Sarah Buss (op. cit.) suggests such a view, as has J. David Velleman in correspondence. Elijah Millgram's complex discussion of what he calls the "clear-headed addict" may also point toward such a challenge, though he does seem to allow that such an addict might treat his "urge," if not strictly speaking his "desire," as

instead that such an addict, though perhaps he does treat his desire for the drug as reason-giving, does not *decide* so to treat it. I am, however, skeptical that these strategies will work for all cases. This is no argument, though, and I am unsure how to settle this issue convincingly. What I propose, instead, is to sketch an alternative strategy in defense of the idea that identification involves a decision to treat as reason-giving. I think we can learn from this strategy even if it turns out that it is not the only one available.

The key, I think, is to notice that a decision to treat as reason-giving might itself be incompatible with the agent's *other* standing decisions or policies concerning what to treat as reason-giving. The grudging addict might have a general policy against treating his desire for the drug as reason-giving, and yet, in the face of the present urgency of the desire, he might decide to treat it as reason-giving this time. It seems to me that such an addict does not identify with his desire for the drug, even though he decides to treat it as reason-giving this time.

We can develop the point by exploiting Frankfurt's terminology of being "satisfied" – only now we focus on satisfaction with a special kind of decision.[38] To identify with a desire, we can say, one needs both to decide to treat that desire as reason-giving in some of one's relevant practical reasoning and to be satisfied with that decision. And what is it to be satisfied with such a decision? We should not require the complete absence of conflict concerning that decision. But we may require that one not have reached and retained a conflicting

---

end-setting. See his *Practical Induction* (Cambridge, Mass.: Harvard University Press, 1997), 29–31.

38 There are similarities between what I say here and Frankfurt's remarks about the wholeheartedness of a decision in "Identification and Wholeheartedness." Frankfurt there alludes to a case in which a "decision, no matter how apparently conscientious and sincere, is not wholehearted: Whether the person is aware of it or not, he has other intentions, intentions incompatible with the one the decision established . . ." (174). Elsewhere, though, Frankfurt seems to indicate that wholeheartedness can be undermined not only by conflicting intentions but also by conflicting desires (ibid., 175) or by a conflict with what the person cares about ("The Importance of What We Care About," 84). My approach, like that suggested in the above quote from Frankfurt, but unlike some of Frankfurt's remarks elsewhere, sees a conflict of intentions, decisions, or policies as basic.

decision, intention, or policy concerning the treatment of one's desire as reason-giving. If one has a general policy of not treating a certain desire as reason-giving, and yet, in a particular situation and in the face of the urgency of the desire, decides to treat it as reason-giving this time, one's will would be divided.[39] To identify with a certain desire one needs to decide to treat it as reason-giving in some relevant practical reasoning and to be satisfied with that decision. One is satisfied with such a decision when one's will is, in relevant ways, not divided: The decision to treat as reason-giving does not conflict with other standing decisions and policies about which desires to treat as reason-giving.[40]

VII. A SUCCESS CONDITION

We need one final addition to the basic account of what it is to identify with a desire. In "The Importance of What We Care About," Frankfurt emphasizes that one can decide to care about

---

39 Frankfurt says that "choosing not to do X . . . is incompatible with choosing to do X" (Frankfurt, "Concerning the Freedom and Limits of the Will," *Philosophical Topics* 17 [1989]: 119–130; the quotation appears on 127). In the case I am describing, however, one decision concerns a general policy (not to treat the desire as a reason) and one concerns a particular instance (of treating it as a reason). Such a general policy is a "self-governing intention" of the sort I discuss in my *Intention, Plans, and Practical Reason*, esp. p. 159.

40 As suggested in notes 33 and 38, the idea that identification with a desire involves a decision to treat that desire as a reason, along with being satisfied with the decision, may be one interpretation of Frankfurt's view in "Identification and Wholeheartedness." However, as is also suggested in these notes, it is not clear that this is an interpretation he would welcome.

In *The Sources of Normativity* (Cambridge: Cambridge University Press, 1996), Christine Korsgaard also connects, but in a different way, identification with treating as a reason. Like Frankfurt, Korsgaard emphasizes the reflective structure of our conscious agency. (Korsgaard refers to Frankfurt's 1971 paper – at 99 n. 8 – but does not try to chart Frankfurt's later views.) Korsgaard believes that when a reflective agent acts on a desire, that agent "must say to itself that the desire is a reason" (94). To see a desire as a reason is, for Korsgaard, to see it as fitting with a relevant normative conception one has of one's identity: The connection with one's conception of one's identity is what makes the desire a reason. I discuss Korsgaard's views in essay 14.

something and yet "when the chips are down" fail to care about it.[41] Perhaps, similarly, I might decide to treat my desire, say, to seek a reconciliation with an old acquaintance as reason-giving and yet, when the chips are down, find myself unable to treat it this way. I might find that, despite my decision, and despite the fact that I am satisfied with that decision, I do not care enough about reconciliation.

In such a case it seems that I have not fully succeeded in identifying with my desire for reconciliation. For one to identify with a desire one normally not only would reach an appropriate decision to treat that desire as reason-giving but would also treat it that way. We need, however, to be careful to allow for cases in which one identifies with a desire but, as it happens, does not find oneself in those circumstances with respect to which one has decided to treat it as reason-giving. Though one does not, in fact, find oneself in such circumstances, one is fully prepared to treat the desire as reason-giving in such circumstances.

I think we can do justice both to these complexities and to Frankfurt's insight about the limits of decision in the following way: To identify with one's desire is (a) to reach a decision to treat that desire as reason-giving and to be satisfied with that decision, and (b_1) to treat that desire as reason-giving or, at least, (b_2) to be fully prepared to treat it as reason-giving were a relevant occasion to arise.

We can now return to Velleman's concern about "unwitting" decisions. The decision in Velleman's example is a decision to (execute the desire to) sever the friendship. It is not a decision to treat the desire to sever the friendship as reason-giving. It seems to me that when we turn to a decision to treat that desire as reason-giving, when we add that this is a decision with which the agent is satisfied, and when we also add that the agent does treat that desire as reason-giving, it will no longer be plausible for the agent to insist that "it was my resentment speaking, not I."[42]

---

41 Frankfurt, *The Importance of What We Care About*, 84–85. See also his remarks in "Identification and Wholeheartedness," 174. Thoughtful comments from Sarah Buss helped me see the need to address issues raised by this aspect of Frankfurt's views.

42 This is a good point at which to reflect briefly on Velleman's positive proposal in

VIII. EXTENDING THE MODEL

Recall that I might unreflectively treat a desire of mine as reason-giving without actually deciding to treat it that way. This suggests an objection:[43] Suppose I routinely and as a matter of course treat a given desire of mine as reason-giving. Suppose I have not actually decided to treat it this way but have made no decision to the contrary. Do I not identify with that desire?

---

his "What Happens When Someone Acts?" and its relation to the view I am sketching here. Velleman seeks a component of the agent's motivational machinery that plays what is seen by common sense as the role of the agent. Velleman argues that what plays this role is "the desire to act in accordance with reasons" (478). More specifically, it is the desire "to see which [motives] provide stronger reasons for acting, and then to ensure that they prevail over those whose rational force is weaker" (ibid.). In a sense, the agent is to be identified with this particular desire as it functions in her psychology: "the agent *is* [this] motive, functionally speaking" (480). My approach, in contrast, understands identification in terms of deciding to treat, and of treating, a desire as a reason, rather than in terms of a desire to act in accordance with the strongest reasons. This allows my approach to provide what seems a more natural treatment of identification with desires on the losing side. My approach can also see both the motives with which there is identification, and the decisions and policies which help ensure such identification, as the agent's "own." That said, my view is in the spirit of Velleman's (as he helped me see in correspondence) in understanding identification in part by appeal to a way in which one may bring one's desire into one's practical reasoning.

Another useful comparison may be with Sarah Buss's treatment in "Autonomy Reconsidered"; for Buss also appeals to how one brings, or does not bring, one's desire into one's practical reasoning. Buss writes that a "person's desires . . . can figure in her practical reasoning as some of the things she considers . . . Sometimes, however, these very same states exert a *non*rational influence on a person's reasoning" (106). Buss argues that this distinction is crucial to the idea that some desires are external: "their status as external influences depends on how they relate to her practical reasoning. Rather than being *constituents of* this reasoning . . . they influence reasoning from without" (107). (Buss goes on to say that not every such "nonrational influence is autonomy undermining" [108].) I am agreeing with Buss that it is important whether or not one treats one's desire as a reason – as Buss puts it, a thing *"considered"* in one's reasoning (107). But I am also emphasizing that we make decisions and have policies about such matters and that such decisions and policies are important to identification.

43 This objection is due to Nomy Arpaly and Timothy Schroeder.

Frankfurt considers a related issue in his discussion of satisfaction:

It is possible, of course, for someone to be satisfied with his first-order desires without in any way considering whether to endorse them. In that case, he is identified with those first-order desires. But insofar as his desires are utterly unreflective, he is to that extent not genuinely a person at all. He is merely a wanton.[44]

Though it is not completely clear from this passage, I take it that the view here is that such an agent, while "identified with" the first-order desire, does not identify with that desire; for to identify with a desire one must reflectively consider that desire. My initial response to the present objection is along similar lines. If one is unreflective about whether to treat one's desire as a reason, one does not yet face the kind of problem to which identification is a response. If, however, one is to some extent reflective about this desire, then one needs to decide, however inchoately, in order to settle the issue. So there will be intentional actions whose motivating desires are ones which the agent treats as reason-giving and does not treat as external but with which, strictly speaking, he does not identify.

That, as I said, is my initial response. But I want also to note a natural way in which, in response to the present objection and in light of Frankfurt's remarks, we might find it useful to extend the account. We might go on to say that a person is, in an extended sense, identified with a desire if (*i*) she treats it as reason-giving, (*ii*) she does not treat it as external, and (*iii*) she would decide to continue to treat it as reason-giving, be satisfied with that decision, and continue to treat it as reason-giving if she were to reflect on the matter.[45] One may, in this extended sense, be identified with a desire even if one has not reflected on that desire in ways that are needed for one to identify with it.

---

44 Frankfurt, "The Faintest Passion," 14.

45 Though there will be cases in which there is no clear answer to the question of what an agent would decide if she were to reflect on the matter. Jennifer Rosner explores related issues about what she calls "counterfactual stability under reflective evaluation" in her *Reflective Evaluation, Autonomy, and Self-knowledge* (Ph.D. thesis, Stanford University, 1998).

IX. THREE CONCERNS

Let us see how this approach would respond to a trio of concerns.

First, suppose an addict is so depressed and resigned to his addiction that he does not try to resist.[46] Instead, he decides to treat his desire for the drug as reason-giving, proceeds to do so, and, because of his resignation to his addiction, has no policy to the contrary. But he still sees the desire as criticizable.

I think such an example shows that one can identify with a desire one thinks is criticizable if one really does arrive at, and is satisfied with, a decision to treat it as reason-giving and does in fact treat it that way. Perhaps this is a result of resignation or depression, but that is a different matter.[47]

Second, suppose my decision to treat my desire for money as reason-giving is motivated by a bet I make with you.[48] I win the bet if I spend the next ten years treating this desire in this way, even though I think so acting is, to say the least, undignified.[49] I am satisfied with this decision, but only because I want to win the bet. Do I identify with my desire for money? I think that it is plausible to say "yes": I identify with it in order to win the bet. This is a nonstandard ground for identification and may be a bad way to live one's life, but that is a different matter.

Third, what about Watson's "perverse" cases? A person might identify with her desire in favor of something "thrilling" without

---

46 This example is due to John Fischer.

47 Note that this example differs from the one noted earlier in which one's depression prevents one from making any decision about whether to treat one's desire as reason-giving. Now, in "Identification and Externality," Frankfurt writes: "A person may acknowledge to himself that passions of which he disapproves are undeniably and unequivocally his . . ." (65). I am suggesting that there are two different versions of the case to which Frankfurt here alludes: one in which the person is simply resigned to the passion of which he disapproves; another in which the person goes on, perhaps out of resignation, to decide to treat that passion as reason-giving. On my view, this difference matters to identification.

48 This example is due to Alfred Mele.

49 If I win the bet, I get something other than money that I value highly. Perhaps I get to marry Turandot.

thinking this best or caring most about it. But if she really does identify with it, she endorses it in some way, and the present proposal seems a plausible story about what that way is. Though she thinks so acting is not best, she still decides to treat her desire for the thrilling thing as reason-giving; and she goes on to treat it this way. If she is satisfied with her decision to treat that desire as reason-giving, she identifies with that desire.

X. CONCLUSION

I have tried to understand identification by appeal to phenomena of deciding to treat, and of treating, a desire of one's as reason-giving in one's practical reasoning, planning, and action. Is identification, so understood, "fundamental," as Frankfurt says, "to any philosophy of mind and of action"? Well, we have seen reason to include in our model of intentional agency such phenomena of deciding to treat, and of treating, certain of one's desires as reason-giving. Identification, at bottom, consists in such phenomena – or so I have proposed. Given that such phenomena are important in our practical lives, we may agree with Frankfurt that identification is, in this sense, "fundamental."

PART FOUR

CRITICAL STUDIES

11

Davidson's Theory of Intention

In an important and fascinating series of papers, spanning a decade and a half, Donald Davidson has sketched a general theory of intention, a theory that tries to explain what it is to do something intentionally, what it is to intend to do something later, and how these two phenomena are related.[1] In this paper I say what this theory is, argue that it faces a pair of serious difficulties, and diagnose these difficulties as rooted in an overly limited conception of the role of intentions and plans in practical reasoning.

I. DAVIDSON'S THEORY: MAIN IDEAS

Davidson begins with intentional action. In his classic paper 'Actions, Reasons and Causes',[2] he sketches the following general view. Intentional action is action that is explainable, in the appropriate way, by appeal to the agent's reasons for action. The reasons that explain intentional actions are appropriate pairs of the agent's desires (and other 'pro-attitudes') and beliefs. When one acts *for* a certain reason

---

I want to thank Robert Audi, Myles Brand, John Dupré, Dagfinn Follesdal, John Perry, Howard Wettstein, and members of a spring 1982 Stanford seminar, given jointly by John Perry and me, for their helpful comments and criticisms.

1 These papers are all reprinted in *Essays on Actions and Events* (Oxford: Oxford University Press, 1980). Hereafter *EAE*. The crucial papers for my purposes here are 'Actions, Reasons and Causes', 'How is Weakness of the Will Possible?', and 'Intending'.

2 In *EAE*, pp. 3–19.

an appropriate desire–belief pair *causes* one's action. Suppose, for example, that I intentionally go to Davies Hall because I want to hear Pavarotti sing and believe going to Davies Hall would be a way of doing this. Since I act *for* this reason, the pro-attitude and belief *cause* my action.

This conception of intentional action makes no essential appeal to any distinct state or event of *intending* to go to Davies Hall that intervenes between my desire–belief pair and my action. The intentionality of my action lies, rather, in its relation to my desire–belief pair.

This is a compromise position. On the one hand it insists that in explaining actions in terms of their reasons we are citing *causes* of those actions. So it rejects radical suggestions to the contrary – typically rooted in strong behaviouristic assumptions – offered by Anscombe, Melden, and others.[3] On the other hand, in seeing the intentionality of action as solely a matter of its relation to the agent's desires and beliefs, Davidson rejects the *volitional* conception that frequently accompanies causal theories. On a volitional conception of, for example, an intentional arm-raising, a volition in favour of so acting is, as Davidson says, 'an event that is common and peculiar to all cases where a man intentionally raises his arm' ('Actions, Reasons and Causes', p. 13). Further, on such a conception this volitional event plays a crucial causal role in the arm-raising. While embracing a causal theory of the relation between reason and action, Davidson explicitly denies that there is any such volitional event involved in the causation of intentional arm-raisings.

Now, even granting that when I act for a reason my reason is a cause of my action, there will also be some sort of *logical* relation between my reason and my action. In 'How is Weakness of the Will Possible?'[4] Davidson tries to characterize this logical relation in terms of a general conception of practical reasoning.[5] The guiding idea is that the reason for which I act provides me with premises from

---

3 For references, see Davidson's initial footnote in 'Actions, Reasons and Causes'.

4 In *EAE*, pp. 21–42.

5 The main ideas of this conception are also usefully discussed in 'Intending'. In what follows I draw on that discussion as well.

which I could have reasoned to a conclusion which corresponds to my action.

Consider again my intentionally going to Davies Hall because I want to listen to Pavarotti. This pro-attitude provides one premiss for my potential reasoning, and my belief that going to Davies Hall is a way of doing this provides another. The premiss provided by my belief is just *what* I believe: the proposition that going to Davies Hall is a way of listening to Pavarotti. The premiss provided by my pro-attitude is not, however, so easily arrived at. What I want is *to listen to Pavarotti* or, perhaps, *that I listen to Pavarotti*. But, on Davidson's view, the relevant premiss is neither of these, but rather the prima-facie *evaluative proposition* that any act of mine would be desirable in so far as it is an act of listening to Pavarotti. Davidson supposes that such an evaluative proposition is the 'natural expression' of my pro-attitude.[6] Finally, my intentional action corresponds, on the theory, to an 'unconditional' (or, as he later says in 'Intending', 'all-out') – rather than a merely prima-facie – evaluative proposition that my action is desirable. This unconditional evaluative proposition can, on the theory, be represented as a non-deductive conclusion of an argument whose premisses are provided by my pro-attitude and belief. In

6 Davidson's explanation of this prima-facie evaluative proposition leans on a supposed parallel with inductive-statistical explanations, as they are understood by Hempel in *Aspects of Scientific Explanation* (New York, 1965), pp. 376–403. While I am convinced by Davidson that there is some important parallel here, I am unsure about the details of his treatment of this parallel. As Hempel emphasizes, inductive-statistical explanations involve two distinct concepts of probability: statistical probability, and inductive probability. The former is used in the major premiss of such explanations, the latter characterizes the *relation* between premisses and conclusion of the explanation. Davidson's main idea is to treat 'prima facie' as relating premisses and conclusion of practical syllogisms. In this respect, 'prima facie' is seen as analogous to inductive probability. But Davidson also understands the major premisses of such practical syllogisms as using the concept of prima facie. Given the analogy with probability, this suggests that there is a notion of prima facie analogous to that of statistical probability. But the problem is that we seem to have only a *single* notion of prima facie, in contrast with the probabilistic case. This disanalogy between the two cases does not emerge clearly in Davidson's discussion, because the distinction between two concepts of probability is lost in his formalism. (See 'How is Weakness of the Will Possible?', p. 38.)

intentionally going to Davies Hall I accept this all-out evaluative conclusion.

This signals a modest retreat from the rejection of a volitional conception. On this later version of Davidson's theory, there *is* an element 'common and peculiar to all cases' of intentional concert-going, namely the acceptance of an all-out evaluation that the concert-going being performed is desirable.[7] But this retreat is not a capitulation, for Davidson supposes that when I intentionally go to the concert my acceptance of this all-out evaluative proposition in favour of my action need not be distinct from my very act of going. This is why he says that on his theory 'Aristotle's remark that the conclusion (of a piece of practical reasoning) is an action remains cogent'.[8] And, of course, if my acceptance of this all-out conclusion is not distinct from my action, it cannot be a cause of my action.[9]

My all-out evaluative conclusion has two further features it is important to note. First, it is at least implicitly comparative. It assesses my action favourably in comparison with the other options I actually considered (which in some cases may only include the option of refraining from so acting).[10]

---

7 'Evaluation' is ambiguous between the evaluative proposition accepted, and the acceptance of that proposition. So I will only use this term when the context clearly disambiguates.

8 'How is Weakness of the Will Possible?', p. 39.

9 Given Davidson's metaphysics of action as presented in 'Agency' (*EAE*, pp. 43–61), however, my acceptance of this conclusion *could* cause the upshot in terms of which the action is described. Thus, my acceptance of an all-out conclusion in favour of raising my arm may cause my arm's rising. This suggests that Davidson's theory *is* compatible with a volitional theory in the spirit of Prichard's 'Acting, Willing, and Desiring' (in A. R. White (ed.), *The Philosophy of Action* (Oxford, 1968)).

10 As I urged in 'Practical Reasoning and Weakness of the Will', *Noûs* 13 (1979), 153–70, I think that at this point the theory encounters serious difficulties with weak-willed intentional conduct. But here I am interested in other matters.

The implicitly comparative nature of these all-out evaluations is clearer in Davidson's earlier discussion in 'How is Weakness of the Will Possible?' than in his later discussion in 'Intending', where he typically uses the apparently non-comparative predicate 'is desirable'. Suffice it to say here, in defence of my interpretation of these all-out evaluations as implicitly comparative, that if they really

Second, my all-out evaluation is about the *particular* act of concert-going I am now performing. In this respect it differs from my initial pro-attitude, which was in favour of actions in so far as they were of a certain *type* (for example, concert-going). Davidson's view seems to be that desirability is, strictly speaking, always a property of particular actions, rather than of types of actions.[11] Different instances of a given type of action may well vary in their desirability. Some ways of going to the concert (for example, by hijacking a cab) will be quite undesirable. Only when we are given a particular action are we given something which is either desirable or not (relative to the agent's values).

We have so far seen the main outlines of Davidson's theory of intentional action. A theory of intentional action cannot, however, stand alone. It needs to be related to a plausible conception of future intention – intending (or, having an intention) now to do something later. After all, both phenomena in some sense involve *intent*; our theory needs to say in what sense.

I may now have various reasons – appropriate desire–belief pairs – in favour of going to the concert tomorrow. But such desires and beliefs do not suffice for an intention to go. What is the nature of the new state I am in when I come to intend to go?

Davidson's strategy here is to *extend* his account of the role of all-

---

were non-comparative the problem of agglomerativity, discussed below, would arise even more immediately. It would be immediately clear that one could have future-directed all-out evaluations both in favour of going to the concert and in favour of not going.

11 Davidson's main discussion of this feature of all-out evaluations is in 'Intending', pp. 96–7. In this discussion he seems to me not to separate two different issues. First, there is the issue of when there can be *demonstrative reference* to a particular action. Here Davidson supposes that there can be no demonstrative reference to an event in the future. Second, there is the issue of what the property of desirability is a property *of*. Here Davidson's view is, I take it, that it is always a property of *particular* acts. As I see it, it is this second view that is critical to his discussion of future intention.

What about an all-out *comparison* that my action is better than certain alternatives? what does such a comparison compare my particular act *to*? The answer, I take it, is that it compares my particular act to other particular acts *of different types*, where the relevant types are determined by the alternatives I have considered.

out evaluations in intentional action to the future-directed case. In just having reasons for acting in a certain way I only accept certain prima-facie evaluative propositions. When I actually act for those reasons – and so act intentionally – I accept an appropriate all-out evaluative proposition. Similarly, on Davidson's theory, when I come to intend to go to the concert tomorrow I come to accept a future-directed all-out evaluative proposition in favour of going to the concert then: my future intention is this all-out evaluation. By extending his theory of intentional action in this way Davidson can ensure that future intention, like intentional action, can be a conclusion of practical reasoning. And he can exhibit a common feature in the two cases of intent.

However, Davidson sees a problem with this strategy. As we have seen, in the case of intentional action the involved judgement of all-out desirability is about a particular action; desirability is a property of particular acts, not of types of acts. But when I intend to go to the concert tomorrow I have in mind no single, particular act of concert-going. And there may well never be in the world an actual, particular concert-going to judge desirable. So, how could my intention be an all-out evaluation?

Granted, I could judge that *any* particular act of concert-going would be desirable; for such a judgement would still only ascribe desirability to particular acts.[12] But this would normally be an insane judgement. Some concert-goings – for example, those that involve hijacking a cab – will surely be undesirable. Future intention should not require insanity.

Davidson's solution to this problem is couched in terms of a different example – that of intending to eat a sweet in a moment. Here is what he says:

It would be mad to hold that any action of mine in the immediate future that is the eating of something sweet would be desirable. But there is nothing absurd in my judging that any action of mine in the immediate future that is the eating of something sweet would be desirable *given the rest of what I believe about the immediate future*. I do not believe I will eat a poisonous candy, and

12 As John Perry has emphasized to me in conversation.

so that is not one of the actions of eating something sweet that my all-out judgement includes. ('Intending', p. 99, emphasis in the original).

Returning to our example, when I intend to go to the concert I judge that any act of mine that is both a concert-going and *whose other features are all consistent with my beliefs* would be desirable. I believe that I would not go to the concert by hijacking a cab. So the undesirability of going that way does not stop me from holding that any concert-going of mine that *is* consistent with my beliefs would be desirable. And that is just what I hold when I intend to go.

II. DAVIDSON'S THEORY: BELIEF CONDITIONS ON INTENTION

We have now seen the main features of Davidson's theory of intentional action and future intention. On the latter theory, my beliefs provide a critical background for the all-out evaluations which are my future intentions. As Davidson puts it, my future intentions are 'conditioned by my beliefs' ('Intending, p. 100). But having said this it remains unclear just what these beliefs must be. So let us ask just what I must believe for me to intend to go to the concert tonight.

Consider three candidates for necessary conditions for such a future intention:

(1) My going to the concert is consistent with my beliefs.
(2) I believe I will be able to go.
(3) I believe I will go.

Davidson sees his theory as imposing (1) as a requirement on my intention. He says that 'wishes for things that are not consistent with what one believes' cannot be intentions, for that is 'ruled out by our conception of an intention' ('Intending', p. 101). His reasoning seems to be that if, in our example, my going to the concert is inconsistent with my beliefs, then there 'can be no judgement that such an action consistent with [my] beliefs is desirable. There can be no such intention' ('Intending', p. 101).[13]

13 I am puzzled by this, for it seems that in such a case there *can* be a judgement that

What about (2)? Note that (2) is not entailed by (1). It *is* necessary for (1) that I do not believe I will not be able to go. But my going may be consistent with my beliefs even though I do not actually believe I will be able to go. So we need to ask whether, on the theory, (2) is also required for intention.

I find Davidson's remarks on this issue unclear. At times he seems to think that (2) is indeed required.[14] But this cannot be his considered view. Let me note three reasons why.

The first concerns Davidson's discussion of (3). Grice[15] and Harman[16] have both argued that (3) is necessary for my intention. In Grice's example I think I may well be in jail by tonight, and for that reason do not believe I will go to the concert. Grice claims that I then do not intend to go, but only, perhaps, hope to go or intend to go if I can.

Davidson disagrees. He claims that in such a case I still may intend to go, though it might be misleading for me simply to report this intention without mentioning my worries about jail. Now in such a case I surely will not satisfy (2). The whole point of the example is that I believe I may well be in jail, and for that reason do not actually believe I will be able to go to the concert. At most, I will not believe I will not be able to go, and so be in a position to satisfy (1). Since Davidson insists that in such a case I may still intend to go, he must not see (2) as necessary for my intention.

Second, in his discussion of Grice's paper Davidson seems to com-

---

any concert-going act consistent with my beliefs would be desirable. Indeed, if this is ordinary universal quantification, it seems that the theory is in danger of saying that, once I believe I will not go, I get an intention to go by default. This suggests that Davidson is *adding* to his account of my future-directed all-out evaluation in favour of *A*-ing, the further condition that my *A*-ing be consistent with my beliefs. In any case, in what follows I will assume Davidson's interpretation of my future-directed all-out evaluation in favour of *A*-ing as requiring that my *A*-ing be consistent with my beliefs.

14 For example, at one point he describes a future intention as a judgement in favour of 'something I think I can do' ('Intending', p. 101).

15 In 'Intention and Uncertainty', *Proceedings of the British Academy* 57 (1971), 263–79.

16 In 'Practical Reasoning', *Review of Metaphysics* 29 (1976), 431–63.

mit himself to the view that future intention cannot be subject to a stronger belief requirement than is intentional action.[17] So, for Davidson to accept (2) as a condition on my future intention he would also have to suppose that to *A* intentionally I must believe, while I am *A*-ing, that I can *A*. But Davidson himself has an example that shows that this latter view is not plausible. I might try to make ten carbon copies of a paper on my typewriter while doubting that I can. Nevertheless, if I actually do make ten copies, if my success is due to my relevant skills, and if making ten copies is also my goal in acting[18] then I *intentionally* make ten copies. This shows that intentional action does not require a belief that one can so act. So, given his assumption about the relation between belief requirements on intentional action and future intention, Davidson cannot accept (2) as a condition on my future intention.

There is, finally, a third reason why Davidson must reject (2) as necessary for my intention. To explain this I need to touch on Davidson's approach to the distinction between simple and conditional intentions.

III. DAVIDSON'S THEORY: SIMPLE AND CONDITIONAL INTENTION

Suppose my going to the concert is consistent with my beliefs, but I do not actually believe I will be able to go. Perhaps I just do not know whether there will be any tickets left. I ask myself: would any concert-going act, consistent with my beliefs, be desirable?

There is an initial problem in answering this question. Let us call a condition whose presence I believe to be required for my being able to *A* an *enabling condition for A-ing*. In our example, the availabil-

---

17 See his remarks at 'Intending', p. 92. Let me note that in my view this assumption is not obvious. It seems to me likely that I need a stronger belief about my ability to *A* to intend now to *A* later, than I do just to give *A* a try when the time comes.

18 These last two qualifications are mine, not Davidson's, but I think they are needed to make the example convincing. I was convinced of the need for the second qualification by Harman's discussion in 'Willing and Intending' (in R. Grandy and R. Warner (eds.), *Philosophical Grounds of Rationality* (Oxford: Oxford University Press, 1986)).

ity of tickets is an enabling condition of my going to the concert. This condition is consistent with my beliefs, but not guaranteed by them. So among those future situations which are consistent with my beliefs there will be some in which this enabling condition will hold, and some in which it will not. When I try to answer my question, do I consider all of these future situations, or only those in which the appropriate enabling conditions obtain?

I think Davidson must suppose that I need consider only those future situations in which I *can* go to the concert. After all, there will be no *un*desirable concert-goings in those other situations, consistent with my beliefs. In answering my question, then, I limit my attention to futures consistent with my beliefs *and* in which obtain all enabling conditions for going to the concert. I limit my attention, for example, to those cases in which there are tickets left and ask whether, in such cases, my going would be desirable. I do this even if some enabling conditions, though consistent with my beliefs, are not guaranteed by my beliefs.

Suppose I conclude that any such concert-going act, consistent with my beliefs, would be desirable. And suppose I reach this conclusion even though some enabling conditions for my going – for example, the availability of tickets – are not guaranteed by my beliefs. Do I *simply* intend to go; or do I have only the *conditional* intention to go if I can?

I think it is clear that Davidson's answer is that I simply intend to go; for consider his remarks about 'genuine conditional intentions':

Genuine conditional intentions are appropriate when we explicitly consider what to do in various contingencies; for example, someone may intend to go home early from a party if the music is too loud. If we ask for the difference between conditions that really do make the statement of an intention more accurate and bogus conditions like 'if I can' . . . it seems to me clear that the difference is this: bona-fide conditions are ones that are reasons for acting that are contemporary with the intention. Someone may not like loud music now, and that may be why he now intends to go home early from the party if the music is too loud. His not being able to go home early is not a reason for or against his going home early, and so it is not a relevant condition for an intention . . . ('Intending', pp. 94–5).

On Davidson's view, then, mere enabling conditions are not 'bona-fide' conditions for 'genuine conditional intentions', for they are not 'reasons for acting that are contemporary with the intention'. The availability of tickets is, by itself, no reason for my going to the concert, though it is an enabling condition for my going. Of course, to intend to go I cannot believe such enabling conditions will *not* be present; for then I would not satisfy (1). But even if I do not actually believe they will all be present I may still have a simple intention to go.

In our example, then, I simply intend to go to the concert, despite my lack of belief in the availability of tickets. But then (2) cannot be necessary for my future intention.

IV. THE BURIDAN PROBLEM

I now want to consider two interrelated problems for Davidson's theory. The first problem is an analogue of the old problem of Buridan's Ass. Buridan wondered how an ass, midway between two piles of hay judged equally desirable, could intentionally go to one.[19] Our problem concerns the possibility of *future* intention in the face of equally desirable future options.

Suppose I know I can stop at one of two bookstores after work, Kepler's or Printer's Inc., but not both. And suppose I find both options equally attractive. I judge all-out that any act of my stopping at Kepler's would be just as desirable as any act of stopping at Printer's Inc., given my beliefs. Does it follow from Davidson's theory that I have both intentions? Neither intention?

These questions highlight an unclarity in Davidson's discussion. An all-out desirability judgement in favour of *A*-ing is implicitly comparative. But there are weak and strong comparisons. A *weak* comparison would see *A*-ing as at least as desirable as its alternatives; a *strong* comparison sees *A*-ing as strictly more desirable than its alter-

---

19 For a useful discussion of such cases see E. Ullmann-Margalit and S. Morgenbesser, 'Picking and Choosing', *Social Research* 44 (1977), 757–85. I was first led to consider the relevance of such cases to Davidson's theory by a remark of Saul Kripke.

natives. Which sort of comparison does Davidson's theory require for future intention?

There is a dilemma here. If all that is required is a weak comparison, then in the present case I both intend to go to Kepler's and intend to go to Printer's Inc. But this seems wrong. Recall that I know I cannot go to both stores. So I cannot, on Davidson's view, intend to go to both. But then, if I were to have each intention, I would be in a position in which I (rationally, we may suppose) intend to A and intend to B, but cannot intend to do both.

This violates a natural constraint on intention. Rational intentions should be *agglomerative*. If at one and the same time I rationally intend to A and rationally intend to B then it should be both possible and rational for me, at the same time, to intend to A *and* B. But if all that is required for future intention is a weak comparison, then intentions will not be agglomerative in this way.

Granted, many practical attitudes are not agglomerative. I might rationally desire to drink a milk shake for lunch and rationally desire to run four miles after lunch, and yet find the prospect of doing both appalling. But this is one way in which intentions differ from ordinary desires. Rational intentions are agglomerative, and this fact should be captured and explained by our theory.

This suggests that Davidson should insist that to intend to A I must hold a strong comparative evaluation in favour of A. Thus I neither intend to go to Kepler's, nor intend to go to Printer's Inc. So, in the present case, agglomerativity is not threatened.

But now we have our Buridan problem. It seems that I can just decide on which bookstore to go to, while continuing to see each option as equally desirable. Such a decision provides me with an intention which does not correspond to a strong comparative evaluation. I might just decide to go to Kepler's even though I do not judge all-out that so acting would be strictly more desirable than going to Printer's Inc. But the intention I thereby reach does not satisfy the demands of Davidson's theory as we are now interpreting it. In trying to avoid the horn of agglomerativity, Davidson's theory is threatened by the horn of a Buridan problem.

V. A FURTHER PROBLEM WITH AGGLOMERATIVITY

The second problem is that even if future intention requires a strong comparative evaluation, Davidson's theory still will not ensure that rational intentions are agglomerative. This results from the weak belief condition on intention.

An example will make my point. I have for a long time wanted to buy copies of *The White Hotel* and *The Fixer*, and know I will be at a bookstore this afternoon. Further, I know the bookstore will have one or other of these novels in stock, but not both. Unfortunately, I do not know which one will be in stock.

I ask: would any act of my buying *The Fixer* be desirable, given my beliefs? In answering this I limit my attention to possible futures consistent with my beliefs and in which all enabling conditions – including the condition that *The Fixer* is in stock – obtain. And, let us suppose, I reasonably judge that any such act of buying *The Fixer* would be strictly better than its alternatives, and so, in the relevant sense, desirable. Note that the relevant alternatives here will include buying no novel, but will not include buying *The White Hotel*. This is because the latter is not open to me in any future which is both consistent with my beliefs and in which I can buy *The Fixer*. In this way I reach a simple intention to buy *The Fixer* this afternoon.

By an analogous route I might also reasonably judge that any act of my buying *The White Hotel* that is consistent with my beliefs would be desirable, thereby reaching an intention to buy *The White Hotel*.

Of course, in each case I do not believe all the required enabling conditions will obtain. But on Davidson's account that does not turn my intentions into mere conditional intentions to buy *The Fixer* / *The White Hotel* if I can. Rather, I both intend to buy *The Fixer* and intend to buy *The White Hotel*. And on Davidson's account both intentions might be perfectly reasonable.

But recall that I believe I cannot buy both novels. So it is not possible for me to intend to buy both. We are led to the result that though I rationally intend to buy *The Fixer*, and rationally intend to buy *The White Hotel*, it is not even possible for me to intend both to buy *The Fixer* and to buy *The White Hotel*. On Davidson's theory rational intentions may fail to be agglomerative. And that seems wrong.

VI. INTENTION AND PRACTICAL REASONING

I now want to try to diagnose the source of this pair of difficulties. My conjecture is that both difficulties are in large part rooted in Davidson's conception of just what facts a theory of future intention must account for. In particular, I think Davidson's theory is constrained by an overly weak conception of the role of future intentions in further practical thinking.

To my knowledge, Davidson says almost nothing about this role. His picture seems to be that the basic inputs for practical reasoning about what to do – either now or later – will just be the agent's desires and beliefs. Such reasoning, when concerned with the future, can issue in future intentions. And these intentions are fundamentally different sorts of states from the desires and beliefs on which they are based. But there is no significant further role for these intentions to play as inputs into one's further practical thinking. Future intentions are, rather, mere spin-offs of practical reasoning concerning the future.

This is an attenuated conception of the role of intention in practical reasoning. It receives support from Davidson's *strategy of extension*: the attempt to extend the materials present in his account of intentional action to an account of future intention. In intentional action, there is no temporal interval between all-out evaluation and action. So there is no room for further practical reasoning in which that all-out evaluation can play a significant role as an input. When we extend the notion of an all-out evaluation to the future-directed case, it will then be easy to overlook the possibility that *future* intentions *will*, at least typically, play such a role.

I believe that this limited conception of the role of future intentions in practical reasoning fails to accommodate the facts; for such intentions typically play an important role in our practical thinking. Moreover, I suspect that Davidson's acceptance of this limited conception may well account for his failure to be concerned with the pair of problems I have emphasized.

Let us begin with my first point. A theory of future intentions needs to explain why we ever *bother* to form them. Why do we not just cross our bridges when we come to them? One answer is that we want to avoid the need for deliberation at the time of action. But, more importantly, we form future intentions as parts of larger plans whose role is to aid *co-ordination* of our activities over time. Further, we do not adopt these plans, in all their detail, all at once. Rather, as time goes on we add to and adjust our plans. As elements in these plans, future intentions force the formation of yet further intentions and constrain the formation of other intentions and plans. For example, they force the formation of intentions concerning means, and constrain later plans to be consistent with prior plans.[20] This means that they play a significant role in our further practical thinking, in the on-going creation and adjustment of our plans – a role Davidson neglects.

My second point is that Davidson's neglect of this role may well account for his neglect of the pair of problems I have emphasized. This is because this neglected role is a major source of the facts about future intentions that generate these problems.

Let us call the role my future intentions play in constraining and influencing the further construction and adjustment of my plans in pursuit of co-ordination, their *co-ordinating role*. Rational intentions will be capable of playing this role well. To do this they must be capable of being part of an overall plan that can successfully co-ordinate the agent's activities. So rational intentions are to be agglomerative.

Further, the search for co-ordination of my activities over time may sometimes require me to settle in advance on one of several options judged equally desirable. Perhaps in order to get on with my plans for the day I must settle now on one of the bookstores, despite their equal attractiveness. Or, having settled on a bookstore I must settle on a means to getting there, even if there are several equally desirable routes.

20 I discuss these and related ideas further in 'Taking Plans Seriously', *Social Theory and Practice* 9 (1983), and in 'Two Faces of Intention'. *Philosophical Review* 93 (1984).

So, the co-ordinating role of future intentions underlies the further facts about future intentions that have been the basis of my pair of criticisms. This co-ordinating role both imposes a demand for agglomerativity and creates a need for the ability to settle in advance on one of several options judged equally desirable. If one's conception of the facts to be explained about future intention does not include this co-ordinating role, it may be easy for it also not to include these further facts.

My conjecture is that this is what happens to Davidson's theory. He begins with an attenuated conception of the role of intention in practical reasoning, a conception partly supported by his strategy of extension. This attenuated conception blocks from view the facts about agglomerativity and Buridan cases which I have emphasized, and allows Davidson to accept a theory that does not accommodate these facts. If this is right, Davidson's difficulties with agglomerativity and the Buridan problem are symptoms of a deeper problem. They are symptoms of an overly limited conception of the role of intentions and plans in rational motivation and practical reasoning.

12

Castañeda's Theory of Thought and Action

In a variety of papers and books – most especially in his recent work *Thinking and Doing* ([6])[1] – Hector-Neri Castañeda has developed and refined one of the most subtle and thorough philosophical theories of the relation of thought to action to be published in recent years. I begin this paper by laying out some of the main features of this theory. I then raise some questions about this theory, which lead up to a challenge to Castañeda's basic conception of practical thinking.

I

A central case in which thinking issues in intentional conduct is the case in which one's practical reasoning concludes with an appropriate intention and, as a result, one acts accordingly. Castañeda focuses on this central case. He wants a theory of practical reasoning which explains how various mental elements enter into such reasoning and how they are related to its conclusions.

Castañeda supposes that among the basic elements in such reason-

A version of this essay was presented at a conference on the philosophy of Hector-Neri Castañeda at the University of Cincinnati, November, 1979. I learned much from Myles Brand's and Hector-Neri Castañeda's comments on my paper at that conference, as well as from the probing remarks of many of the other participants. I have also benefitted from comments by Bruce Aune and John Perry. Work on this essay was partially supported by a Graves Award in the Humanities.
1 All parenthetical page references in the main text are to Castañeda's book.

ing are one's beliefs and intentions, and that both believing and in-tending can be understood as the endorsement (acceptance) of a certain thought-content (noema). For example, to believe it will rain is fully to endorse the proposition that it will rain. Analogously, to intend to run is also fully to endorse an appropriate noema. It is not, however, to endorse the proposition that one will run, but rather what Castañeda calls the *intention* canonically expressed by 'I to run'. The difference between intending to run and believing one will lies not in a difference in attitude towards the same proposition (that one will run) but in the different contents of the same generic attitude of endorsement. Believing and intending are not different types of propositional attitudes but, rather, the same type of attitude – namely, full endorsement – directed at different types of noemata: in the one case propositions, in the other case intentions.

Castañeda supposes that in reasoning one typically proceeds from certain thought contents one already endorses to other thought contents one thinks are implied by the former thought contents. (58) A theory of practical reasoning must specify what types of thought contents are involved, and what are the implicational relations in which such contents stand. The contents of practical reasoning will include at least propositions and intentions – the contents of believings and intendings respectively. But in practical reasoning we also consider the various things we want or desire, the various ends and goals we care about to some extent, and so on. Such wants, desires and carings are patently different from intending and believing. Does this mean we need yet a third type of thought content?

Castañeda's answer is no. Wanting is understood as a complex disposition to intend, and the contents of one's wants are to be understood in terms of the contents of these associated intendings.[2] So intentions remain the basic first-personal[3] practical contents.

What are intentions? The main outlines of Castañeda's answer lie

---

2 Strictly, wants also involve dispositions to endorse appropriate prescriptions as well. See pp. 228–9.

3 The reason for this qualification will become clear below. Note that this is not to say that *reports* of wants do not play an independent role in practical reasoning. As we will see, on Castañeda's theory they do.

along lines sketched by philosophers like Hare ([8]) and Kenny ([11] and [12]). Such philosophers look to speech acts like commanding, ordering, requesting and the like to find the conceptual machinery with which to understand the basic link between cognition and action. I notice that I am late for the meeting, so I run. How does my belief issue in action? The answer suggested by Hare and Kenny is, very roughly, that it leads me to accept something like a self-addressed command to run, and that leads to my running. The central idea is that the link between cognition and action is importantly analogous to the link between a command (order, request) and its execution. Of course, commands and the like are typically addressed to *other* people, whereas the basic link at issue concerns the first-person case, so to speak. Nevertheless, we can understand the first person link in part by looking at commands and the like in second- and third-person cases, and then generalizing from those cases to the first-person case.[4]

An important rationale for this approach lies in the striking parallel between the relation between a command (order, request) and its execution, on the one hand, and the relation between an intention or decision and an action based on it, on the other hand. Just as the command is a cause of the act of carrying it out, so the intention is a cause of one's intentional action. And just as the execution of the command is at fault if it differs from what is commanded, so the action in which the intention issues is at fault if it differs from what is intended.[5] In these respects these relations differ from the analogous relations involved in perception – the other main arena of interaction between mind and the world. In this case the causality goes from perceived object to perceptual state, and if there is a difference between the perceived object and the way it is represented in the perceptual state, it is the latter state that is at fault.

Now, Castañeda's version of this conception of the link between

4 Kenny, for example, summarizes his theory with the remark that the "relation between Volition and action has throughout . . . been explained by analogy with the relation between a command and its fulfillment." ([11]:238) Compare Hobbes's remark that "the Language of Desire, and Aversion, is *Imperative*; as *Do this, forbear that*" ([10]: Part 1, Chap. 6)
5 This last point is made by Anscombe ([1]:55–6), and endorsed by Kenny ([11]:216).

227

cognition and action diverges from accounts like Hare's and Kenny's in a variety of ways which I will not try to chronicle here. Still, Castañeda retains a version of the analogy between commands and intentions. He distinguishes the *speech-acts* of commanding, and so on, from the *thought contents* expressed in such acts. It is the latter that provide the key to understanding the cognition-action link. Castañeda calls the various thought contents specifically expressed in commanding Jones to run, requesting him to run, and so on, *mandates*. The mandate expressed in a command will differ from that expressed in a request. But there also is a common core to such contents; and this core Castañeda calls a *prescription*. The contents of the cited command, order and request involve the prescription: *Jones to run*.[6] The different mandates are different "embellishments" of the same prescription. Prescriptions are the basic practical contents of practical reasoning aimed at answering a question about what someone else is to do. For example, I engage in such prescriptional reasoning when I reason about what Carter is to do about running in 1980.

Prescriptions differ in a basic way from their corresponding performance propositions. In the prescription *Jones to run* a certain conception of the subject is joined by a special practical copula with the relevant act-property. This copula differs from the ordinary indicative copula involved in the proposition that Jones runs. A prescription is a "*structure of agent and action connected in a special way*, which could be called a *demanding way*." (40)

It is precisely this special copula that intentions share with prescriptions. This common feature represents Castañeda's version of the analogy between commanding and intending. Since intentions and prescriptions share this basic structure they are naturally treated as belonging to the same basic category of practical thought content: *practitions*.

Intentions and prescriptions are, however, different species of this

---

6 Castañeda uses single asterisks around a sentence or locution to produce a name of the proposition, intention or prescription expressed by that sentence or locution in the given context of discussion. He also uses such single asterisks to produce names of propositional, intentional and prescriptional forms. Here and throughout I follow his usage. See [6]:19,54.

genus: they differ in their conception of the agent. An intention has as a "subject constituent the conception of an agent in the first-person way." (170) Prescriptions do not involve this special, first-person conception of the subject. Thus, when Jones endorses the intention ★I (= Jones) to run★ he endorses a different noema than I do when I endorse the prescription ★Jones to run★. We may put the point by saying that whereas intentions are first-person practitions, prescriptions are second- or third-person practitions. The former are not reducible to the latter. No matter what second- or third-person conception of the agent appears in the prescription, we could imagine that that very agent endorses that prescription without knowing that it is *he himself* which that conception is a conception of, and so without endorsing the corresponding intention.

Much of Castañeda's theory is devoted to an account of practitions and, thereby, to an account of the special practical copula shared by prescriptions and intentions. The bulk of this account is in the form of a theory of the implicational structure of practitions, and of the semantic backing for this structure. This theory draws on the basic parallel between intentions and prescriptions: Its logic and semantics for intentions essentially parallels its logic and semantics for prescriptions. That is why the theory can be formulated as a general theory for *practitions*.

On Castañeda's theory, the implicational structure among practitions and propositions is just the natural extension from the purely propositional case in which the distinction between proposition and practition is strictly observed, and there is no implication, in either direction, between a practition and its corresponding proposition. Since practitions are, it seems, neither true nor false, this extension requires a broader interpretation of the ordinarily truth-functional connectives.

On this extension, for example,

(a) ★If it will rain then I to take an umbrella★

(the content of a conditional intending to take an umbrella if it rains) together with

(b) ★It will rain★

implies, by generalized modus ponens

(c) ★I to take an umbrella★[7]

In contrast, (c) together with

(d) ★I will take an umbrella only if I buy one★

does *not* imply

(e) ★I to buy an umbrella★

This is because (c) and (e) are intentions, whereas the antecedent and consequent of (d) are propositions.

To understand Castañeda's account of the semantic backing for this implicational structure we need to return for a moment to Castañeda's conception of believing and intending as the endorsement of certain noemata. Suppose I fully endorse ★It will rain★. What is involved in such an endorsement?

Castañeda supposes that to endorse a proposition one must take it to be *true*. Sometimes one will satisfy this condition by actually having a second-order belief that the cited proposition is true. Sometimes one will satisfy this condition only in a weaker sense. One "place[s] . . . the proposition on the side of true propositions [and has] the attitude of reacting to it as a member of the class of true propositions . . . [though one does] not have an *exact* idea of what the property of truth is." (58) Each case, however, reveals that truth is the "*psychologically preferred value* of propositions" (47): "thinking beings are interested in endorsing" propositions that have that value. (121)

Truth plays a further role in Castañeda's theory of believing. The relation of implication among the propositional contents of believings is to be *truth-preserving*. If several propositions imply a further proposition then if the former propositions are true so is the latter. Casta-

---

7 Castañeda supposes that, in general, the conditional intention ★I to *A* if *p*★ together with the proposition that *p* implies the non-conditional intention ★I to *A*★. This is why he supposes that a rational agent who intends to *A* if *p*, and believes that *p*, will non-conditionally intend to *A*. ([6]:279). For further discussion of this view see [4]; and for reasons to be wary of this view see [3].

ñeda alludes to this dual role of truth by calling it the *"designated value"* of the contents of believings. (58)

To believe is to endorse a proposition and, so, to take it to have the designated value of truth. Castañeda extends this model to practical thinking as well. To endorse a practition is, in part, to take it to have the relevant designated value. This designated value is both the psychologically preferred value of such thinking – its "polar star" (176) – and that which is preserved under implication. What is this designated value – the analogue of truth – for practitions?

It is not truth itself for, as already indicated, practitions seem to be neither true nor false. Still, practitions may be said to be *realized* or not, depending on whether their corresponding performance propositions are true. But Castañeda argues that being realized cannot be the designated value for practitions: If it were, a practition would always imply its corresponding performance proposition. But we cannot infer that Kennedy will run from the prescription ★Kennedy to run★.

Castañeda supposes that for a practition to have the relevant designated value is not for it to be realized, but (roughly) for the indicated action to be required, in the situation, by the relevant ends and institutions. Castañeda labels this designated value *Legitimacy* and explains it in two stages. First, there is Legitimacy *relative to a limited context*. Such a context consists of certain ends together with certain facts about the situation of the relevant agent(s) and the relevant natural laws. The basic case in which an atomic practition is Legitimate relative to such a context is one in which the agent's acting in the indicated way is logically or naturally necessary, in the context, for the achievement of those ends. For example, ★Jones to pay the fine★ is Legitimate relative to a context involving the end of obeying the law if in his situation Jones must pay the fine if he is to obey the law.

Second, there is Legitimacy relative to an "absolute context." To explain this we need to fill in Castañeda's model of a human agent. Castañeda sees an agent as having a variety of "non-blind wants" which are the product of many factors. Some emerge from basic needs, some from explicit choices, and some from the "internalization" of various institutions. (294–5) These non-blind wants constitute a rough ordering of things one wants, desires, cares about, has as goals and ends, and so on. Castañeda calls this the agent's "motivational hierarchy." This ordering is, I take it, not merely a matter of the brute motivational strength of one's various desires, but is rather in some way thoughtful and reflective.[8] It reflects how much the agent cares about these various ends, where the degree to which one cares about an end is a complex matter of one's dispositions to act in certain ways, feel pride or regret about one's actions, and so on.

Now, the "absolute context" relative to which the Legitimacy of an intention is to be assessed is, roughly, the agent's hierarchy of ends adjusted (if necessary) to "harmonize" with the ends of others he seriously considers as "co-persons." The absolute context relative to which the Legitimacy of a prescription is to be assessed is, roughly, a hierarchy of ends in which the ends of the prescriber *and* the "prescribee"[9] are suitably harmonized. (143–5) The basic case of Legitimacy relative to such an absolute context is just the case in which the agent's acting in the indicated way is necessary for the achievement of the most favored, relevant ends in that context.

To this basic case of Legitimacy are added two more cases so as to guarantee bi-valence. The details, as well as a difficulty they raise, I confine to a footnote.[10]

Legitimacy *in the relevant absolute context* is the designated value of

---

8 Otherwise Castañeda's theory of when an overriding-ought conclusion is true, to be described below, would not be plausible. See section IV.

9 As well as the ends of other agents seriously considered as "co-persons."

10 To explain this I need to explain the basic case of Legitimacy a bit more precisely. For an atomic prescription $\star S$ to $A\star$ the absolute context consists in part of truths about S's situation and relevant natural laws, as well as a set of agents. These agents include both S and the person issuing the prescription, as well as agents considered as "co-persons" by either of these two persons. In the case of an atomic intention we need only consider the agent and his co-persons. We are then to consult the ends of these different people and construct a "harmonized" hierarchy of these ends. In general, some of each person's ends will *not* get into this hierarchy, though the more important an end is to a person the greater its claim to inclusion in the harmonized hierarchy. We then add to the absolute context the supposition that this harmonized hierarchy is realized. In the basic case the prescription or intention is Legitimate in this absolute context if the truths in the context supplemented by this supposition imply the performance proposition corresponding to that prescription or intention. (*continued*)

practitions. It is, first, the psychologically preferred value. To endorse a practition is to take it to be Legitimate in the relevant absolute context. At the least one "place(s)" it "on the side of" absolutely Legitimate practitions; and many times one actually has the second-order belief that it is absolutely Legitimate. Second, such Legitimacy is to be preserved by practitional implication.

Sometimes, however, neither S's X-ing nor S's not X-ing will be so implied. In this case, $\star S$ to $X\star$ is Legitimate if, nonetheless, an agent in the context endorses it and no agent in the context endorses its negation. Finally, if neither S's X-ing nor his not X-ing is so implied, and if no one in the context endorses $\star S$ to $X\star$ in the absence of an endorsement of its negation, then $\star S$ to $X\star$ is Legitimate iff S in fact X's. Legitimacy values for compound practitions are then determined by the Legitimacy values of their atomic components in accordance with "Legitimacy tables" which are the analogues of standard truth-tables for truth-functional connectives. Thus $\star I$ to jump and I to shoot$\star$ is Legitimate in my absolute context iff both $\star I$ to jump$\star$ and $\star I$ to shoot$\star$ are.

This raises a problem for practitions concerning, so to speak, compound acts, as in: $\star I$ to shoot a jumpshot$\star$. It seems that this intention should be Legitimate in my absolute context iff $\star I$ to jump and shoot$\star$ is; for (we may assume) for me to shoot a jumpshot is for me to jump and (then) shoot. (We could put in all the relevant temporal qualifiers if we wanted.) But suppose you and I are playing basketball against each other, and we are both co-persons for each other. Each of us wants to win but, we may assume, neither end of winning gets into the "ideal harmonization" of our ends that characterizes my absolute context. My situation is this: I have the ball and I know that to win I must shoot now. So I endorse $\star I$ to shoot now$\star$. Though I do not notice it, a dog is about to bite me; so my safety requires that I jump now. You think the ball has rolled away and your attention is on the dog; so you endorse no prescription concerning my shooting now.

In this case $\star I$ to jump now$\star$ is Legitimate in my absolute context in the basic way: My jumping now is necessary for my safety. Also $\star I$ to shoot now$\star$ is Legitimate in my absolute context by way of the second condition: Neither my shooting now nor my not shooting now is necessary for the ends in my absolute context. But I endorse $\star I$ to shoot now$\star$ and you do not endorse the negation of its corresponding prescription. So it must be that $\star I$ to jump now and I to shoot now$\star$ – i.e., $\star I$ to jump and shoot now$\star$ – is Legitimate in this context.

Now consider the intention $\star I$ to shoot a jumpshot now$\star$. Expressed in this way it seems to be an atomic intention to which the initial three-part account of Legitimacy can be applied. But when we do that it turns out in our case that the intention may well be Non-Legitimate. My shooting a jumpshot now is not necessary for the relevant ends, and neither of us endorses the cited intention or its

233

I want to turn now to a feature of practical reasoning that we have so far ignored. In such reasoning one is often concerned with what one *ought* to do. Practical reasoning often involves *deontic* contents. What sorts of contents are these?

Castañeda answers with a systematic theory of deontic implication and truth. To any given institution or system of ends or goals is associated a corresponding ought$_i$, where the index indicates the relevant institution or system of ends. A particular ought$_i$ content is a proposition which results from applying an ought$_i$-operator to an appropriate *practition* (*not* to a proposition). For example, ★Jones legally ought to pay the fine★ is rendered as

★Ought $_{legally}$ (Jones to pay the fine)★

Such an ought-content is a prima facie, or *qualified* one. It only says what one ought to do *insofar as* certain considerations (in this case, those of legality) are concerned. In addition to the various qualified ought-contents, there is a special *overriding*-ought-content. This says what one ought to do, everything relevant considered. In practical reasoning one is commonly presented with conflicting qualified oughts which one must "weigh" in determining what one ought overridingly to do. As we will see, this overriding ought provides the essential link between deontic thinking and intending.

Castañeda provides a deontic logic which makes essential use of the practition-proposition distinction in avoiding traditional paradoxes. A serious discussion of this logic is beyond the scope of this paper. Of more direct interest here is the associated theory of deontic truth, which builds on the theory of Legitimacy for practitions.

---

corresponding prescription. So it may be that ★I to jump and shoot now★ is Legitimate, even though ★I to shoot a jumpshot now★ is not!

The upshot is that the Legitimacy values of certain practitions will depend on whether we think of the relevant action as simple, or as a compound. In a later discussion in [5] Castañeda grants this point and replies that this shows that contexts of Legitimacy must include a specification of what actions are to count as "prime actions." Doubtless, this is technically possible. But when we do this which context will be the "absolute context" involved in specifying the designated value of practitions? Whichever choice we make may seem to have a kind of arbitrariness which threatens Castañeda's claim to have articulated the "psychologically preferred value" of practitions.

A deontic proposition will, in the simplest case, have the form
★Ought$_i$ (S to A)★. The index "i" alludes to the relevant ends or
institutions which qualify this ought-content. On Castañeda's theory
such an ought-content is true iff (roughly) the practition ★S to A★ is
"necessarily Legitimate" in the context involving the ends or institutions indexed by "i." By "necessarily Legitimate" is not meant, as
one might have thought, Legitimate in all contexts. Rather, by "necessarily Legitimate" is meant Legitimate in the basic way (i.e., as a
logically or naturally necessary condition of the achievement of the
relevant ends) and not merely by way of the further conditions of
Legitimacy added to insure bi-valence. Finally, the overriding-ought
conclusion ★Ought $_{overriding}$ (S to A)★ is true iff (roughly) the included
practition is necessarily Legitimate in the relevant absolute context.
So when I think that I ought overridingly to pay the fine, what I
think is true iff ★I to pay the fine★ is necessarily Legitimate relative to
my absolute context. And when you think I ought overridingly to
pay, what you think is true iff the associated prescription is necessarily
Legitimate in the absolute context involving both our ends.[11]

Actually, I have so far ignored yet a further element of Castañeda's
theory that should be mentioned here: We can meaningfully ask
whether ★S to A★ is Legitimate in a given context only if S's A-ing is
a "practical action" in that context. (135) This means both that the
context specifies S's A-ing as something S can do, and that the question
of whether or not S A's is not settled by the propositions in that context
that describe S's situation. The context includes S's A-ing in its "Future Zone of Indeterminacy" rather than its "Fixed Future Framework." This qualification is essential to Castañeda's theory of deontic
truth. Without it the theory would be threatened with the paradoxical
result that if in fact S will A then S ought overridingly to A.[12]

---

11 Note that on this theory the truth value of an overriding-ought proposition is
relative to who endorses it. It is possible that when endorsed by Tom ★Dick ought
overridingly to run★ is true, but that when endorsed by Harry it is false. In
contrast, the truth values of qualified-ought propositions are not relativized in this
way. This is because the qualifying index, included in the proposition itself, fully
determines the relevant ends.

12 Suppose S will, in fact, A. Without the cited qualification we could then include,
in the description of S's situation which appears in the relevant absolute context,

Castañeda's theory of deontic truth provides the semantic backing for two crucial features of his account of practical reasoning. The first concerns the way in which one reasons from one's various non-blind wants, together with beliefs about how one must act to satisfy them, to intentions to act. Such reasoning typically involves implicational relations that go beyond the basic logic of practitions.

Castañeda supposes that such reasoning will typically involve contents that fit into roughly the following schema (299):

(a) I want$_i$ to A
(b) I A only if (as a causal factor) I B
(c) I can B
So: (d) I ought$_i$ to B

Here one's initial want is *reported* in the content of a belief. The *content* of that want does not itself enter into this argument. The index *"i"* shows that the ought-conclusion is qualified precisely by the want cited in the premises. That is why it follows directly from Castañeda's account of deontic truth that if (a)–(c) are true so is (d). Thus Castañeda calls this a "valid schema." So, by way of his theory of deontic truth, Castañeda provides an account of how one may reason from one's relevant wants and beliefs to a view about what one ought qualifiedly do.

Of course, such qualified ought-conclusions will frequently conflict. It might be true that I ought to drink the milkshake insofar as I love ice cream, and also that I ought not to drink it insofar as I want to lose weight. In practical reasoning one must weigh such conflicting, qualified oughts to reach a conclusion about what one ought to do, everything relevant considered. This is an *overriding*-ought conclusion. Castañeda's theory of deontic truth provides for an implicational link between such an overriding-ought conclusion and its con-

---

the true proposition that S will A. But once the proposition $\star S$ will $A\star$ is allowed to enter into the absolute context in this way, the practition $\star S$ to $A\star$ is, trivially, necessarily Legitimate in that context. So if S will A, and if this fact can be included in the description of S's situation in the relevant absolute context, then it will be true that S ought overridingly to A.

tained practition. For example, suppose I conclude that I ought overridingly not drink the milkshake. This conclusion is true only if the intention *I not to drink the milkshake* is necessarily Legitimate in my absolute context. So my overriding-ought conclusion implies the contained practition. Going from the former to the latter involves merely a kind of semantic descent. So Castañeda has an axiom which sanctions such inferences and says that "to think firmly that one ought overridingly to do A is in fact to endorse the practition to do A [and so, to intend to A]." (304)

Thus, Castañeda's theory of deontic truth provides for an essential link between deontic thinking and intention, as well as for an essential link between wants and deontic judgments. It is a kind of naturalistic theory of truth for deontic judgments which retains the essential link between oughts and action typically cited by emotivist and prescriptivist critiques of such naturalism.

In partial summary: Basic to Castañeda's theory of practical thinking are his conception of practitions as the fundamental contents of practical thinking, his theory of Legitimacy as the designated value of these practitions, and his associated theory of deontic truth. These basic elements all involve, among other things, the analogy between, on the one hand, the contents of commands, orders, and the like, and on the other hand, the contents of intending and deciding. The theory draws on this supposed analogy in providing parallel treatments of the logic and semantics of intentions and prescriptions, and of their relations to deontic propositions.

I want now to raise some questions about this theory. In section II I begin with some problems for the account of deontic truth. In sections III and IV I raise some questions about the theory's conception of the relation between intending and certain associated attitudes. This leads to a challenge to Castañeda's conception of practical thinking.

II

On Castañeda's main account deontic truth is necessary Legitimacy. But Castañeda also offers a pair of alternative accounts of deontic

237

truth. In *Thinking and Doing* Castañeda claims these accounts are equivalent. A useful first step in exploring Castañeda's conception of deontic truth is to see that this equivalence claim is incorrect.

Castañeda's second account (246–8) explains deontic truth in terms of practitional implication. On this account, a deontic proposition ★S ought to A★ is associated with an appropriate set of practitions, namely: those practitions included in the context *i*. For example, suppose I promise to meet Hector. This promise sets up a context relative to which certain qualified ought-claims will be true. The practition in this context is just the practition ★I to meet Hector★. (198). This practition will, together with other true propositions, imply other practitions, for example: ★I to meet the editor of NOÛS★.

Now, Castañeda says that ★S ought to A★ is true iff the associated practition(s), together with some true propositions, imply the practition ★S to A★. (248) But this account of deontic truth diverges from the main account in terms of necessary Legitimacy. To see why, suppose that having promised to meet Hector I discover that I can do this only by taking a bus. On the main account of deontic truth it is true that I ought _{promise to Hector} to take the bus, since my taking the bus is a necessary means to meeting Hector. On the present theory of deontic truth, however, this qualified ought claim is true iff the practition

(a) ★I to meet Hector★

together with some true propositions, implies the practition

(b) ★I to take a bus★.

But note that (a), together with the conditional proposition that I will meet Hector only if I take the bus, does *not*, on Castañeda's system, imply (b). This is because the antecedent and consequent of this conditional are *propositions*, whereas (a) and (b) are *intentions*. So on the theory of deontic truth as practitional implication it may be *false* that I ought _{promise to Hector} to take the bus. A deontic proposition may be true on the theory of deontic truth as necessary Legitimacy and yet false on the theory of deontic truth as practitional implication.

In contrast, though I will not stop to show this here, if a deontic proposition is true on the practitional implication theory, it is true on

238

the theory of deontic truth as necessary Legitimacy. The theory of denotic truth as necessary Legitimacy is more inclusive than the practitional implication theory.

It seems clear that Castañeda should prefer the more inclusive theory. This is because this theory is required to provide the semantic backing for his account of reasoning from wants to qualified oughts. Recall that on this account the following is a valid schema:

   I. *S* wants$_i$ to *A*
      If *S A*'s then, as a causal factor, *S B*'s
      S can *B*
So: *S* ought$_i$ to *B*

But if deontic truth were just a matter of practitional implication this would not be so, since the practition ⋆*S* to *A*⋆ together with the proposition ⋆If *S A*'s then *S B*'s⋆ does *not* imply ⋆*S* to *B*⋆.

But this more inclusive account of deontic truth is *too* inclusive. To see why note that Castañeda himself carefully distinguishes schema I from the following similar schema which he says is *in*valid (300):

   II. *S wants$_i$* to *A*
      If *S A*'s then, *as an effect, S B*'s
      S can *B*
So: *S* ought$_i$ to *B*

Castañeda is surely correct in being skeptical about the validity of II. If II were valid then, given that I want to go to sleep and believe that if I do I will snore and annoy my wife, I could derive the conclusion that I ought (qualifiedly) to annoy her. And this seems incorrect.

But given the theory of deontic truth as necessary Legitimacy, Castañeda is not entitled to this skepticism. On this theory ⋆*S* ought$_i$ to *B*⋆ is true iff ⋆*S* to *B*⋆ is necessarily Legitimate in context *i*. This will be so if *S*'s *B*-ing is naturally necessary, in the situation, for the relevant ends indexed by"*i*." But the premises of II tell us that *S*'s *B*-ing *is* naturally necessary for the satisfaction of the cited want$_i$. So if the premises of II are true so is its conclusion. Castañeda must say, implausibly, that II, like I, is a valid schema.

While the practitional implication view of deontic truth is too exclusive, the theory of deontic truth as necessary Legitimacy is too inclusive. Working within Castañeda's framework, the following seems a natural compromise:

(DT) $\star S$ ought$_i$ to $A\star$ is true iff (roughly)
    (i) The practitions included in context i, together with some true propositions included in i, imply $\star S$ to $A\star$
or
    (ii) (a) The performance propositions corresponding to the practitions in context i, together with the true propositions included in i about S's situation and the relevant natural laws, imply $\star S$ A's$\star$ *and*
        (b) S's A-ing would be necessary *as a causal factor* for at least one of the ends in i.

Finally we would want to revise the account of necessary Legitimacy accordingly, in order to retain the tight connection between deontic propositions and practitions that is central to Castañeda's theory. On such a revision, the fact that S's A-ing is a naturally necessary condition for the achievement of an end on context i would *not* guarantee that $\star S$ to $A\star$ is necessarily Legitimate in that context; for S's A-ing might not be necessary as a causal factor for that end.

In these revisions we are, of course, working with a notion of causal factor that is by no means perspicuous. And there remain puzzling cases in which the direction of causality seems not to be the same as the direction of the means–end relation.[13] Such cases would be mishandled by (DT). Still (DT) steers clear of the more straightforward objections I have raised. So if we wanted to revise Castañeda's theory of deontic truth in light of these objections but within his framework, (DT) might be a good place to start. Whether we should seek such revisions within his framework depends in part on our assessment of the underlying conception of practical thinking – to which I now turn.

---

13 As when my end is the firing of certain neurons and my means is my raising my arm.

III

A theory of intending should explain its relations to certain associated attitudes. First, we want to know how intending to A is related to believing one will A. Second, we want to know how intending to A is related to thinking that A best promotes, or is a necessary means for one's most favored, relevant ends. I want to argue that Castañeda's theory makes the former relation too loose and the latter relation too tight. These difficulties are traceable, in part, to the basic parallel between intention and prescription. And at least the second of these difficulties leads to a fundamental challenge to Castañeda's extension of his conception of thinking to the case of intending.

Suppose I fully endorse both

(a) ★I to finish this essay★

and

(b) ★I will not finish this essay★

I both intend to finish this essay and believe I will not. It seems to me that I am thereby guilty of a kind of irrationality. This is not to say that by virtue of (rationally) intending to finish I must believe I *will*, as Grice ([7]) and Harman ([9]) maintain. It is only to say that if I am fully rational I will not both intend to finish and believe I will *not*.

The irrationality I have in mind is partly grounded in the role which intending and believing are to play in further practical reasoning. My intendings and believings together are to constitute a kind of background framework within which my further planning about the future is to take place. For example, further plans are to be consistent with this dual framework of plans and beliefs. And my plans about what to do are to be filled in with plans about how to do it. But I cannot coherently treat the relevant part of my framework of plans and beliefs in this way if it includes both an intention to A and a belief that I will not.

This constraint on rational intention and belief seems to be a deep feature of the way in which a rational agent's practical and theoretical attitudes combine in his further practical reasoning. A theory of practical thinking should take account of this constraint in a way that is not *ad hoc*, and that embeds it in a natural way in its general conception of such thinking. Does Castañeda's theory do this?

It is clear that (a) and (b) are *consistent* in Castañeda's logic of practitions and propositions. So if his theory is to provide a natural account of what is wrong with my endorsing both (a) and (b) it must be by virtue of some other, central feature of that theory. But as far as I can see there is no such feature.

Castañeda does suppose that to endorse (a) I must see my finishing the essay as a "practical action." I must think I *can* finish. But the sense of 'can' here is one that allows for failure even if one intends and/or tries to finish – it is the sense of 'can' in which Austin's golfer can sink his putt.[14] In this sense of 'can' the following propositions are consistent: ★I *intend* to finish★, ★I *can* finish★, and ★I will *not* finish★. So the requirement that to intend to finish I must believe I can does not by itself explain why I cannot rationally intend to finish while believing I will not.

It may seem that Castañeda's diagnosis of what is wrong with my endorsing both (a) and (b) is rooted in his theory of Legitimacy. On his view, if I endorse (a) I take it to be Legitimate in my absolute context. My absolute context involves a description that includes: (i) certain truths about my situation, (ii) the achievement of my ends, and (iii) true formulations of laws of nature. Now if I believe that I will *not* finish then I should include my not finishing in (i). But for the notion of Legitimacy in one's absolute context to be coherent, (i)–(iii) must be consistent. So I cannot also include my finishing this essay in (ii). So if I endorse (b) and think the matter through I cannot then endorse (a): To endorse (a) I must take it to be Legitimate in my absolute context and, so, suppose that context to be consistent. But the very endorsement of (a) would make that context *inconsistent*.

But this way of explaining what is wrong with my fully endorsing both (a) and (b) is not available to Castañeda. This is because, as noted

---

14 See [2]. That this is the sense of 'can' here is clear from the fact that Castañeda supposes I can rationally intend to finish while being agnostic about whether I will. ([6]:41–2).

in section I, he supposes that propositions about whether or not I will *A* are *not* to be included in the absolute context relative to which the Legitimacy of my intention of *A* is to be assessed. In that context my *A*-ing is to be a "practical action": The question of whether I *A* is not settled by the propositions in that context that describe my situation. So even if I endorse (b), (b) will not get into the context relative to which the Legitimacy of (a) is to be assessed.

Nowhere in Castañeda's logic or semantics for practical thinking do we find an explanation of what is irrational about my intending to finish while believing I won't. Since this logic and semantics, together with the underlying conceptions of thinking and reasoning, constitute the main framework of Castañeda's theory of practical thinking, there is at least a lacuna in that theory: It does not say enough about the relation between intending and believing. But I suspect the point goes deeper. The lacuna is rooted in the basic parallel between intention and prescription.

Consider a prescriptional analogue to the case of intending to *A* while believing one won't: I endorse ★Kennedy to run★ while believing he won't. Clearly, there need be no irrationality here. The two noemata I endorse seem logically independent. This independence must be reflected in our logic for prescriptions. But the logic of practitions is to be a generalization of the logic of prescriptions. So it will be obliged to see ★I to finish★ and ★I won't finish★ as independent. So our logic will not discriminate between the acceptable case of thinking that Kennedy will not run while endorsing the prescription that he run, and the unacceptable case of intending to finish while believing one won't.

The same point holds concerning Castañeda's semantic theory. So long as the Legitimacy semantics for intentions parallels that for prescriptions it will not be able to explain the cited difference how one's beliefs constrain one's intendings, and how they constrain one's prescriptional thinking.

Castañeda sees intending and believing as endorsing appropriate noemata, and endorsing a noema as, in part, taking it to have the relevant designated value. On this conception we would expect rational constraints on intending and believing to come primarily from the logical relations among these noemata, and from features of the relevant designated values. But, given the parallel between intention and prescription, neither of these sources will explain the special way in which belief constrains rational intending. Of course, Castañeda could just *add* the requirement that a rational agent not intend to *A* while believing he will not. But this would be *ad hoc*. What I have been unable to find in Castañeda's theory is a basic feature of the conception of practical thinking which could ground such a requirement.

IV

For Castañeda, if I intentionally drink the wine then I intend to drink it. To intend to drink it I must endorse ★I to drink it★. So I must take the intention ★I to drink it★ to be Legitimate in my absolute context. In the basic case this is (roughly) to take my drinking it to be necessary for my most favored, relevant ends. At the least I "place" my intention "on the side of" intentions which are Legitimate in this sense; sometimes I have the second-order belief that my intention is Legitimate in this sense.

Now suppose I think that what is really necessary for my most favored, relevant ends is that I put the wine down rather than drink it. For example, I think I must do this if I am to perform well in tomorrow's interview. I see that a good performance in the interview is much more important to me, in the long run, than the pleasure and relaxation of drinking. Still, my will is weak and my desire for pleasure and relaxation wins the day. I proceed intentionally to drink the wine. So, on Castañeda's theory, I endorse the intention ★I to drink it★. But do I take this intention to be Legitimate in my absolute context? It seems clear I do not. The intention I take to be Legitimate in this context is, rather, ★I to put the wine down and not drink it★.

It seems that Castañeda must deny that such weak-willed intentional action is possible; for in such cases the link, between intending and taking the associated content to have the relevant designated value, is broken. But it seems clear that this variety of weakness of the will is possible.

A reply might be that if I intentionally drink the wine then I "really" favor the ends of present pleasure and relaxation over the end of a good performance. So there is no bar to my seeing my intention to drink as Legitimate in my absolute context.

This reply is not very forceful. Granted there is *a* sense of 'favoring an end' in which if I plump for the wine it follows that I favored present pleasure and relaxation over a good performance – that I ranked the former ends over the latter. But the ranking of my ends that constitutes my absolute context – and so determines which intentions are Legitimate in that context – cannot be merely a matter of which desires happen, at the moment, to be motivationally strongest. Presumably the relevant ranking, while tied in part to my present dispositions to choose one end over another, is also tied to other dispositions: for example, dispositions towards pride and regret, towards making an effort to change myself in various ways, towards bringing up my children in certain ways, and so on. If something like this were *not* the ranking in my absolute context, then the fact that the ranking in that context requires a certain action could not plausibly play the role it is supposed by the theory to play. The theory supposes that (roughly) the idea of being required by this ranking is the "polar star" of intending; it is that in which I am "interested" in forming my intentions. It also supposes that, in the basic case, it is what is required by this ranking that determines the truth or falsity of my conclusions about what I ought overridingly to do. Each supposition is plausible only if the ranking is more than a matter of which desires happen, at the moment, to move me more.

I conclude, then, that Castañeda's semantics of Legitimacy forces him into a kind of Socratic skepticism about weakness of the will. If – pace Socrates – we think such cases possible we cannot be content with this feature of Castañeda's theory.

One aspect of Castañeda's theory which such cases of akrasia challenge is, again, the parallel between intention and prescription. The analogue of weak-willed intentional action – "prescriptional akrasia" – is, when properly understood, plausibly disallowed by the theory. This suggests, in turn, that prescriptional thinking of the sort in which Castañeda is interested is more naturally treated within the framework of his basic conception of thinking than is intending. I turn now to an elaboration of these suggestions.

In a case of *prescriptional* akrasia one endorses a prescription $\star S$ to

$A^\star$ and yet thinks it is S's *not* A-ing, and *not* S's A-ing, that is necessary for the relevant ends in the appropriate, joint context. As for the case of *intentional* akrasia (i.e., akratic intending), such *prescriptional* akrasia must be disallowed by Castañeda's theory. This is because the theory holds that to endorse $^\star S$ to $A^\star$ one must, in the basic case, see S's A-ing as necessary for the relevant ends. But, in contrast with the denial of intentional akrasia, this denial of prescriptional akrasia turns out to be plausible when correctly understood.

We need to look more closely at what it is to endorse a prescription. Begin by recalling that on Castañeda's theory the ends relevant to the Legitimacy of a prescription are determined by the ends of *both* the prescriber and the "prescribee." This may seem implausible from the start. When I order a trespasser off my property it seems I endorse a prescription that he get off. Yet the ends I have in mind as relevant may well *not* include those of the trespasser. I might not see him as a "co-person" at all, but see only *my* ends as relevant. So one might suppose that Castañeda is wrong when he says that such prescriptions are endorsed "under the *implicit assumption* that a consideration of everything pertaining to both of them [i.e., prescriber and prescribee] would uncover no reason against the agent's doing that act." (145)

Castañeda's reply here would be that we are confusing the Legitimacy of the expressed prescription with the Legitimacy of the *intention* I endorse when I intentionally express this prescription in a command. (39, 133–4) The ends in the absolute context relative to which the Legitimacy of the latter *intention* is to be assessed are, indeed, determined primarily by *my* end.[15] I can intentionally issue this command without seeing the commanded act as necessary for ends common to me and the trespasser. But in such a case I intentionally issue the command without *endorsing* the *prescription* that the trespasser leave; though I do *express* that prescription. For me to *endorse* that prescription I must see it as Legitimate in our joint context.

This conception of endorsing a prescription creates, so to speak, a buffer between such an endorsement and intentional conduct. The buffer is constituted by one's own intendings and, so, by one's own ends. On this conception endorsing a prescription is rather a cognitive

---

15 And my conception of "co-persons."

affair: It involves seeing that S's A-ing stands in a certain relation to certain ends – one's own and S's. To be sure, it also involves a kind of approval of S's A-ing. *But this is a kind of approval that cannot directly motivate conduct.* It cannot even directly move one to express the endorsed prescription.

Seen in this way, the endorsement of a prescription generally involves (roughly) taking the indicated action to be necessary for the relevant ends in the appropriate, joint context. This fact is captured by the view that Legitimacy is the designated value of prescriptions. Prescriptional akrasia does not seriously threaten this view. Now that we have properly understood what (on Castañeda's theory) it is to endorse a prescription, such akrasia really does not seem possible. If I do not think S's A-ing is (roughly) necessary for the relevant ends, I do not *endorse* *S to A* – though I may still *intentionally express* this prescription, for example by ordering S to A.

What makes the theory's rejection of prescriptional akrasia plausible is the way in which it buffers the endorsement of a prescription from action. It is precisely because of the tighter connection between intending and action that the rejection of *intentional* akrasia is *im*plausible. Intending – and so endorsing an intention – has a special relation to conduct. When I form an intention to A I come to be in a state which will, in the normal course of events, lead to my A-ing. Further, it at least *seems* that this state which I get myself into by forming an intention to A can diverge from my view of what is required by my most favored ends. These are two pieces of "data" about intending to which a theory of intending must do justice. In contrast, we do not have an analogous pair of data concerning prescriptional thinking, when that thinking is understood in the indicated way. Since it need not cope with such data, Castañeda's theory of prescriptional thinking can plausibly rule out prescriptional akrasia. But his theory of intending must come to terms with this data. If we extend the view that Legitimacy is the designated value of prescriptions to the analogous view about intentions, we must test this extension against this new data. If one is overly impressed with the parallel between intention and prescription one may be tempted to explain *away* the appearance of akratic conduct, rather than allow for its real possibility. But in that case, I think, one is in danger of being misled by a theoretical commitment. When one actually notes the difference between prescriptional thinking and intending, and tries to see whether the data peculiar to *intending* fit the extension, one will be troubled. The possibility of intentional akrasia neither fits the theory that results from the extension, nor is easily denied. Weakness of the will shows that the extension of the Legitimacy semantics from prescriptions to intentions is at least problematic and, I think, probably a mistake.

This raises the fundamental question of whether Castañeda's basic conception of thinking can plausibly be extended to the case of intending. On Castañeda's conception, to think is, in the basic case, to endorse a certain noema. Of course, not all thinking involves the endorsement of a noema: One may merely entertain a thought-content without endorsing it. On Castañeda's conception, the basic difference between merely entertaining a thought-content and endorsing it is that in the latter case one takes the content to have the relevant designated value. There may well be deep problems in applying this conception even to believing. But suppose for now we grant the conception as it applies to theoretical thinking. Can it be, as Castañeda supposes, plausibly extended to practical thinking?

We have seen reason to think it can be extended to prescriptional thinking. But weakness of the will challenges its extension to that which provides the basic link between cognition and action: intending. Applied to intending the conception requires that in intending to *A* one takes the associated intention to have the relevant designated value. This designated value is the "polar star" of intending: It is that in which we are "interested" in forming intentions. As Castañeda supposes, the natural candidate for that in which we are interested in forming our intentions really does seem to be some sort of appropriateness in light of our favored ends, values, and the like. But the phenomenon of weakness of the will warns us against construing such appropriateness as *the designated value*, in Castañeda's sense, of intentions.

This suggests that we may, in the end, be forced to give up, or radically modify, the application of Castañeda's model of thinking to the case of intending. We may be forced to see intending not as the mere endorsement of a special kind of thought content, but as itself a special kind of attitude, an attitude which differs in basic ways from that involved in believing. Weakness of the will grins up at us from the bottom of the wine glass, like Austin's frog.

REFERENCES

[1]   Anscombe, E., *Intention* (Oxford: Blackwell, 1957).

[2]   Austin, J. L., "Ifs and Cans," in *Philosophical Papers* (London: Oxford University Press, 1961):153–180.

[3]   Bratman, M., "Simple Intention," *Philosophical Studies* 36 (1979):245–259.

[4]   Castañeda, H. N., "Intentions and Intending," *American Philosophical Quarterly* 9 (1972):139–149.

[5]   —, "The Theory of Questions, Epistemic Powers, and the Indexical Theory of Knowledge," in P. French et al., eds., *Midwest Studies in Philosophy V* (Minneapolis: University of Minnesota Press, 1980):193–237.

[6]   —, *Thinking and Doing* (Dordrecht, Holland: Reidel, 1975).

[7]   Grice, P., "Intention and Uncertainty," *Proceedings of the British Academy* 57 (1971):263–279.

[8]   Hare, R. M., "Wanting: Some Pitfalls," in R. Binkley et al., eds., *Agent, Action, and Reason* (Toronto: University of Toronto Press, 1971):81–97.

[9]   Harman, G., "Practical Reasoning," *Review of Metaphysics* 29 (1976):431–463.

[10] Hobbes, *Leviathan*.

[11] Kenny, A., *Action, Emotion and Will* (London: Routledge & Kegan Paul, 1973).

[12] Kenny, A., *Will, Freedom and Power* (Oxford: Blackwell, 1975).

13

Cognitivism about Practical Reason

I. REASONING: THEORETICAL AND PRACTICAL

In theoretical reasoning our concern is with what to believe, in practical reasoning with what to intend and to do. In the former we are trying to find out how the world is; in the latter we are concerned with how to (try to) change it. These can seem to be two different – though no doubt importantly related – enterprises. J. David Velleman argues otherwise. His view is "that practical reasoning is a kind of theoretical reasoning, and that practical conclusions, or intentions, are the corresponding theoretical conclusions, or beliefs" (p. 15).* These twin identifications – of practical reasoning with a kind of theoretical reasoning, and of intention with a kind of belief – are at the heart of this wide-ranging, imaginative, and important study of autonomous agency, rationality, and value. Let us call this pair of identifications

An earlier version of this essay was presented at a symposium on Velleman's book at the 1990 Pacific Division Meetings of the American Philosophical Association, Los Angeles, March 31, 1990. There I benefited from Velleman's replies to my presentation, from the remarks of my cosymposiast Alison McIntyre, and from the general discussion. I have also been aided by discussion with David Chan, Philip Clark, Neil Delaney, Jr., Fred Dretske, Tommy Lott, and Michael O'Rourke. My work on this essay was supported in part by the Center for the Study of Language and Information and by the Stanford University Humanities Center.

*This essay is a review of J. David Velleman, *Practical Reflection* (Princeton, N.J.: Princeton University Press, 1989). References to his book appear parenthetically in the text.

"cognitivism about practical reason."[1] Velleman's cognitivism about practical reason lies at the foundations of his book. I want to know if it is defensible.

II. SPONTANEOUS SELF-KNOWLEDGE

Velleman's route to his main conclusions begins with reflection on the special kind of knowledge and understanding we normally seem to have of our own intentional conduct. When I act intentionally I usually know what I am doing and I usually know at least a rudimentary explanation of why. Further, I seem to know this in a distinctive way. As Velleman puts it, there is a kind of "spontaneity" in my knowledge: I do not need to step back and observe what I do and infer what my motives are in the way you would need to for you to have such knowledge about me. But how is such spontaneous knowledge of what we are doing and why we are doing it possible if our actions are themselves effects of antecedent, motivating causes?

Imagine a motivational system that consisted solely of ordinary desires and beliefs about how to satisfy those desires. It might want to eat, drink, and be merry; and it might have beliefs about, say, where the wine and crumpets are. These desires and beliefs would provide motives that would tend to cause appropriate behavior – reaching for the crumpets, for example. But so far this is an overly simple model. While possible, such a simple motivational system is not yet a self-conscious, autonomous agent of the sort we take ourselves to be.

What is missing? We cannot answer by appeal to a little person inside who keeps track of these desire-belief motives, totes them up, and proceeds to act; for that would just push our problem one step back. Velleman's idea is instead to appeal to certain special desires and their role in practical reasoning and motivation. Which desires? We might try appealing to some sort of overarching desire for harmonious satisfaction of one's first-order desires, or something similar. But this is not the tack Velleman takes. Instead, he supposes that a self-

---

1 Note that, as defined, cognitivism about practical reason does not entail that desires are a kind of belief.

conscious autonomous agent will have certain intrinsic desires for knowledge and understanding about herself. These desires are *intellectual* desires, since they are desires for self-*knowledge*. But, Velleman argues, their presence will have a deep impact on the agent's motivational system. Velleman's claim is that "we can transform a rudimentary model of human motivation into a sophisticated model of autonomous agency merely by positing desires for reflective knowledge" (pp. 241–42).

Velleman eventually appeals to a number of different intrinsic desires for self-knowledge and self-understanding, but we can focus here on the two closest to present action: the desire to know what one is doing while one is acting and the desire to understand why one is acting as one is. In Velleman's terminology these are, respectively, intrinsic desires for "self-awareness" and for "self-understanding." Velleman argues that a system which has these intellectual desires for self-knowledge will be moved to "reflective theoretical reasoning," reasoning aimed at achieving self-understanding and self-awareness. And he argues that when such theoretical reflection on one's own actions and motivations runs its course it will generate both spontaneous self-knowledge and autonomy. The practical reflection that gives the book its title is, it turns out, theoretical reflection on one's own actions and motives.

How is this supposed to work? Ignoring many complexities, and focusing on an agent's present action, the main picture is this. Given one's desire for self-understanding one will be averse to acting in ways that one does not understand. So one will screen one's actions "in advance for their apparent intelligibility" (p. 35). An action will seem intelligible if one believes one has some motive(s) or other that would explain it if one were to do it. An action will not seem intelligible if one does not see oneself as having a motive for doing it.[2] If option A does not seem to one intelligible there will be a strong desire, rooted in one's desire for self-understanding, not to A. So even if, unbeknownst to oneself, one in fact had a strong desire to A, it is not likely that, when the causal machinery works its way, one will A. In contrast, if one believes that one has a motive that would make B-

2 Here I ignore other explanatory factors considered by Velleman, such as habits.

ing intelligible if one were to B, then the desire for self-understanding will not stand in the way of B-ing. So, one will tend to perform only those actions for which one has available some explanation. And that is why one will tend to understand what one does.

One frequently has different motives for conflicting courses of action. I have motives for playing basketball, and I have motives for writing this essay. As far as I can tell, I have no motives for calling up George Schultz. My desire for self-understanding will tend to filter out my calling up George Schultz. But, given my knowledge of my motives, my desire for self-understanding will be neutral as between basketball and working on this essay. At this point are we then back to the simple causal picture: a tug of war between my desires for basketball and for essay writing? No; for I also desire "self-awareness" – I desire to know what I am doing while I am doing it. I do not want just to wait to see how the tug of war works out – I don't want just to wait to see whether I head toward the playground or the word processor. But how can I, as Velleman charmingly says, "prevent [my] actions from outrunning [my] awareness" (p. 48)? Velleman's answer is : I just forecast my action in advance. I jump to the conclusion that I will, say, play ball. This expectation that I will play ball will then combine with my desire for self-awareness to provide me with a new motive for playing ball, namely: I will thereby know what I am doing while I am doing it, whereas if I were instead to start writing the essay I would, at least for a moment, be surprised (to say the least). In this way, as Velleman says, "the desire to know what [I'm] doing . . . disposes [me] to undertake only those actions which [I'm] aware of expecting [myself] to perform" (p. 49).

There are, however, limits on all this. I cannot jump to just any conclusion about what I will do and depend on my desire for self-awareness to make my conclusion true. My desire for self-awareness is just one desire among many. If I concluded that I would jump into the icy river my deep aversion to cold might keep me back even at the cost of a temporary loss of self-awareness. Further, if I knew of this deep aversion I would see my so jumping as not intelligible, and so my desire for self-understanding would also get in the way. Still, there might well be several conflicting options each of which is apparently intelligible and for each of which my motivation is enough to prevail if it were reinforced by my desire for self-awareness. As Velleman puts it: "there are usually several different actions toward which you're antecedently inclined, each inclination being capable of prevailing over the others if it is reinforced, while the others are suppressed, by your inclination to do what you expect" (p. 58). In such cases you can jump to a conclusion in favor of any one of these options, for your resulting expectation will, in tandem with your desire for self-awareness, make itself true. (At least it will if the world cooperates with your efforts, an assumption I am making here.) Your conclusion, in such a case, is not determined by your antecedent evidence, evidence that does not include the conclusion itself; for this evidence is compatible with either of several conclusions. But once you reach this particular conclusion it is justified by your present evidence, for now the evidence includes the conclusion itself and its expected impact, by way of your desire for self-awareness, on your conduct.

This reflective prediction of your action will tend to be self-fulfilling because of the way in which it engages the desire for self-awareness. And you will see this, for it is its contribution to your motivation that makes it justified by present evidence even though it was not dictated by prior evidence. It will be adopted not because it was dictated by prior evidence but out of your preference for the relevant option. In such a case you believe as you do because of what you want and not because of what the prior evidence dictates. Your belief (and if things go well, your knowledge) about your action is in this way "spontaneous": it exhibits what Velleman calls "epistemic freedom."

This, in broad outline, is Velleman's account of how spontaneous self-knowledge of what one is doing is possible, even given that our actions are embedded in a motivational, causal order. Velleman takes as given – as part of a "rudimentary model of human motivation" – the idea of desire–belief motivation of action, motivation that is shaped by the contents of those desires and beliefs but which need not be self-conscious and can even be effective in ways that surprise the agent. (See, e.g., p. 193.) His concern is not to explain how such content-shaped motivation is possible, an issue that has tended to dominate recent work in the philosophy of mind. Instead he asks,

Given that content-shaped, desire–belief motivation is possible, how is spontaneous self-knowledge possible for an agent whose actions are motivated, in this content-shaped way, by his desires and beliefs? And his answer is that spontaneous self-knowledge – as well as a kind of autonomy – is made possible not by a break in the chain of desire–belief motivation nor by the presence of some special practical concern on the part of the agent but, rather, by the introduction of certain intellectual desires and the ensuing reflective theoretical reasoning. This reflective theoretical reasoning typically issues in a special kind of prediction about one's own action, a prediction that tends to be self-fulfilling, represents itself as such, and is adopted on the basis of one's desires or preferences.

In this way we arrive at Velleman's twin identifications: First, practical reasoning is this special sort of reflective theoretical reasoning; and, second, an intention to act is this special sort of reflective self-prediction:

Intentions to act . . . are the expectations of acting that issue from reflective theoretical reasoning. These are self-fulfilling expectations of acting that are adopted by the agent from among potentially self-fulfilling alternatives because he prefers that they be fulfilled, and they represent themselves as such. . . . I shall summarize the relevant features of these expectations by saying that they are,[3] and represent themselves as being, self-fulfilling expectations of acting that the agent adopts out of a desire for their fulfillment. . . . These features of the expectations cast them in the role of the agent's intentions to act. (p. 98)

This leads Velleman to an associated view of reasons for action. Reasons for action are provided by the premises of such reflective reasoning, premises whose acceptance puts the agent in a position to increase his self-knowledge by acting so as to satisfy some reflective prediction or explanation: *"reasons for an action are those things belief in which, on the agent's part, would put him in a position to enhance his self-knowledge, in this distinctively practical way, by intending or performing that*

3 Sometimes Velleman says only that intentions are expectations that tend to be self-fulfilling (pp. 95, 136). But the quoted passage seems to be his official, stronger view.

action" (p. 198, italics in original). Velleman then claims that the propositional content of an intention to act provides a reason for so acting and that in this sense intentions are reasons for action. For example, the content of my intention to turn on the light is that I will turn on the light as a result of this very intention. In believing this I am in a position to enhance my self-awareness by just going ahead and turning on the light. So the content of my intention – and in this way the intention itself – gives me a reason to do what I intend (pp. 198–201).[4]

Velleman claims, then, that we can model the kinds of agents we take ourselves to be within a desire–belief framework so long as we assume the presence of special intellectual desires for self-understanding and self-awareness. These special intellectual desires will drive reflective theoretical reasoning. Such reasoning will yield special self-predictions. This reflective theoretical reasoning is practical reasoning. And these special self-predictions are intentions and provide reasons for action. This is cognitivism about practical reason.

A crucial idea here is that practical reasoning and intention derive from our theoretical interest in self-knowledge. This makes the desire for self-awareness a critical component of the theory. But just what is the desire for self-awareness a desire for? What if I see that I am about to do something that I would rather not do? To use Velleman's own example, what if I see that I am about to walk in front of a car (p. 55)? Does this expectation combine with my desire for self-awareness to give me a motive for doing so? Velleman explicitly considers this query and answers in the affirmative, though he is quick to point out that such motivation will likely be overwhelmed by my desire for safety. As Velleman understands the desire for self-awareness, then, it is a straightforward desire for "concurrent knowledge of [one's] actions" (p. 215). This desire is frustrated if one fails to do now what one now expects oneself to do now – for example, if one surprises oneself and fails to step in front of the car. The theory assumes that this desire for "concurrent knowledge of [one's] actions" will be

---

4 Velleman later says that intentions are *"procedural* rather than *evaluative* reasons" (p. 299).

present in any agent capable of spontaneous self-knowledge and intention.

III. A DILEMMA

This is an impressive, thoughtful, systematic contribution to foundational issues in the theory of action. But I believe the theory faces a dilemma. On the one hand, if we understand the desire for self-awareness along the lines of Velleman's official interpretation, then the identification of intentions with special beliefs, and the associated account of intentions as reasons for action, are both subject to difficulties. On the other hand, if we modify our understanding of the desire for self-awareness in ways that aim at blocking these difficulties, we undermine the central idea that this desire is both present in all agents capable of intention and is, at bottom, a theoretical desire for a kind of self-knowledge. In neither case does cognitivism about practical reason survive unscathed. I proceed to a discussion of this dilemma.

The First Horn

We have lots of beliefs about our own actions. Many of these beliefs do not function in our lives in ways characteristic of intentions to act. If we want to say, with Velleman, that intentions to act are a kind of belief about one's own actions, then we must be able to say why beliefs of this kind do function as intentions. And we must be careful that our explanation does not have as a consequence that other beliefs, though not intentions, come to function as if they were intentions. I will discuss two ways in which Velleman's theory seems not to satisfy these demands.

INTENTION AND MERE EXPECTATION OF SIDE EFFECTS. Consider first the distinction between intention and the mere expectation of side effects.[5] I arrive home late at night and wonder whether to turn on the light even though that will, unfortunately, wake up Susan. On reflection I decide to turn it on, for I worry I will otherwise trip over something. I intend to turn on the light and expect – but do not intend – that I will thereby wake up Susan. I have an intention and a related self-prediction that is not an intention.

Why say that I expect but do not intend to wake up Susan, even, though I made my decision in full awareness that I would wake her by turning on the light? The answer is that I do not satisfy any of a trio of conditions, satisfaction of which seems characteristic of intention: I am not at all disposed to pursue alternative means to waking Susan if it turns out that the light bulb isn't working; nor am I disposed to rule out other options because of their incompatibility with my waking of Susan; nor do I see myself as faced with a problem of what means to use in order to wake Susan.[6] On Velleman's theory, however, both my intention to turn on the light and my expectation that I will thereby wake Susan are self-predictions. Can the theory nevertheless say that I intend to turn on the light, but do not intend to wake Susan?

It may seem that the theory has available to it the following treatment of this example:[7] My first conclusion is my belief, adopted out of my relevant preferences, that

(1) I will turn on the light as a result of my belief that (1).

Given my belief that (1), I then infer that

(2) I will wake up Susan as a result of my belief that (1).

My belief that (1) is an intention, for it represents itself as being self-fulfilling, and it is adopted out of relevant preferences. My belief that

5 The questions I raise here about Velleman's account are similar to some discussed by Gilbert Harman in his earlier exploration of a belief theory of intention ("Practical Reasoning," *Review of Metaphysics* 29 [1976]: 431–63, at pp. 453–57).
6 I defend this way of distinguishing intended and merely expected effects in my *Intention, Plans, and Practical Reason* (Cambridge, Mass.: Harvard University Press, 1987), chap. 10.
7 Compare Harman, p. 454.

(2), in contrast, neither represents itself as self-fulfilling nor is adopted out of relevant preferences. So it is a self-prediction that is not an intention.

But why is (1) the conclusion I initially reach? I explicitly considered the side effect in reaching my initial decision to turn on the light. I am clear that what I will do is turn on the light and thereby wake up Susan. So why don't I include the side effect in my conclusion? That is, why don't I conclude that

(1') I will turn on the light and wake up Susan as a result of my belief that (1')?

Perhaps the answer will be that I will not see my belief that I will wake Susan as playing any causal role in my action. So I will not accept that it is my belief that I will turn on the light and wake up Susan that will result in my turning on the light and waking Susan. It is, instead, simply my belief that I will turn on the light that will do the causal work. Thus I reach (1) and (2), rather than (1').

The problem is that, given Velleman's account of the desire for self-awareness, this way of blocking conclusion (1') is unstable. Consider my belief that I will wake up Susan. If I acted and failed to satisfy this prediction I would be surprised. Given that I desire self-awareness, then, my belief that I will wake up Susan will induce motivation to ensure that I wake her up. After all, as Velleman puts it, "expecting an action causes your desire for self-awareness to reinforce your motives for it" (p. 54). If this is true of my expectation (in Velleman's example) that I am about to walk in front of a car, it is true of my expectation that I am about to wake Susan. So, on the theory, my belief that I will wake Susan will tend to cause my waking her. And we may assume that this will be known to me in just the way in which, on Velleman's theory, the motivational impacts of my self-predictions tend to be known to me. So Velleman's theory cannot appeal to the causal impotence of my belief that I will wake Susan to explain why I don't just conclude that (1').

Granted, I know that I would wake Susan even if I had not noticed that I would; for I would still have turned on the light. But I do not think that Velleman can appeal to this fact to explain why I do not reach conclusion (1'). To see why, change the example slightly. Suppose that once I notice that I will wake Susan I greet this upshot with enthusiasm and form the intention not only to turn on the light but also thereby to wake her. On the theory my intention will be my belief that (1'). And I will have this intention even though I know that I would have woken Susan up even if I had not noticed that I would; for even if I had not noticed her sleeping I would have turned on the light. So we are still without an explanation of why I don't just conclude that (1') in the original example.

Perhaps it will be said that though I might well reach (1') in the original example, I do not adopt this conclusion on the basis of my preferences; for I would rather not wake Susan. But though I would rather not wake Susan, I do prefer turning on the light and waking her to not doing either. And it would be that preference that would be the basis for my conclusion that (1').

So it is unclear why, on Velleman's theory, I do not in the original example just reach conclusion (1') on the basis of my relevant preference. But if I do that then, on the theory, I will intend to wake Susan. And that seems wrong.

This difficulty would not get a foothold if my expectation that I will wake Susan did not engage the desire for self-awareness; for if it did not engage this desire it would not tend to cause its own self-fulfillment. As we are presently understanding it, however, the desire for self-awareness will be satisfied to the extent that one acts as one expects. And this motivational mechanism is promiscuous, being engaged by self-predictions such as my expectation that I will wake up Susan. This leads to instability in the account of the difference between intention and the mere expectation of side effects.

A possible response – sketched by Velleman in his reply[8] to an earlier version of this essay – is to concede that in the cited example I reach conclusion (1'). So I intend to wake Susan, though I do not satisfy the trio of conditions cited earlier as characteristic of intention. But, the response continues, this is an acceptable consequence. Granted, I do not treat my waking her as a goal of mine. But we can nevertheless include my waking her in what I intend.

---

8 Presented at the 1990 Pacific Division Meetings of the American Philosophical Association, Los Angeles, March 1990.

This response leans on Velleman's efforts in his book to specify the target of his account of intention. Velleman says that ordinary uses of 'intention' and 'intend' are ambiguous: "They are used to denote both plan-states and goal-states of the agent" (p. 112). One's plan-states are states of "being decided upon" (p. 112) an option; and one can have an option as a goal without being decided upon it: "Attaining his goal is often something that the agent can desire but cannot be decided upon, since whether he attains his goal may not be sufficiently within his control for him to decide" (p. 112). Velleman makes it clear that he uses 'intention' and 'intend' to refer to "plan-states," not "goal-states." The suggestion, then, is that my belief that (1') is an intention in the sense that it is a plan-state; and this is acceptable so long as we distinguish plan-states from goal-states.

Distinguish two different claims. There is first the claim – suggested in the passage just quoted – that one can have something as a goal without including it in what one intends. This claim seems to me correct.[9] But the response at issue here requires the further claim that one can intend something without either having it as a goal or seeing it as a means to a goal one has. This further claim seems to me a high price to pay. Intention is a practical attitude, one that potentially guides and controls conduct. When we divorce intentions from goals in this way we are in danger of changing the subject. I have my turning on the light as a goal, but I do not have as a goal my waking Susan. It seems to me that this difference is reflected in a difference in intention, and that we should resist the collapse of the distinction between intention and the mere expectation of side effects.

INTENTIONS AS REASONS FOR ACTION. Velleman says that "the belief constituting an intention puts us in a position to increase our self-knowledge by satisfying that very belief. The content of this belief therefore qualifies as a reason for acting" (p. 200). But again we have a problem of promiscuity; for on this account some beliefs which are not intentions will also qualify as reasons for action. A

9 I argue, on different grounds, for a similar thesis in my *Intention, Plans, and Practical Reason*, chaps. 8 and 9.

pessimistic actor, for example, might be on stage with the purportedly self-fulfilling belief that

(3) I will stumble on my next lines as a result of this very belief.[10]

This belief that (3) puts the pessimistic actor "into a position to increase [his] self-knowledge by satisfying that very belief." After all, if he does stumble on his lines as a result of his belief that (3), this will be as he expects. He will be in a position to think: "Just as I thought, I am stumbling on my lines because I believed I would. Next time I'd better focus more on my lines and less on self-prediction." The belief that (3) is not, on the theory, an intention to stumble, for it is not appropriately based on the actor's desires. And the actor's stumbling would still not be intentional. Still, once the pessimistic actor has this belief he is in a position to "increase [his] self-knowledge by satisfying that very belief." So the belief that (3) gives the actor a reason to stumble on his lines in the sense in which, according to the theory, an intention to act gives a reason for so acting.

This seems wrong. A plausible story of how intentions give reasons for action should explain how they give reasons in a way in which the pessimistic actor's purportedly self-fulfilling prophecy does not. Velleman can explain why the actor's belief that (3) is not an intention. But this difference between this belief and an ordinary intention does not, on the theory, prevent the belief that (3) from playing the reason-giving role of an intention.

The Second Horn

So we have two problems for Velleman's version of cognitivism about practical reason: a problem about the distinction between intention and the mere expectation of side effects; and a problem about the way in which intentions provide reasons for action. In each case the theory has difficulty with an aspect of intention that seems part of its practical character.

---

10 This example is modeled on the case, introduced into this literature by Derek Parfit and Harman, of the insomniac who believes she will stay awake as a result of her very belief (see Harman, p. 448).

However, both difficulties depend on a straightforward understanding of the desire for self-awareness. Perhaps Velleman could respond by modifying his account of this desire, interpreting it more narrowly so that it is not engaged by the mere expectation that I will *A*. On this narrower interpretation, what is needed to engage the desire for self-awareness is an expectation that I will *A* as a result of this very expectation, when this expectation is adopted on the basis of my preferences. Let us see how this might work.

The first problem about side effects occurred because my belief that I will wake Susan engaged the desire for self-awareness and thereby led to motivation to wake her. But suppose we say that what engages my desire for self-awareness is only an expectation that I will *A* as a result of this very expectation, when that expectation is adopted on the basis of relevant preferences. Since my expectation that I will wake Susan is not at first self-referential in this way, it doesn't engage the desire for self-awareness so understood. So the pressure to arrive at conclusion (1') is blunted.

Again, since the pessimistic actor's belief that (3) is not adopted on the basis of his preferences, it will not engage a desire that is understood in this more limited way. So the actor does not, by stumbling on his lines, satisfy this more narrowly interpreted desire for self-awareness. So his belief does not give him a reason for stumbling on his lines.

In each case the problem is blocked by understanding the desire for self-awareness at issue more narrowly than before. On this understanding Velleman's expectation that he is about to walk in front of a car would not engage the desire for self-awareness. While this is not the understanding of the desire for self-awareness that Velleman endorses, it does help block my objections.

But it does this only by throwing us from the frying pan into the fire. We now must suppose that all agents capable of intention will have a very special desire, a desire that favors *A*-ing precisely when one expects one will *A* as a result of that expectation and when that expectation is itself based on one's preferences. It is difficult enough to suppose that all agents capable of intention have an intrinsic desire for self-awareness when that desire is interpreted in the straightforward way assumed by Velleman. But what reason would we have to suppose that any agent capable of intention must have such an intrinsic desire for self-awareness narrowly construed?

Perhaps the answer is that we desire to do what we intend, and such expectations are, on the theory, intentions. But now what is doing the work is no longer an intrinsic intellectual desire for self-knowledge but a distinctively practical desire. What is doing the work is, at bottom, a desire for success in action rather than a theoretical concern with self-knowledge. And this puts into jeopardy the central idea that practical reasoning and intention derive from our theoretical interest in self-knowledge.

IV. CONCLUSION

So we have the promised dilemma. On the one hand, we can interpret the desire for self-awareness in a straightforward way. So interpreted, this desire ignores many of the complexities that, on the theory, are needed to turn self-prediction into intention. Such a desire for self-awareness engages promiscuously a wide range of predictions of one's own actions. This leads to problems both about the distinction between intention and the mere expectation of side effects and about the reason-giving role of intention. On the other hand, we could tailor our interpretation of the desire for self-awareness so that it is engaged only by special self-predictions, namely: those self-predictions that satisfy the further conditions that, on the theory, are necessary for intention. But then we need to explain why such a complex desire can be presumed to be present in any agent capable of intention. The answer seems to be that we desire to do what we intend, and so we desire to satisfy those expectations that are, on the theory, intentions. But this is to give pride of place to an overarching desire for success in action and so to give up the idea that practical reflection is, at bottom, theoretical reflection.

Velleman has provided us with a lucid, forceful, and detailed defense of cognitivism about practical reason; and he has explored the implications of this doctrine with insight and ingenuity. But if I am right there remain serious difficulties for this brand of cognitivism.

14

Review of Korsgaard's *The Sources of Normativity*

The Sources of Normativity derives from the 1992 Tanner Lectures and Seminar in Cambridge, England.* It consists of a brief introduction by Onora O'Neill, a "Prologue" and four lectures by Christine Korsgaard, separate discussions of these lectures by G. A. Cohen, Raymond Geuss, Thomas Nagel, and Bernard Williams, and a concluding "Reply" by Korsgaard. It is a major work of the first importance.

We have beliefs and intentions, and we perform actions. In each case we make ought judgments that purport to say what to believe, what to intend, what to do. In making claims on what we believe, intend, or do such judgments are *normative*, and we can ask what the source, the justification, of this normativity is. Morality, in particular, makes normative claims – sometimes quite demanding – on (at least) what we intend and do. We can ask what the grounds are for the normativity of such moral demands.

Korsgaard's main question – which she labels "the normative question" (10) – is this last question about the "claims morality makes on us." (10). But her answer involves a general approach to grounds for

Thanks to Rachel Cohon, David Copp, John Fischer, Harry Frankfurt, Elijah Millgram, Arthur Ripstein, and Timothy Schroeder for their help. This essay was written while I was a Fellow at the Center for Advanced Study in the Behavioral Sciences. I am grateful for financial support provided by The Andrew W. Mellon Foundation.

*This essay is a study of Christine M. Korsgaard's *The Sources of Normativity* (Cambridge: Cambridge University Press, 1996). References in the text to this book appear in parentheses.

normative claims on what we intend and do.[1] Her answer – which she sees as Kantian, and notes (99n) has similarities to views of Harry Frankfurt – is that the basic ground of practical normativity is "the reflective structure" of our minds (100). We – normal, mature human beings – have the capacity to be reflectively aware of the desires and inclinations that tend to move us to intention and action. The answer to the normative question lies in the basic structure of this reflective capacity; or so Korsgaard maintains.

I. OVERVIEW OF THE ARGUMENT

Let me begin by sketching the main outlines of Korsgaard's argument.[2] Suppose I find myself faced with some desire or inclination to act in a certain way. As a reflective agent, I have the capacity to be reflectively aware of this desire, D, and of its support for action A. Once I am reflectively aware I am faced with the question: "Should I act in the way D indicates?" To answer this query I need to decide whether or not to *endorse* acting on D in the present circumstance. But for a reflective agent to endorse acting on D is for that agent to endorse some general principle that sanctions so acting. As a fully reflective agent I will be aware of the principle I endorse. But that reflective awareness leads to the question: Should I endorse that principle? which then leads to the question: Should I be the sort of person who endorses such a principle? Intentionally to go ahead with A in full reflectiveness I need to endorse being such a person, which is to say I need to endorse a certain conception of what Korsgaard calls my "practical identity" (120). Examples of such conceptions include being a Quaker, a teacher, a scholar, a thief, a citizen of Brazil, a friend

1 Korsgaard leaves it open whether her views are extendible to judgments about what to believe. See p. 232, n. 16.

2 The bulk of this argument is in her third and fourth lecture and her "Reply." She sets the stage in her first two lectures by criticizing a trio of alternatives: a form of "voluntarism" in the spirit of Hobbes; a form of realism associated with, for example, Prichard; and an approach that tries to proceed by showing that "morality is good for us" (19), an approach she associates with Hume and, in contemporary work, with Bernard Williams.

of Gregory. It is in general a contingent matter which such conceptions a particular person endorses. But now consider the fact that I am the kind of reflective agent who has been led from the awareness of D to a reflective endorsement of a relevant conception of my practical identity. If I am fully reflective I will be aware of that fact. But then I am led to ask whether to endorse that fact, whether reflectively to endorse my own reflectiveness. Not to do so would, Korsgaard avers, undermine my agency: I would "lose [my] grip on [myself] as having any reason to do one thing rather than another" (121). The continued application of the pressures of reflection lead, then, to my endorsement of a conception of myself as a reflective being. Since reflectiveness is a basic characteristic of normal human agents, this is an endorsement of my humanity. Korsgaard then argues that this involves a commitment to endorsing the value of reflectiveness (humanity) generally, not simply *my* reflectiveness, *my* humanity. But to endorse reflectiveness (humanity) generally is to endorse the source of the normativity of morality. So we reach the conclusion that the continued pressure on a reflective agent to bring her practical thinking within the reach of reflection leads ineluctably to her endorsement of the source of moral claims on us: The claims of morality are grounded in our reflectiveness. Since "the laws of morality are" on this account "the laws of the agent's own will" Korsgaard calls this view "The Appeal to Autonomy" (19).

II. INITIAL ANALYSIS OF THE ARGUMENT

This is a powerful and deep line of argument. In this section I try to disentangle its steps in a bit more detail.

The argument begins by supposing that

(1) I am throughout a fully reflective agent.

The idea behind this supposition is not that I am in fact always fully reflective, or, given the press of events and the limits on our mental resources, should always be. We are interested in what is involved in being fully reflective because the capacity for full reflection is a basic feature of our agency. Fully reflective activity is the paradigm case of human action – it is human action "par excellence."[3] The argument will be that the pressure imposed by this paradigm or archetype is the source of practical normativity.[4]

We now place the reflective agent in a circumstance calling for practical reflection. We suppose that

(2) I am faced with desire D in favor of my now performing action A.

Since I am fully reflective I am reflectively aware that (2). This is not like being aware of a sudden urge to sneeze; for I see my potential action on the basis of D as an exercise of my agency, and not merely the output of a causal process. Given that I see my acting on D as a case of my agency, I am faced with the question of whether to endorse my so acting.[5] That is:

(3) I am faced with the questions: Should I now act on D? Should I endorse my now acting on D?

In fully reflective agency I act on D only if I endorse my so acting. Korsgaard sometimes seems to identify such an endorsement with a judgment that D "really is a reason" to A (108). But this is not quite

---

3 The quote is from J. David Velleman's discussion of a related idea in his "The Possibility of Practical Reason," *Ethics* (1996): 694–726, at p. 714.

4 This is a slightly deflationary understanding of Korsgaard's concluding remark: "the activity of reflection has rules of its own. . . . And one of them . . . is the rule that we should never stop reflecting until we have reached a satisfactory answer, one that admits of no further questioning" (258). Harry Frankfurt, who also emphasizes the significance of reflective endorsement, is more concerned with the fact that such reflection can stop, and the agent can be fully satisfied with her reflective endorsement, even though a further question might be raised. See his "The Faintest Passion," *Proceedings and Addresses of the APA* 66 (1992): 5–16, esp. pp. 13–14. Korsgaard acknowledges that an agent can act for reasons even if the process of reflection is in fact only "partially carried out" (256) in her concluding discussion of the Mafioso (256–257).

5 As noted, Korsgaard's argument is driven by the continued iteration of the demand for reflection. Implicit in my remarks in this paragraph is the point that each new application of the demand for reflection involves the assumption that the target of the required reflection is itself an activity. This is one of the ways in which the category of action plays a fundamental role in the argument.

right, for one might see a desire as a reason and still be unsettled about whether, in a case of conflict, to act on it. For me to endorse my now acting on D is, I take it, for me to endorse it all things considered, and not merely to judge there is something to be said for it. Korsgaard also seems to identify such an endorsement with willing so to act.[6] This raises issues about weakness of will and what Gary Watson has called "perverse cases" of agency;[7] for it seems that one can, in full awareness, act contrary to what one endorses all considered. But I will pass over this worry here.

The next piece in Korsgaard's argument is the claim that the endorsement called for in (3) needs to involve a general principle:

(4) If I reflectively endorse my acting on D now, then I endorse a general principle that supports my so acting.

But why must reflective endorsement of a particular action involve the endorsement of an associated general principle? Consider G. A. Cohen's challenge:

The reflective structure of human consciousness may require . . . that, on pain of reducing myself to the condition of a wanton, I endorse the first-order impulses on which I act. . . . But it does not follow, and it is not true, that the structure of my consciousness requires that I identify myself with some law or principle. . . . sometimes the commands that I issue will be singular, not universal. . . . [They will be] singular edicts. . . . (176)

Korsgaard's main response to this challenge occurs in her "Reply."[8] What requires the endorsement or willing of a general principle is not, she thinks, simply that "thought traffics in the general," for

[t]his by itself . . . does not quite commit me to reaching the same conclusion about what it would be appropriate to do on all relevantly similar occasions as I reach now. (228)

Rather, what is crucial is that "I need to will universally in order to see my action as something which I *do*" (228–229). Again:

6 I think this idea is implicit in her remarks on pp. 108 and 113.
7 Gary Watson, "Free Action and Free Will," *Mind* 96 (1987): 145–172, at p. 150.
8 Section 1, esp. pp. 227–233.

if I am to regard *this* act, the one I do now, as the act of my *will*, I must at least make a claim to universality, a claim that the reason for which a claim which I act now will be valid on other occasions, or on occasions of this type – *including this one, conceived in a general way.* (231–32)

That this is something I, in the full sense, *do* – that is, is an act of my *will* (Korsgaard treats these as the same idea) – requires "a claim to universality." Or so Korsgaard avers. I return to these matters below.

Korsgaard wants to go from (4) to

(5) The general principle that supports my acting on D now is part of or grounded in a conception of my practical identity that I endorse.[9]

Why, though, can't I endorse a principle that is not about me? Of course, I am the one who endorses it; but that does not make it a conception of myself.[10] Even if I endorse acting on D by way of an endorsed principle *of mine*, it does not follow that this is a principle that concerns *my identity*.

The reply, I take it, is to appeal again to reflectiveness. Suppose I endorse acting on D by appeal to principle P, which I endorse. I can be reflectively aware of all this. So long as this complex process of practical thinking is itself an activity of mine, I need to ask whether I endorse *it*. But to endorse it is to endorse being a person who endorses P. So it seems I do need to endorse a practical conception of my identity, at least in this attenuated sense, even if P itself is not about my identity.[11]

We can now apply the demand for reflectiveness to the entire complex of being reflective about D and thereby arriving at a supporting conception of one's practical identity. In full reflectiveness I am aware of all this and – assuming this entire process of practical thinking is itself an activity of mine – I am faced with a question of whether or not to endorse it. To reject this entire structure, however, would preclude acting with full reflection. If I were to reject this

9 See, e.g., pp. 100–101.
10 See G. A. Cohen, p. 185.
11 Cohen anticipated this response. It matches his "trivial sense" (185) in which I may endorse a self-conception.

270

structure of reflection I would not see D as giving me reason to act;[12] and if I were nevertheless to be moved by D I would not, in the full sense, be acting. To act with full reflection, then, I must endorse my reflective nature as a conception of my practical identity.[13] So given that I am an agent who acts in full reflection we arrive at

(6) I endorse my reflectiveness (my humanity) as a conception of my practical identity.

The endorsement in (6) is a general endorsement of my reflectiveness, not simply an endorsement of my reflective activity on this particular occasion. Why? Part of the argument that is to get us to (6) is the application of the demand for reflective endorsement to one's present activity of reflectively endorsing acting now on D. Taken by itself, however, this argument may only show that a fully reflective agent who reflectively endorses acting now on D will need also reflectively to endorse being reflective on this occasion. That is, the iteration of the demand for reflection by itself does not seem yet to show why the resulting endorsement cannot be limited to one's reflectiveness on this particular occasion. Korsgaard's reply here, I take it, would be to appeal to the argument that took us from (3) to (4), the argument that reflective endorsement, of necessity, involves endorsement of a general principle. Applied to the present case, the argument supports a general endorsement of my reflectiveness.

Having arrived at (6) Korsgaard assesses her position as follows:

to value yourself just as a human being is to have moral identity, as the Enlightenment understood it. So this puts you in moral territory. Or at least, it does so if valuing humanity in your own person rationally requires valuing it in the person of others. (121)

---

12 See p. 121.

13 Could I instead merely think my reflectiveness is unavoidable, though unwelcome? The answer, I take it, would be that I then would not see myself as fully active. What if I simply endorse my reflectiveness as a mere means to other ends? (A question of Simon May.) The answer here, I suppose, would be that I must then examine my endorsement of those ends, and so the pressures for continued reflection are not yet at an end.

271

In her fourth lecture Korsgaard tries to show that "valuing humanity in your own person rationally requires valuing it in the person of others." She tries to show, that is, that from (6) and the assumption of full reflection we can infer

(7) I endorse (and so value) reflectiveness (humanity) in general – in the person of others as well as in my own person.

There is an obvious worry here, nicely articulated by Raymond Guess:

I may well come to see *my* mere humanity as a source of value for *me*, your mere humanity as a source of value for *you;* how does it follow from that that *your* humanity must be a source of value for *me*? (197)

Korsgaard's answer draws on Wittgensteinian themes.[14] Since reasons are essentially "public" (135), my humanity is reason-giving only if humanity is reason-giving. So (6) commits me to (7). Or so Korsgaard claims.

The issues raised in the effort to move to (7) are difficult; I will not try to sort them out here.[15] Instead I want to focus on a pair of issues that arise at earlier stages in the argument.

III. IS THERE A REGRESS?

Suppose I have arrived at the stage of reflection described by (6): I endorse my own reflectiveness. Do I need to continue to reflect

14 See esp. pp. 132–145.
15 Even if we get to (7) there remain issues about the priority to be given to one's endorsement of humanity. (7) does commit me not to endorse other conceptions of my practical identity that are *inconsistent* with my endorsing the value of reflectiveness (126). But there will be self-conceptions that, while not themselves inconsistent with valuing humanity, can come into conflict with it. Perhaps, for example, my endorsed self-conception as a researcher supports conducting medical research in which, given the special features of the case, human subjects are treated as a means merely. So far as I can see, Korsgaard does not here provide an argument that "humanity" has priority in such cases of conflict. She argues that the normative force of particular practical identities *depends on* one's general endorsement of humanity. But it does not follow that the latter has *priority over* the former in a case of conflict.

about whether to endorse this endorsement? If so, is there a vicious regress?[16]

The concern here is familiar from Frankfurt's seminal paper, "Freedom of the Will and the Concept of a Person."[17] Suppose I have (as Frankfurt in that essay would describe it) a second-order desire that my desire for X be my will. Do I desire that that second-order desire be realized? If so, does an analogous question await concerning this third-order desire? If not, why does my second-order desire have authority? The question for Korsgaard is whether there is a similar worry that I need to endorse my endorsement of my reflectiveness and, if so, whether a regress threatens.

I suspect that Korsgaard's answer would be that my reflective endorsement of my reflectiveness is in part about itself: I reflectively endorse my reflectiveness, including this very reflectiveness.[18] My reflective endorsement of my reflectiveness is in part an endorsement of itself, and in this way it blocks a further regress.

This seems to explain why my endorsement of my reflectiveness itself engenders no regress. But it may not block a different regress. Suppose my practical conceptions of my identity include my conceptions of myself as a father and as a faculty member. Suppose each conception is compatible with my endorsement of my reflectiveness. But suppose my self-conceptions as father and as faculty member come into conflict on a particular occasion.[19] Suppose I step back and endorse the priority, on this occasion, of the former conception. (Perhaps this means being with my son and missing a colloquium.) Since (as we are supposing) I am fully reflective I need to reflect on this endorsement of the priority of my self-conception as father. Do I endorse this conflict-resolving endorsement or not? Whichever way I answer, will I then be faced with an analogous question concerning my answer?

16 This section benefited from comments from John Fischer and Elijah Millgram, and discussion with Arthur Ripstein.
17 In his *The Importance of What We Care About* (Cambridge: Cambridge University Press, 1988): 11–25.
18 This may be suggested by remarks on p. 154.
19 Jennifer Rosner discusses a similar example in her *Reflective Evaluation, Autonomy, and Self-Knowledge* (Ph.D. thesis, Stanford University, 1998).

If the issue of priority were settled by my endorsement of my reflectiveness, then there would be no regress. But many conflicts are not settled in this way. For these cases Korsgaard might try to say that my conflict-resolving endorsement is itself a decisive commitment that stops the regress.[20] But then we need an explanation of why this is so, of why full reflection does not require yet further reflection on whether to endorse this conflict-resolving endorsement.[21]

IV. AGENCY AND UNIVERSALITY

Turn now to the move to (4). Cohen's challenge to this move was that a reflective agent could act on "singular edicts." Korsgaard's response was that agency requires universality. Why?

Korsgaard emphasizes the significance of the first-person, practical perspective of deliberation. From within this perspective I see myself as a chooser who is distinct from his desires:

When you deliberate it is as if there were something over and above all your desires, something which is *you*, and which *chooses* which desire to act on. (100)

Korsgaard believes that this perspective is essential to our understanding of agency. As she says elsewhere:

it is only from the practical point of view that actions and choices can be distinguished from mere "behavior" determined by biological and psychological laws.[22]

---

20 This would be in the spirit of work of Harry Frankfurt. See his "Freedom of the Will and the Concept of a Person," at p. 21, and his "Identification and Whole-heartedness" in *The Importance of What We Care About*, pp. 159–176, at p. 170. I discuss related matters in my "Identification, Decision, and Treating as a Reason," *Philosophical Topics* 24 (1996): 1–18 [this volume, essay 10].

21 Korsgaard might perhaps say that the conflict-resolving endorsement is in part about itself: It is an endorsement both of the priority of the first conception and of itself. But it is not clear that this would solve the problem. It seems there could be other endorsements that bootstrap themselves in this way and yet are in conflict with this endorsement.

22 "Personal Identity and the Unity of Agency," in her *Creating the Kingdom of Ends* (Cambridge: Cambridge University Press, 1996): 363–397, at p. 378.

From the standpoint of practical deliberation I am convinced of *my* causality as an agent, an agent who is "something over and above" his desires. I can reasonably see myself in this way only if my relevant motivational structures are sufficiently unified. There needs to be sufficient motivational organization and integration so that it is reasonable to conceive of the situation as one in which there is a single agent acting, rather than merely a play of event-causal forces – so that there is an agent acting and not just an undifferentiated mix of motivational forces, of pushes and pulls. Korsgaard believes that this is what imposes a demand for a general principle that says that "the reason for which I act now will be valid on other occasions, or on occasions of this type" (232). Endorsement of such general principles of action is needed "to bring integrity and therefore unity – and therefore, really, existence – to the acting self" (229).

Distinguish two different interpretations of this idea. First, there is the idea that what is needed for there to be sufficient unity at the time of action is an endorsement, at that time, of a general principle concerning other possible but nonactual ways this present occasion might have been. Second, there is an interpretation that requires that the agent see the activity on which she has decided as an activity that extends into the future. For such cases the idea, on this second interpretation, is that what is needed for there to be sufficient unity is an endorsement of a principle that specifies general conditions in the anticipated future under which one is committed to sticking with one's activity.

Korsgaard sometimes suggests this second interpretation:

when I will an end, I must *ipso facto* will that even on another occasion, even when I am tempted not to, I will stay on the track of that end. (230–231)

And she elsewhere notes that "most of the things we do that matter to us take up time."[23] But she also seems sometimes to guard against this interpretation. She cautions that "the argument does not really require the possibility of a temporally later occasion" (231). And she

---

23 "Personal Identity and the Unity of Agency," p. 371, though it does not strictly follow from this remark that most of the time we *intend* the later parts of those things that matter to us.

suggests that what is needed "if I am not merely the place where an impulse is operating" is reference "to *this* occasion, regarded as possibly other, and so regarded in general terms" (231).

The first interpretation focuses on unity of agency at the time of action. Here it is important to note that there can be substantial motivational integration with respect to present action without the endorsement of a general "claim that the reason for which I act now will be valid on other occasions, or on occasions of this type." Suppose I desire to *A* now. Suppose I endorse acting now on this desire, and that this endorsement is itself part of the explanation of my so acting. Suppose that I endorse both this endorsement and its role in my agency. And suppose that there is not, in fact, any other present endorsement of mine that is incompatible with these endorsements.[24] My relevant endorsements could be specifically concerned with my *A*-ing now in this particular circumstance; they could be "singular edicts" without a commitment to a universal principle of action. Yet such a structure of endorsements seems to provide some traction for talk of an agent who is not simply a place where desires push and pull. It seems to provide resources for the project of constructing the "active self."

Korsgaard sometimes seems to suppose that there are only two main possibilities in the theory of action: a broadly Humean view that sees acts as events that are the upshot of the causal operation of impulses and desires, and the will as at most a mere by-product of these processes; and a broadly Kantian view that sees agency and the will as "over and above" the operation of event-causal forces, as tied to universal principles, and as accessible only from within the standpoint of deliberation.[25] This may tend to hide from view more complex structures of motivation that do not fit comfortably within either picture. In the present case the more complex structures I have cited

---

24 Cp. Frankfurt, "The Faintest Passion."
25 While I think this two-option picture is detectable in *The Sources of Normativity*, it is also present in "Personal Identity and the Unity of Agency." See, e.g., p. 387 in *Creating the Kingdom of Ends*. See also Korsgaard's "The Normativity of Instrumental Reason" in Garrett Cullity and Berys Gaut, eds., *Ethics and Practical Reason* (Oxford: Oxford University Press, 1997): 215–254, at p. 234, note 42.

involve endorsements that, though they may be "singular," neverthe-less provide resources for unity of agency at the time of action.[26]

Consider now the second interpretation, an interpretation which highlights decisions concerning future action. Are there additional resources here for supporting the inference to (4)? A fully reflective decision now to A at some later time, on the basis of desire D, would involve a reflective, present endorsement of that decision concerning the future. What endorsement? Well, in reaching this decision I an-ticipate a temporal gap between decision and action, a gap during which there is the real possibility of reconsideration. Reflectively to endorse the decision I normally need to endorse its persistence from now until the time of action – not, of course, its persistence no matter what, but its persistence in circumstances in which it is reasonable not to reconsider. This will normally involve the reflective endorsement of the continuation of the endorsement of the priority of D over its relevant competitors.

So there is further structure introduced when we consider a pres-ent decision concerning future action. This further structure may seem to introduce a kind of generality that is relevant to the unity of agency over time, and so help support a version of the inference to (4). A reflectively endorsed decision concerning future action seems to involve an endorsement of a principle that "the reasons for which I [decide] now will be valid on" future occasions in the interim between the time of this decision and the time of its execution.

There is a problem here, however. The relevant principle, when fully spelled out, will be that "the reasons for which I [decide] now will be valid" on relevant later occasions *unless I should then reconsider my decision*. What is not clear is whether the agent must be able to

---

26 This may be a way to see Harry Frankfurt's work on identification. See, e.g., his "The Faintest Passion" and his "Autonomy, Necessity and Love," in *Vernunftbe-griffe in der Moderne*, ed. Hans Friedrich Fulda and Rolf-Peter Horstmann (Klett-Cotta, 1994): 433–447. I also see my own views about intention as, in a different way, an effort to avoid either extreme. See my *Intention, Plans, and Practical Reason* (Cambridge: Harvard University Press, 1987). Both Frankfurt and I would em-phasize the significance of future-directed decisions, so we both have a stake in the status of Korsgaard's argument on the second interpretation. But, as I go on to argue, this interpretation still leaves room for theories in this middle ground.

provide a relevantly general specification of those conditions under which she should (or should not) reconsider. Why couldn't I reach a decision about the future and trust that I would make a reasonable judgment about reconsideration if the issue arose, without endorsing some nontrivial general principle that says when to reconsider and when not to?[27] Even on the second interpretation, then, the step from (3) to (4) remains problematic. Unity of agency, both at a time and over time, may not ensure commitment to universal principles.

This raises the question of whether the demand for universality could be postponed in Korsgaard's argument. Even without an appeal to universality the iterated demand for reflection will, it seems, lead to my endorsement of my reflectiveness on the present occasion. This would be a highly particularized version of (6). It is possible, for all that I have said here, that appeal to the idea that reasons are "public" could then be applied to this particularized version of (6) in a way that led to (7). But this would be to ask appeals to the public nature of reasons to do more work, and appeals to unity of agency less work, than they are asked to do on Korsgaard's official version of her argument.

This is a fine book, full of insights and challenges. It deserves and rewards careful study.

27 These last two sentences benefited greatly from correspondence with David Copp and Elijah Millgram.

Index

Prepared by Peter J. Graham

culpability, *see* planning agency

Davidson, Donald, 2, 5, 10–12, 31n.21
Davidson's theory of intention, 10–11, 209–24; strategy of extension, 213–14, 222, 224. *See also* agglomerativity; evaluative propositions; intention; intentional action; planning agency; practical reasoning
decision, 7, 30–3, 36; vs. choice (Frankfurt), 192–3; about desires, 190–3; unwitting decisions (Velleman), 193–5, 202. *See also* acceptance; belief; identification; intention; cognitive background
decision theory, 11, 16–17; discounting, temporal, 38–40, 75n.29; expected utility, 38–9, 41, 43; matching law, 39. *See also* standard model; standard view
deep responsibility (Wolf), *see* responsible agency
DeHelian, Laura, 54, 56n.31, 70n.20
deliberation, 16, 20, 30, 31, 61, 64; first-person, practical perspective (Korsgaard), 274–6
Dennett, Daniel, 172n.18
deontic content and truth (Castañeda): deontic propositions, 235–7; deontic thinking and intending, 234; deontic truth as necessarily Legitimate, 235–40; deontic truth as practitional implication, 238–40; overriding ought-contents, 234, 235n.11, 235–7, 245; qualified ought-contents, 234, 236, 238, 240. *See also* designated value; practitions; prescriptions; weakness of will
designated value (Castañeda): belief and truth, 231, 243–4, 248; Legitimacy, relative to an absolute context, 231–2, 235, 237, 242–5; Legitimacy, relative to a limited context, 231; "polar star," 231, 245, 248; and practitional implication, 233, 236–40. *See also* practitions; prescriptions
desire, 15; conflict of desires, integration/ordering, 191–2, 195; conflict of desires, segregation/rejection, 191–2,

195, 197n.33; first-order vs. second-order, 53–4n.26, 167, 187, 193, 273; hedonistic, 38n.3; intrinsic, 60n.4, 63n.11, 68n.17, 252ff. *See also* decision; hierarchical models of motivation; identification; preferences; spontaneous self-knowledge and understanding
determinism, 166. *See also* responsible agency
discouragement, 49. *See also* temptation; willpower
Donagan, Alan, 109, 110n.4, 114, 114n.12, 119, 147n.9
Döring, Frank, 48n.19
Dretske, Fred, 185n.2
drug addict case: clear-headed addict (Milgram), 199n.37; unwilling (grudging) addict (Frankfurt), 168–9, 186, 188–9, 192, 195, 198–200, 205
duet case, 9, 93–4, 97, 103, 106, 110, 122; cautious singers, 126–8, 133–4, 137–8; coercive singer, 132–3, 137–8; unhelpful singers, 103–5, 107
Dummett, Michael, 25

Elster, Jon, 82n.40
emotivism, 237
endorsement (Castañeda), 226, 230–1, 233, 244; and practitions, 231, 233, 237, 244–5; and prescriptions, 246–8
endorsement (Korsgaard), *see* reflective endorsement
evaluative propositions (Davidson): all-out/unconditional, 211–12, 222; implicitly comparative, 212; particular acts, not types, 213–14; practical reasoning, 210–14; prima facie, 211, 214. *See also* inductive-statistical explanations; intention; intentional action
evaluative rankings, 61, 65, 69–70; functional account of, 75–6; vs. mere preferences, 76; regret, 83, 86–8; temporary reversals, 73–77, 80. *See also* preferences; temptation; stability of intention
examples, *see* cases
exclusionary reason (Raz), 196n.32

inductive-statistical explanations (Hempel), 211n.6

information, 2, 4, 8; unanticipated, 61–2, 88; no-unanticipated, 65, 70, 79, 88–9. *See also* stability of intention

instrumental rationality, 60, 60n.5, 63n.11, 64, 67–70, 76, 80, 85, 89; and the good, 6–7, 60. *See also* decision theory; intention; planning agency; standard model

intending as endorsement of an intention/noema (Castañeda), 10, 226, 230, 243. *See also* intention

intention, 1–4, 8 15, 31–3, 36–7, 41, 50–1, 62–3; analogy with speech acts (Castañeda), 227, 237, 241, 243–7; as basic/distinct mental state, 185, 210; as belief, 250, 255, 257, 258n.5; belief-conditions on, 215–19 (vs. connected beliefs about means and ends, 241ff); and commitment, 2–4, 7–8, 11; and decision, 32, 190; vs. desire, 220; future-intention/future-directed intention, 3, 10n.17, 50–2, 213–15, 217–19, 222–3, 220, 277n.16 (as all-out evaluation (Davidson), 214–15); vs. goal, 260–1; vs. hope, 216; and intending, 3n.5; as involving acceptance, 32–3; as involving belief, 31–2; vs. mere expectation of side-effects, 257–64; rational intention, 70–79, 87, 241–44; as reasons (Velleman), 256, 261ff. (procedural vs. evaluative reasons, 256n.4); as self-fulfilling reflective prediction (Velleman), 254–9, 262–4; self-referential character, 167n.5. *See also* cognitivism about practical reason; conditional intention; Davidson's theory of intention, strategy of extension; evaluative propositions; instrumental rationality; planning theory of intention; practical reason; reasons; shared intention; stability of intention; standard model

intentional action, 209–14, 217, 222; behaviorist conception, 210; volitional conception, 210, 212, 212n.9. *See also* Davidson's theory of intention, strategy of extension; evaluative propo-

sitions; intention; intentional agency; shared cooperative activity

intentional agency, 190–1, 205

intentional joint goal (Toumela), 117n.21

intentional stance (Dennett), 172n.18

interlocking web of intentions, *see* shared intention

interpersonal relationships, 167, 172, 175–8, 180–2, 183n.48, 194; culturally idiosyncratic character of relationships objection (Fischer), 180–1; and interpersonal communication, 177–8, 180–1; resenting a stranger (Bennett), 176–7; and responsibility, 171–2, 178; temporally extended character of, 177–8. *See also* planning agency; reactive attitudes; responsible agency

Israel, David, 3n.5

Kaplan, J., 170n.8

Kavka, Gregory, 8, 55, 62, 62n.9, 63, 63 n.10, 63n.12

Kenny, A., 227–8

Korsgaard, Christine, 10–11, 201n.40: *Sources of Normativity,* 265–78

Kutz, Christopher, 146, 148n.10

Legitimacy (Castañeda), *see* designated value

Lehrer, Keith, 167n.4

Levesque, Hector J., 96n.7, 104n.17, 110n.6

Levi, Isaac, 28–9, 29n.18

Lewis, C. I., 39n.4

Lewis, David, 102n.15, 111n.7, 127n.29, 143–4

linking principle, 52, 55, 63–6, 68–70, 80

Livingston, Paisley, 60n.6

Loomes, Graham, 80n.38

McClennen, Edward, 54, 56n.31, 69n.19, 70, 70n.20

Maher, Patrick, 31n.23

matching law, *see* decision theory

means–end coherence, 3, 97n.8, 103, 113, 115, 123–4, 241. *See also* coordination; plans; practical reasoning

Melden, A., 210

plan-state vs. goal-state (Velleman), 261
Plato, 40n.8
plural-subject concepts (Gilbert), 108n.25
policy, 7, 9, 41n.10, 52, 191n.22, 200–1
Pollack, Martha, 3n.5
Postema, Gerald J., 86n.47, 153n.13
practical action (Castañeda), 235, 242–3.
    See also intention; intentional action;
    practical reasoning; practitions; pre-
    scriptions
practical identity (Korsgaard), 266, 270–1,
    272n.15
practical reasoning, 4, 10–11, 15–16,
    21, 26, 28–9, 33, 52, 187, 250–2;
    Aristotelian conception (Davidson),
    210–12; decision theory, 16; and in-
    tentions as inputs, 222–3; three-stage
    model, 16; and treating a desire as rea-
    son-giving, 196–8, 200–1, 205. See also
    cognitivism about practical reason; Da-
    vidson's theory of intention; intention;
    intentional agency; instrumental ration-
    ality; planning agency; weakness of will
practitions (Castañeda), 228–9, 236–40;
    implicational structure of, 229–30, 235–
    7; and intendings as first-person, 229;
    Legitimacy of, 231–2, 232n.10, 234,
    237ff., 245ff., 248–9; and prescriptions
    as second- /third-person, 229; vs.
    propositions, 226, 229–30, 234–8; spe-
    cial copula, 228–9. See also deontic
    contents and truth; designated value;
    endorsement; intending; intention;
    practical reason; prescriptions; weakness
    of will
praise and blame, see reactive attitudes
predictability, 16–7, 59, 155–6; See also co-
    ordination
preferences: intransitive, slippery slope, 77–
    9, 81–2 (see also self-torturer case);
    planning theory of intention, 53–5;
    preference reversal, 38–40, 44n.13, 50–
    1 (vs. losing control, 38); sophistica-
    tion, 73–7; vs. values, 55, 70, 77–8;
    vanishing point preferences, 89n.53.
    See also evaluative rankings; temptation
premeditation, see planning agency
prescriptions (Castañeda), 228, 235; Legiti-

macy of a prescription, 232, 243–4,
    246–8; mandates, 228; as practical con-
    tents of practical reasoning, 228; and
    performance propositions, 228; and
    practical copula, 228. See also deontic
    content and truth; designated value; in-
    tending; intention; Legitimacy; practi-
    cal reasoning; practitions
prescriptivism, 237
Price, H. H., 25
Prichard, 212n.9, 266n.2
Principle F (Scanlon), 136–41; value of as-
    surance, 135, 137, 139. See also mutual
    obligation
Principle of Double Effect, 3n.5
prisoner's dilemma, 45–50; Ainslie's anal-
    ogy, 45–50; disanalogy, 47–9
pro-attitude, 209, 211. See also reasons
promises, 2, 7, 135. See also intention; mu-
    tual obligation; Principle F
Putnam, Hilary, 129n.34, 144

quality of will, see reactive attitudes
Quinn, Warren, 77, 77n.32–3, 78n.35, 80

Rabinowicz, Wlodek, 60n.4
rational irrationality (Parfit), 40n.9
Rawls, John, 6n.9, 39n.4, 80n.38, 87n.50
Raz, Joseph, 23n.12, 138n.21, 196n.32
reactive attitudes (Strawson), 171–4, 176–7;
    praise and blame, 166, 172; quality of
    will, 173–4, 181–2; resentment and
    gratitude, 166–7, 176; self-reactive atti-
    tudes, 172. See also interpersonal rela-
    tionships; objective attitude; planning
    agency; responsible agency
realism (Prichard), 266n.2
reason-responsiveness and moral responsi-
    bility (Fischer), 183
reasons: as belief–desire pairs, 209–11, 213;
    as causes, 209–11; and intentional ac-
    tion, 209–211; as public, 272, 278. See
    also treating a desire as reason-giving
reciprocation, 66–70, 82; resolution, 72;
    temptation, 76. See also autonomous
    benefits; planning theory; sophistica-
    tion
reconsideration, see stability of intention

288

DATE DUE

GAYLORD

PRINTED IN U.S.A.